se ret
own a
be re

TRIO

The Rt Hon. Lord Radice was Labour MP for Durham North and Chairman of the powerful Treasury Committee until he became a Life Peer in 2001. His previous books include *Offshore: Britain and the European Idea* (I.B.Tauris), *Friends and Rivals: Crosland, Jenkins and Healey* ('the best political book of the year' – *Independent on Sunday*), *Diaries: 1980–2001* (shortlisted for Channel 4's Political Book of the Year in 2004) and *The Tortoise and the Hares: Attlee, Bevin, Cripps, Dalton, Morrison*. He brings to his works the skills of a historian and the insights of a politician.

TRIO

*Inside the Blair,
Brown, Mandelson Project*

GILES RADICE

I.B. TAURIS
PUBLISHERS

Published in 2010 by I.B.Tauris & Co Ltd
6 Salem Road, London W2 4BU
175 Fifth Avenue, New York NY 10010
www.ibtauris.com

Distributed in the United States and Canada Exclusively by Palgrave Macmillan
175 Fifth Avenue, New York NY 10010

ISBN: 978 1 84885 445 1

A full CIP record for this book is available from the British Library
A full CIP record is available from the Library of Congress

Library of Congress Catalog Card Number: available

Typeset in Garamond Premier Pro by Ellipsis Books Limited, Glasgow
Printed and bound in Great Britain by CPI Antony Rowe, Chippenham

FSC
www.fsc.org
MIX
Paper from
responsible sources
FSC® C013604

To Lisanne without whose love, inspiration and help
this book would not have been written

CONTENTS

Contents

PICTURE CREDITS

The photographs included in the two plate sections of this book are reproduced by kind permission of the following:

PLATE SECTION ONE – located between pages 76 and 77

Plate 1: *top*, SCPL/Camera Press London, *middle*, Topfoto, *bottom*, Topfoto

Plate 2: *top,* Topfoto, *bottom*, Topfoto

Plate 3: *top,* Getty Images, *bottom*, Getty Images

Plate 4: *whole page,* Enrico Oliverio/AP/Press Association Images

Plate 5: *top,* Topfoto, *bottom left*, Getty Images, *bottom right*, Rex Features

Plate 6: *top,* Rex Features, *bottom*, Rex Features

Plate 7: *top,* Sean Dempsey/PA Archive/Press Association Images, *bottom*, PA/PA Archive/Press Association Images

Plate 8: *whole page,* Russell Boyce/Corbis

PLATE SECTION TWO – located between pages 172 and 173

Plate 9: *top*, Stefan Rousseau/PA Wire/Press Association Images, *bottom*, Gerald Herbert/AP/Press Association Images

ix

Picture Credits

Plate 10: *top*, Getty Images, *bottom*, Getty Images

Plate 11: *top*, Rex Features, *bottom*, Martin Rickett/PA Wire/Press Association

Plate 12: *top*, Getty Images, *bottom*, Topfoto

Plate 13: *top*, Jeff Moore/Empics Entertainment/Press Association Images, *bottom*, Getty Images

Plate 14: *top*, Press Association Images, *bottom*, Rex Features

Plate 15: *top*, Ken McKay/AP Press Association Images, *bottom*, Lewis Whyld/PA Wire Press Association Images

Plate 16: *whole page*, Alastair Grant/AP/Press Association Images

ACKNOWLEDGEMENTS

This is my third comparative biography of leading Labour politicians. The first, *Friends and Rivals*, was a critique of my revisionist heroes, Tony Crosland, Roy Jenkins and Denis Healey, whose failure to combine weakened the social democratic cause inside the Labour Party in the 1970s and early 1980s. The second, *The Tortoise and the Hares*, was an assessment of the relationships between the giants of Clement Attlee's 1945–1951 governments. *Trio* is a study of Tony Blair, Gordon Brown and Peter Mandelson. They helped to create New Labour and then dominated British politics for over a decade.

I have long been fascinated by these outstanding members of Labour's 1980s' generation. I have known Mandelson since the 1970s; I was a Durham constituency neighbour of Blair; and I was Chairman of the Commons Treasury Committee during Brown's first and most creative period as Chancellor of the Exchequer. I have benefitted from the discussions that I have had with all three over many years.

For this book, I have had interviews and conversations with over fifty people, including former ministers, MPs, peers, civil servants,

Acknowledgements

academics and journalists. I am very grateful for their help.

I would like to thank Roger Liddle, Patrick Diamond, Simon Latham, Geoffrey Norris, Peter Riddell and, above all, Lisanne Radice for commenting on drafts of the book.

I am grateful to Simon Latham for his research work throughout the book; to Penny Bochum for her assistance on the Brown government; to Richard Heller for his help on 'credit crunch' issues; and to Policy Network for a research grant.

Thanks to the House of Lords Library for their help.

I would like to thank Iradj Bagherzade and Joanna Godfrey for their editorial advice; Patricia Marshall for her copy-editing; Linda Silverman for her assistance with the photographs; and Rohan Bolton for the index.

I write with a fountain pen on a lectern. Special thanks are, therefore, due to Nikki Applewhite for her miraculous deciphering of my hand-writing and Martin Gibbs for repairing my lectern.

Finally, I take full responsibility for the opinions expressed in this book.

INTRODUCTION

In 2010, Labour lost the General Election of 6 May and, following the formation of the Conservative–Liberal coalition under David Cameron, went into opposition. It was the end of the New Labour era.

This is the story of the three politicians – Blair, Brown and Mandelson – who made and sustained New Labour over sixteen years. Inspired by this trio, New Labour, a modernised version of traditional social democracy, was able to dominate politics before and after the turn of the twenty-first century, winning three successive elections in 1997, 2001 and 2005.

Tony Blair was its talisman. Boyish into his early fifties, he was stylish and charismatic, with a winning smile and charm. The best communicator of his generation, he was a master not only of parliamentary debate and party conference but, above all, of television. Unlike many politicians, his style was conversational rather than declamatory. He treated his audiences with respect, trying to present an argument rather than overwhelming with rhetoric.

Although highly intelligent and, like the trained lawyer he was, swift to pick up the kernel of a case, he was an instinctive rather than an intellectual politician. As Prime Minister, he was good at focusing on the main issues confronting his government – when necessary, he made decisions quickly, though he was criticised for the informal way in which he took them. His persuasiveness and persistence enabled him to become an effective negotiator, as his outstanding contribution to bringing peace and democracy to Northern Ireland demonstrated. Whenever possible, he avoided confrontation and rows, sometimes to his cost.

He was an outsider, without deep roots in his party. This was both a strength and a weakness. On the one hand, he could see clearly what needed to be done to reform the party but, on the other hand, when the going got tough, it was more difficult for him to appeal for loyalty.

Blair was as much a Christian Democrat (in the continental mode) as he was a Social Democrat. He believed, above all, in a strong community and a 'one nation' approach to policies. He was a social moralist, who combined a tough line on crime with a liberal attitude on abortion, gay rights and racial equality.

In foreign affairs, Blair was a liberal internationalist. Like Brown, he sustained a concerned interest in Africa. As he said in his Brighton Party Conference speech after 9/11, 'The state of Africa is a scar on the conscience of the world.' He set up the Commission for Africa which put forward a package of debt relief, development aid and good governance which was later adopted at the G8 Gleneagles summit. In May 2000, he instigated the successful UK military intervention to support the recognised government in Sierra Leone.

In his 1999 Chicago speech, he put forward a doctrine of liberal intervention. He argued that acts of genocide could never be a purely internal matter and set out a number of tests that would have to be satisfied before nations intervened. This was a promising initiative which was later undermined by the Iraq imbroglio.

Like a dark cloud, Iraq hung over much of the later part of his premiership. It distorted his foreign policy and diverted his attention away from domestic issues. Blair was a strong supporter of UK member-ship of the European Union while, at the same time, stressing the impor-tance of the so-called 'special relationship' with the United States. He hoped not to have to choose between the European Union and the United States – Britain, he argued, could be a mediator or 'bridge' between the two. This was an over-optimistic strategy which was torn apart by 9/11 and the unilateralism of the Republican President, George W. Bush. When Blair was forced to choose, he sent British troops into Iraq, alongside the Americans. He did so without UN backing and at a high cost to his personal reputation and to the long-term prospects of his party. Labour won the 2005 election but Blair and his party lost the support of the liberal intelligentsia which had been an integral part of the New Labour coalition.

In his last speech in the House of Lords, Roy Jenkins criticised Blair for being too much of a 'conviction' politician. Although Blair, perhaps because of his religious beliefs, had always had a 'conviction' element in his make-up, it had been balanced by a healthy and humane pragmatism. After 9/11 and certainly after Iraq, the idea of commitment became predom-inant, sometimes to the detriment of his effectiveness as a politician.

Gordon Brown was the policy expert of New Labour. He devoured ideas and policies as others devoured food. On holiday, often on the east coast of the United States, he would relax by getting through the piles of books he had brought with him. He was clever – he got a brilliant first in history at Edinburgh University – hard working, energetic and obsessed by politics. When he came to my constituency in March 1990, I wrote in my diary, 'With the glowering good looks of a Heathcliff, he is very much a "driven" politician.'[1]

Brown saw himself as a modern egalitarian. While rejecting the idea of equality of outcome as both undesirable and unrealisable, he stressed the case for a strong version of equality of opportunity. Everyone should have the chance, he said, to bridge the gap between what they are and what they have it in themselves to become – hence the argument for investment in lifelong learning and for minimum standards of living, including a minimum wage, a tax and benefit system that helped people into work, decent health and social services and good provision for pensioners.

Brown had far deeper roots in the party than Blair. Long before he became an MP, he was well dug into the Scottish Labour Party, a member of the party's executive and a leader of the Scottish devolution campaign. In the close friendship which he formed at Westminster with Tony Blair, it was natural that he should be senior partner.

Yet, in the media-driven world of modern politics, Brown had a significant disadvantage. Unlike Blair, he was not a natural communicator. His mother said that he was the shyest of the three Brown brothers. Relaxing with his family and friends, he could be charming and witty. He had a captivating private smile. In small gatherings, particularly of policy experts or intellectuals, he was stimulating and incisive. In Parliament or at party conference, he made eloquent speeches. But, when performing on television, so vital a part of political life, he could seem wooden, even robotic. In the TV debates of the 2010 election, Brown, though well informed, always seemed stiff and ponderous compared to Cameron and Clegg.

Brown was an outstanding Chancellor of the Exchequer, at least until the end of the second term. He introduced a number of creative policy initiatives, including transferring control over interest rates from the Treasury to the Bank of England and the Working Families Tax Credit to help the working poor. Under his management, the British economy grew steadily until 2007, increasing national output by a third, while inflation was kept under firm control. From 2000, substantial extra resources were channelled into health and education, significantly improving the performance of these services, although, by 2007, his spending plans were based on over-optimistic forecasts.

If the chancellorship suited Brown's abilities and temperament, he was less at home as Prime Minister, where there were far more decisions to take. Brown, who was used to weighing all the options at the Treasury, found the flow of business at Number 10 a major problem, especially as he liked to take as many decisions as possible himself. His party and Cabinet grew restive. However, his premiership was rescued by the global banking crisis, in which he played a key leadership role, and by the return from Brussels of Peter Mandelson, who became Business Secretary and de facto Deputy Prime Minister.

The third of the trio was Peter Mandelson. Mandelson had a good claim to be called one of the main architects of New Labour. From the moment he became Neil Kinnock's Director of Communications, he was a committed moderniser – of organisation, policy and overall strategy. After the 1987 election, he threw much of his energy into nurturing the careers of Brown and Blair – he could rightly claim to have picked, schooled and deployed them.

Unlike Brown and Blair, Mandelson was born into the Labour Party. His grandfather was Herbert Morrison, one of the giants of Attlee's post-war Labour government, and his parents were active members of the Hampstead Labour Party. When he was sixteen, he helped set up a Young Socialist branch in the constituency – though, for a year or two, he also had a flirtation with the Young Communist League. He was an 'anorak' about politics, professing to know the names of every Labour MP.

In the early 1980s, in contrast to Brown and Blair, he threw himself into the battle to save the Labour Party, fighting the Trotskyites on Lambeth council, joining the so-called Labour Solidarity campaign and working for the Healey deputy leadership campaign.

From the beginning, he was a committed internationalist, spending a gap year in Tanzania and joining the United Nations Students' Association and the Young European Left at university. A consistent theme in his political career was his sustained support for British membership of the European Union. It was fitting that he should have become a European Commissioner.

Mandelson had a reputation, often exaggerated, as a master of media manipulation. His enemies inside as well as outside the Labour Party called him 'the Prince of Darkness'. Dark haired and immaculately dressed, he sometimes appeared to fit the part but he was always more than a media man. When Mandelson resigned as Secretary of State for Industry at the end of 1998, Philip Stephens, the *Financial Times* columnist, described him as 'the most remarkable political strategist of his generation'.[2] As Labour's campaign manager, he helped to deliver the great landslide triumph of 1997, a victory for which he had worked for over a decade.

He was Blair's consultant in chief, his *consigliere* to whom he turned for advice and support. He was also an excellent Cabinet minister, first at the Department of Trade and Industry and then at the Northern Ireland Office. When Brown brought him back from Brussels to join his Cabinet as Business Secretary, he quickly became the dominant Cabinet minister, effective in his departmental duties and de facto Deputy Prime Minister.

Mandelson was a complex character. Especially in the first part of his political career, he could be arrogant and a risk taker. He would never have advised anyone else to accept, as he did, a loan from a fellow politician, an ill-judged action which led to his first resignation – though, as it is explained later in this book, his second resignation was totally unjustified. At the same time, he was charming and witty, prepared to take responsibility, loyal to his friends and devoted to the Labour Party. The standing ovation which he received for his main speech at the 2009 party conference gave him enormous pleasure.

A key theme of this book is how the relationships between Blair, Brown and Mandelson waxed and waned. Personal relations matter in politics, as elsewhere in life. When exceptionally talented, strong-willed politicians are able to combine together, then it is usually to the benefit of their party and of the nation. When their ambitions collide, it is almost always detrimental.

The celebrated 1994 deal between Blair and Brown ensured Blair a clear and successful run at the leadership of the party, while promising Brown an exceptional role in both opposition and government, as well as hope for the succession. For a number of years, certainly until Labour's second term, the partnership, though with some upsets, worked well. Blair and Brown's complementary skills and abilities, with the addition of Mandelson's strategic direction, provided an unbeatable combination.

However, between 2002 and 2005 and again in 2006, there were explosive rows, usually instigated by Brown, which undermined and weakened the government. The departure of Mandelson for Brussels was also a blow. The conflict between Blair and Brown was, to a considerable extent, a battle of egos in which the two most powerful men in the New Labour government, aided and abetted by their respective entourages, jockeyed for political position. In his heart, Brown continued to believe, mistakenly as it turned out, that he was better qualified to be Prime Minister and kept pressing Blair to stand down. Blair, increasingly vulnerable because of Iraq, prevaricated. In September 2006, Blair was forced by a Brownite rebellion to announce publicly that he would go the following summer. In this way, Brown got his turn at being Prime Minister for three years, before Labour were defeated in the 2010 election.

This is the story of New Labour, the trio who created it and made it work and the central part which their relationships played in the successes and the failures of the project.

PART 1

ORIGINS: NEW LABOUR'S TRIO

1
PROVENANCE
AND UPBRINGING

Tony Blair

Brown, Blair and Mandelson, all second children, were born between 1951 and 1953 – James Gordon Brown in Govan, Glasgow, on 20 February 1951; Anthony Charles Lynton Blair in Edinburgh on 6 May 1953; and Peter Benjamin Mandelson in Hampstead Garden Suburb, London, on 21 October 1953.

The politics of the 1950s were dominated by the Tories. The reforms of the Attlee Labour administrations from 1945 to 1951 – including the formation of the welfare state and the creation of the National Health Service – had changed the nation's social and political landscape. But, by the beginning of the decade, Labour had run out of steam and ideas and, at the October 1951 general election, despite winning more votes than the Conservatives, was narrowly defeated. The Tories, accepting most of what Labour had done and more in tune with post-war affluence, won three successive elections. The Conservative Prime Minister, Harold Macmillan, summed up the

1950s in his celebrated phrase 'Most of our people have never had it so good.'

Though they were probably not aware of it, the three protagonists of this book would certainly have benefited from the rising standard of living of the 1950s and 1960s, especially the end of food rationing in 1954. But more important for their well-being was that they were brought up in middle-class households. Tony's father, Leo Blair, was an ambitious lecturer in law who was also a barrister; Gordon's father, Dr John Brown, was a highly respected minister in the Church of Scotland; while Peter's father, Tony Mandelson, was the well-paid advertising director of the *Jewish Chronicle*.

Tony Blair's background was different from that of Gordon Brown. Whereas Brown was very much a Scot, rooted in the Scottish church, Scottish education and Scottish politics – especially the Scottish Labour Party and its history – Blair's upbringing was far more rootless and diverse. In 1994, he told the *Observer*, 'I never felt myself very anchored in a particular setting or class'.[1]

In part, this was because of the upward mobility of his father, Leo Blair. Leo had been brought up in Glasgow by foster parents, Glasgow shipyard rigger James Blair and his wife Mary. His real parents were English actors, Charles Parsons (whose stage name was Jimmy Lynton) and Celia Ridgway, who played in comedy, music hall and straight plays in the early 1920s. In August 1923, they had an illegitimate child, Leo, whom they fostered out to the Blairs, a couple they had met while on tour in Glasgow. Leo grew up on Clydeside, becoming secretary of the Govan branch of the Scottish Young Communists (his foster mother, Mary, was a lifelong communist) and working for the communist newspaper, the *Daily Worker*.

It was the Second World War which set Leo Blair on an upward trajectory. He became an officer in the Royal Signals and, though he voted Labour in 1945, by the time he was demobilised in May 1947 he had become a Conservative, attributing his conversion to 'the great change from living in a tenement in Govan to life in the Officers' Mess'.[2] In 1948, he married Tony's mother, Hazel Corscaden, whose Protestant family came from Ballyshannon in County Donegal. Anthony Charles Lynton Blair, as he was called (his middle names were those of his paternal grandfather) was born in Edinburgh in 1953, where his father worked as a junior tax inspector, while studying at night for a law degree at Edinburgh University.

Leo's next career move was to take up a lectureship in administrative law at the University of Adelaide in Australia. Tony's first public performance was remarkably early; on the voyage out, aged eighteen months, and wearing only a nappy, he entertained the first-class passengers on the ocean liner *Iberia* by dancing to the band. According to his father, 'the dance ended only when his nappy dropped to his knees.'[3] After three years in Australia, Leo Blair returned with his young family, now two boys (Tony and his elder brother William) and a girl (his younger sister Sarah), to Durham University, where he had been appointed lecturer in law. As well as lecturing, he read for the Bar and then began to practise as a barrister, also becoming chairman of the local Conservative Association and appearing regularly on regional television. Leo drove himself to the limit. 'I had always had the ambition to be a British MP,' he said, adding, 'Furthermore, my ambition was boundless – I wanted to be Prime Minister.'[4]

He earned a good salary, enough to send both his sons to the Durham Chorister School as day boys. Tony Blair was a successful pupil, good at work and games – in his final year, he won the cup for the best rugger player in the school. It was on 4 July 1964, while he was still at the Chorister School, that his mother broke the devastating news to him that his father had had a severe stroke during the night. With the devoted help of his wife, it took nearly three years for Leo to learn to speak again. According to Tony, the day of his father's stroke was when his childhood ended: 'After his illness my father transferred his ambitions on to his kids. It imposed a certain discipline. I felt I couldn't let him down.'[5] Yet, even though his father's stroke was clearly a key event in his early life, it is probably an exaggeration to say, as does one of his biographers, John Rentoul, that 'Tony Blair's political ambition began at the age of eleven, when his father Leo's ended'.[6] Later developments, particularly his time at Oxford and his marriage to Cherie, were more important.

In 1966, Tony Blair joined his brother Bill at Fettes, a public school in Edinburgh. His father had chosen Fettes because he had read in the *Scottish Field* that it was the 'Eton of Scotland' and felt that his sons would benefit from the conservative, strict boarding-school education which Fettes then provided for the offspring of aspiring parents. Tony did not enjoy Fettes. He had won an exhibition (a minor scholarship) in the school's entrance examination and, for his first year or so, things seem to go well for the younger Blair. He was a diligent pupil, good at games – he played in both the under-14 rugby and cricket sides – and a cheerful 'fag'. 'I remember Blair as very popular,' recalled the older boy for whom Tony fagged, 'running everywhere, very active, slightly immature, engaged all the time in some kind of activity.'[7]

However, at the start of his second year, Tony tried to run away from school. When his parents put him on the Edinburgh train at Newcastle Station, he walked through the carriage and got off again at the other end of the platform. He then went to Newcastle Airport and tried to get on a plane before being rumbled by the airport authorities. They rang the headmaster of Fettes who got in touch with his parents. This was the start of Tony's rebellious phase.

Part of it was dislike of boarding school but, as he became an adolescent, it was also a rejection of the old-fashioned Fettes ethos – the petty rules, the fagging and the beatings. According to one of his contemporaries, 'His tie was always slightly undone, he had dirty shoes, he was questioning things the whole time.' Another said, 'Hair was a big issue. It had to be above the collar and behind the ears. He would put butter and crap on his hair, to grease it down inside the back of the collar.'[8] Even though he was a gifted fly half and had an eye for a cricket ball, he gave up the idea of playing rugby and cricket for the school on the grounds that it was too Establishment. Instead, having grown tall, he took up basketball and became captain of the school team.

Tony's career at Fettes was saved from complete disaster by Eric Anderson, a young master who had returned to the school after a spell at Gordonstoun to set up a new house, Arniston, which was to be run without beating or fagging. Blair eagerly volunteered to join Anderson's new house although, even without fagging, he clashed with the new house-master over the enforcement of rules. Anderson said:

> I got used to a knock at my study door, followed by a grinning Blair face and a fifteen-minute argument about some way of doing things which the school ought, he thought, to change at once. Tony was full of life, maddening at times, pretty full of himself and very argumentative.[9]

Anderson's approach was remarkably advanced for the time. To the headmaster's fury, he even took his entire house to see Lindsay Anderson's film *If*, in the course of which boys in a reactionary boarding school blow up the school and machine-gun their teachers. Eric Anderson intelligently succeeded in channelling some of Blair's energies into acting. In his second year, Tony's Mark Anthony in the house play *Julius Caesar* got good notices and, two years later, with Anderson's encouragement, he formed a group to put on contemporary plays, including works by Pinter and N. F. Simpson. His greatest triumph was playing the part of Captain Stanhope in R. C. Sherriff's *Journey's End*. *The Fettesian* said, 'Arniston were fortunate in having so experienced an actor as Blair for this central figure. From his first entrance . . . Blair brought out the febrile intensity of Stanhope.'[10]

Unfortunately, in Blair's last year, Eric Anderson left to become head-master of Abingdon School. His successor as housemaster, Bob Roberts, was far less sympathetic to Tony and, instead of making him a prefect, beat Blair and two friends for 'persistent defiance'. Even for Fettes, caning seventeen-year-olds was unusual and Tony bitterly resented the harsh way in which he felt he had been treated. Only the intervention of Lord MacKenzie-Stuart, Scottish law lord, school governor and father of Amanda, the first girl to be admitted to Fettes (and also Tony's first girl-friend), prevented him being expelled. MacKenzie-Stuart proposed that Blair should spend the last four weeks after A levels doing social work at a boys' camp on the East Lothian coast.

Three years after leaving the school, Blair was visiting Edinburgh with some Oxford friends. 'We were driving past Fettes and Tony hit the floor-boards,' said one of them. 'There must be something about that place.'[11] If, for Tony, Fettes was largely a negative experience, he took a few posi-tives from the school. The first was getting good enough A-level grades to get him into St John's College, Oxford. The second was finding out, through acting, that he could hold the attention of an audience. The third was learning to think and speak for himself. One of his house tutors said, 'He was always interested in pointing out the defects of the institution of which he was a part, and that kind of analytical stance is probably fundamentally some kind of political stance.'[12]

On the face of it, the years between leaving Fettes and coming down from Oxford (from July 1971 to June 1975) seem to be ones in which nothing much happened in Blair's life. Contrast his 'gap' year between leaving school and going up to Oxford with that of Mandelson. Peter spent a year in the Tanzanian bush, teaching in a village school and helping in a village hospital, while Tony, with a friend, Alan Colonette, tried to promote rock bands in London. At university, Gordon Brown got a bril-liant first in history and was elected student Rector of Edinburgh. Tony Blair's Oxford career was in no way outstanding. He got a good second in law (afterwards he wished he had read history) but he did not become an officer of the Oxford Union (though he once went to hear Michael Heseltine speak) or a leading actor or a successful sportsman. He did not even join the Labour or any other political club.

Even so, his time during these years was not wasted. Although his attempt to launch a career as a rock promoter was a failure, he made a lot of friends. As one of them remarked, 'He had immense charm and maturity for his age.'[13] There is general agreement that he did not 'get into' drugs. His friend, Colonette, said, 'He was fun to be around partly because he had few inhibitions and knew how to have fun instinctively without the need for artificial stimulation.'[14]

In his third year at Oxford, he became the lead singer in a rock group of former public school boys called Ugly Rumours. Tony looked the part – 'long hair, cut-off T-shirt, purple loons and Cuban-heeled cowboy boots and used to come on stage, giving it some serious Mick Jagger, a bit of finger wagging and punching the air.' Though opinions differed on his singing ability, all agreed that he put on a great show. A member of the group said, 'He was quite a good frontman, you know, hip-wiggler in chief.' Another remembered thinking, 'This is no ordinary junior love-god lead singer we have here. Where is this guy going to go?'[15] The group did not last long, playing only half a dozen gigs in its brief career, but Tony the showman was born. A contemporary recalls that he had 'an aura about him even then; people noticed him; he stood out . . . [H]e was already deploying the sort of assets – trendiness and charm – which have been in evidence ever since.'[16]

What was more important to Blair were the beliefs and values that he acquired while he was at Oxford. As often happens with students, a group of friends, including Tony, used to meet in college, two or three times a week, sometimes late at night, to discuss ideas. The leading figure was an Australian, Peter Thomson, a priest in the Anglican Church of Australia, who was a thirty-six-year-old mature student, reading theology. Others included another Australian Geoff Gallop, then a revolutionary Marxist who later became Premier of Western Australia, Olara Otunna, a refugee from Uganda who was to be Ugandan Foreign Minister, David Gardner, later the *Financial Times'* Brussels correspondent, Anwal Velani, an Indian postgraduate student, and Blair's closest friend, Marc Palley, son of the only white Rhodesian MP to oppose Ian Smith. 'It was no accident that most were from abroad and not products of the British class system,' said

Blair.[17] He was particularly drawn to the openness of the two Australians, especially Thomson. Tony described Thomson as 'the person who most influenced' him.[18]

It was in large part because of Thomson that Blair became a Christian Socialist. His Christianity and his politics came together at the same time. Thomson was very enthusiastic about the ideas of a Scottish philosopher, John Macmurray, who argued that individuals can only be understood in terms of their relationship to others. 'I'll tell you, mate,' said Thomson in his Australian way, 'Macmurray is the classic. He changed philosophical thinking. All his philosophy had a practical relevance; he changed the reference from the idea to the real. What he was on about was community. It's about fellowship, friendship, brotherly love.'[19] Tony was very excited by Thomson's description of Macmurray's ideas because it seemed to him to bring together the Christian concept of duty to others with left-of-centre politics and thus provide him with a working set of beliefs to underpin his life and provide a rationale for social action. At the end of his second year, Blair was confirmed in the Church of England at the Chapel of St John's College. Graham Dow, then assistant chaplain to St John's and later Bishop of Carlisle, said: 'He was looking for something that was active, to change society. He gave the impression of someone who had just discovered something exciting and new – he didn't know it all, that's why he was such fun to talk to.'[20]

Two weeks after Blair graduated, his mother, Hazel, died of throat cancer. His parents had kept the seriousness of her condition from him because they did not want to worry him during his exams. After meeting him off the train, his father took him straight to the hospital to see her. It was a great shock to Tony who adored his mother. He remarked later, 'For the first time I felt not so much a sense of ambition as a consciousness that time is short. My life took on an urgency which has probably never left it.'[21]

Following his brother's example, he started reading for the Bar, the one-year training course for barristers. In the autumn, he also joined the

Labour Party. This was very much his own decision. His father, after all, was a strong Conservative, who had wanted to become a Tory MP, and his mother had supported his political stance though, in Tony's view, her social attitudes were not basically Conservative ones. Charles Falconer, an acquaintance from Scotland who, soon after Blair came to London, became a close friend and flatmate of Blair and later one of his Cabinet ministers, explained his decision to join the Labour Party as follows: 'During Oxford and immediately after he became utterly immersed in a sort of Christian spiritual approach for the solutions of social problems . . . He concluded the only way forward was by political action within the confines of conventional politics.'[22] So he not only joined the Labour Party but became a branch secretary with a place on the general management committee of the Chelsea Labour Party, the first rung of the political ladder.

However, for the first few years in London, his priority was making his way in the legal profession. In order to practise as a barrister, a student who passes the Bar exams has to gain work experience as a pupil in a barristers' chambers. Here Blair had a stroke of luck. Through a chance meeting at a party, he got an introduction to Alexander 'Derry' Irvine, a brilliant barrister at a well-known chambers. Irvine was a Scot who had stood for Parliament as a Labour candidate in 1970 and was a close friend of John Smith. Smith had been a Cabinet minister in the Callaghan government and was an increasingly important figure in the party. Irvine had already taken on one pupil, the exceptionally gifted Cherie Booth, but he was bowled over by Tony's enthusiasm and charm and took him on as well.

In effect, over the next year, the two apprentice barristers were to be locked in competition for only one permanent place at Irvine's chambers. Cherie got off to a flying start when she came top in the whole country in the Bar finals, while Tony got only an undistinguished third-class. He later commented that he did not treat the exam with the seriousness it deserved – '[W]ell actually I think I did treat it with the seriousness it deserved but anyway I didn't work particularly hard at it.'[23] Blair then spent the summer in France, which enabled him to pick up a good French accent, while Booth started her pupillage straightaway.

However, at the end of the year in pupillage, Blair was not only awarded the tenancy in Irvine's Chambers but had won the girl as well. Under Irvine's guidance, he proved to be a first-rate lawyer. 'He was very good at getting to the point. He was a fast gun on paper, possessing an excellent facility with the English language.'[24]

Cherie, who had another boyfriend at the time, was initially doubtful about this self-confident public school, Oxford-educated young man. But they grew closer at a Christmas party and, a few weeks later, were taken out to lunch in Covent Garden by Derry Irvine to celebrate the end of a case. 'Derry took us out for lunch, and he disappeared after a time,' explained Blair. 'And I remember we were still there at dinner time, so something must have happened along the way.'[25] Cherie's comment was: 'Once you succumb to Tony's charm, you never really get over it.'[26] They got engaged while on holiday in Italy just after the 1979 election and then were married in St John's College Chapel in March 1981.

Cherie Booth and Derry Irvine were the key figures in giving Tony Blair the self-confidence to try for a parliamentary seat. Cherie's father was the actor, Tony Booth, who became a household name in the 1960s' comedy series, *Till Death us Do Part*. However, Booth, an alcoholic and a womaniser, was an inadequate father and Cherie was brought up by her mother in her grandparents' house in Crosby near Liverpool. It was both a strongly Catholic and strongly Labour household. She was educated at a convent school and joined the Labour Party at the age of sixteen. When she first met him, she was more political than Tony Blair – and probably more left wing. She had parliamentary ambitions of her own and her passionate involvement in and knowledge of politics helped to fire Blair's own interest in getting a seat. They made a pact that whoever won a seat first would become the career politician, while the other would remain at the Bar and become the breadwinner.

Between 1976 and 1982, Derry Irvine was Blair's guide and mentor.

In legal cases, he frequently chose Tony as his junior, giving him the opportunity to hone a fluent, persuasive style in court, something which was also to be useful to him in politics. In chambers, he groomed him intellectually, teaching him to concentrate and develop his thinking power. For the first time, law became interesting and practical for the young man. Although most of Irvine's work was commercial, he encouraged Blair to specialise in employment which was not only close to his interests but also brought him in touch with key figures in the trade unions and the Labour Party – Irvine introduced him to his friend, John Smith, and the two men immediately hit it off. Irvine encouraged Tony to look for a seat although it was likely to take him away from the law.

For a prospective middle-class politician with Blair's outlook, it was a difficult time to be looking for a seat in the Labour Party. Following the 'winter of discontent' in 1978–79, the rash of public sector strikes and Callaghan's resignation as party leader, Michael Foot had narrowly defeated Denis Healey for the party leadership though Healey was far better qualified for the position. Meanwhile the charismatic Tony Benn, with his left-wing economic programme of import controls, public ownership, workers' control and withdrawal from the Common Market, combined with a raft of internal party reforms, swept all before him in the constituencies. In 1981, in a bitterly fought struggle, Healey only just beat Benn for the deputy leadership. Disgusted by Labour's antics, Roy Jenkins, former deputy leader, with the support of Shirley Williams, Bill Rodgers and David Owen amongst the brighter and best of the next generation of potential Labour leaders, broke away to form the Social Democratic Party (SDP).

In a speech given in August 1982 to a university seminar in Perth, Australia, which Tony was visiting with Cherie to meet his Oxford friends, Peter Thomson and Geoff Gallop, Blair gave his views on this chaotic situation.[27] He was highly critical of the SDP breakaway, calling its leaders 'the failed representatives of the old mould'. He attacked the right inside the Labour Party as complacent and out of touch. On the other hand, he was hostile to the Bennites and the hard Trotskyite left, whom he saw as anti-democratic. The way forward for Labour, he argued, anticipating the path pursued by Kinnock as leader in the 1980s, was to reconcile the right with the so-called 'soft left'.

Significantly, even speaking in Australia, he did not say that there should be a change in policies – except to allow the sale of council houses. Blair was attempting to win a seat and an attack on his party's policies, even if, as over Europe and unilateralism, he thought they were both ill advised and unpopular, was not the way to go about it. It was hard enough anyway. He was twice nominated and twice failed to be shortlisted for northern seats, while Cherie Blair tried unsuccessfully to become the Labour candidate for the Crosby by-election, which was sensationally won by Shirley Williams for the SDP. Blair was even turned down for the local council nomination by his branch in Hackney, where the Blairs now lived.

In spring 1982, encouraged by Derry Irvine, John Smith and Tom Pendry, Labour MP and friend of Cherie's father, Blair had put his name forward for the Beaconsfield by-election and won the nomination. It was a Tory safe seat and the by-election was fought against the background of the Falklands War so there was no chance of a Labour victory. The Labour candidate kept his head down on policy – even on the European issue though he had voted 'yes' in the 1975 referendum. He did, however, take a stand by ensuring that Tony Benn did not come to speak for him. The result was a poor one with Labour coming in third and losing their deposit. However, nobody blamed Tony. Indeed, he made a highly favourable impression on Labour's leading politicians who came down to support him while the sheer excitement of politics and his ability to handle all the pressure convinced him more than ever that his future lay at Westminster. But the question of how to get there remained.

Then a year later, when the 1983 general election campaign had already begun and against all the odds, Tony Blair was chosen for the safe seat of Sedgefield in County Durham. He had despaired of obtaining a seat and had reconciled himself to acting as consort for Cherie, who had been selected for the unwinnable seat of Thanet North, when he heard that Sedgefield, a constituency which had been recreated by boundary changes, had yet to select a candidate. I was a Durham MP at the time and, when I met Blair in London, he had impressed me. So, following my intervention, the TGWU regional secretary, Joe Mills, decided to give the young lawyer (who was a T&G member) the union's support. However, very few of the union's branches were affiliated to the constituency party and there were even fewer union delegates. Blair could not win with trade union votes alone. If he was to gain the Sedgefield nomination, he would have to get the backing of the ordinary branch members.

In a whirlwind campaign, he proceeded to win their support. To begin with, after gaining the help of five local activists, including John Burton who was to become his constituency agent, he was nominated by the only branch, Trimdon, which had not yet decided. Then the executive, which was dominated by the left, kept Tony, as well as others (including a former Cabinet minister as well as a local MP) off the shortlist. So the next move was to get the larger general committee to add Blair to the shortlist of six which, following a short but effective intervention by Burton, was narrowly achieved. Finally, at the selection meeting, Blair spoke last but with fire and vigour. According to Burton, he was 'brilliant, excellent – energetic and alive with ideas'. The leading left-wing candidate and his main rival, the MP Leslie Huckfield, was bombarded with difficult questions, designed to highlight his connections with the Trotskyite Militant Tendency, and he fluffed his answers to them. When it came to the voting, Blair, whose speech had won over a number of delegates initially committed to other candidates, triumphed on the fifth ballot. At the general election, on 9 June, Blair was returned to Parliament with a majority of 8281. Through a combination of luck, hard work, skill and charm, he had made it to Westminster with a safe seat, very much in extra time, a remarkable achievement for an outsider, who was a complete newcomer to Labour politics.

2

PROVENANCE AND UPBRINGING

Gordon Brown

Gordon's early life was shaped by his father and his father's calling. In 1954, the Browns moved to Kirkcaldy, then a depressed town on the northern shore of the Firth of Forth, where John Brown became minister at St Brycedale Church.[1] The three Brown boys, John, Gordon and Andrew, grew up in a manse which was as much an advice and drop-in centre as a family home. 'There was always a constant stream of people passing through our front door,' said Gordon.[2] Gordon loved his mother, Elizabeth, who was the daughter of a west Aberdeenshire builder, but it was his father who made the greatest impression on him: 'First, for speaking without notes in front of so many people in that vast church . . . But mostly, I have learned a great deal from what my father managed to do for other people. He taught me to treat everyone equally.'[3]

In Scotland, especially for a son of the manse, education was paramount. A year early, at the age of four, Gordon was sent to the local primary school. Murray Elder, a classmate of Gordon, now in the House of Lords, said, 'They taught us to read and write, in the vigorous old way that Scottish schools did quite well before they became trendy.'[4] Gordon was an exceptionally precocious pupil, being rapidly promoted up the school. At the age of ten, he went on to Kirkcaldy High School where, together with Murray Elder, he was put in the so-called 'E stream', an experimental scheme of fast-track development for the brightest boys and girls which, a few years later, Gordon described in an essay as a 'ludicrous experiment in education'.[5]

At the age of twelve, he had to decide in which subject he should specialise and Gordon Brown chose history. At fourteen, he passed eight O levels and, at fifteen, he got five straight As in his Highers (the Scottish equivalent of A levels). At sixteen – when, according to Gordon, he had 'more problems than he had years'[6] – he passed the Edinburgh University entrance exam, being placed first in history in the bursary competition. The gifted young Brown was able to benefit, at least academically, from the experiment but other pupils fell by the wayside. In his essay, he asked the question: 'Surely it is better for children to succeed at school, and leave with some qualifications for work, rather than endure failure, ignominy, rejection and at the least strain, for the ironic reason of averting failure at university?'[7]

If this judgement reveals a sixteen-year-old with a social conscience, his classmates remember a lively, gregarious, friend: '[I]n our class it was Gordon who set the pace, and the rest of us would do our best to keep up . . . socially, as well as academically. He was so sharp . . . Gordon was always the quickest to come out with a funny line and would soon have the rest of us doubled over in laughter.'[8] Brown was also a good all-round athlete, excelling at tennis, running, football and rugby.

It was during a rugby match between the Kirkcaldy School XV and the old boys that he received a kick on the head that led to him becoming blind in one eye. For some months, he unwisely tried to ignore the injury. Then, three days after he went up to university, he went to a doctor who referred him immediately to a specialist. He was taken into the Edinburgh

Royal Infirmary for a lengthy operation to reattach a detached retina but it was too late to save the sight of the left eye and, over the next eighteen months, he had to have two further operations to save his right eye.

It is difficult to assess the long-term impact of such a traumatic experience on Brown. Immediately, he was forced to miss the whole of his first term and was forbidden to read. A less determined person might have allowed the accident to affect the course of his life. Instead, Gordon became more rather than less single-minded – a young man very much in a hurry. He was awarded a general arts degree at the age of nineteen and, in 1972, aged twenty one, he graduated with first-class honours in history with, according to one of his tutors, the best collection of papers the department had ever seen.[9] It was to be nine years, however, before he completed his doctoral thesis on the rise of the Labour Party in Scotland between 1918–29, which he later expanded into a biography of James Maxton, the left-wing Labour MP and romantic rebel.

At Edinburgh University, he began his ascent to political stardom by becoming a celebrated, long-haired student activist, one much feared by the university Establishment. The period of the late sixties and early seventies was a time of student unrest across Europe and, at Edinburgh, Brown was in the thick of it. In his second year, he became editor of the student magazine, *The Student*. As editor, he soon found himself in possession of a major scoop. The principal, Professor Michael Swann, a prominent supporter of the Anti-Apartheid Movement, had recently assured the University Court that the university did not invest in companies known to have links with apartheid. But a report of its investments, leaked to the student magazine, revealed half a million pounds in shares in South African mining companies, such as De Beers. A four-page 'Student Special' was quickly distributed round the campus and an energetic campaign launched. Swann was forced to change stockbrokers and sell the shares. Brown later commented on his first political victory, 'It was exposure that got results; you didn't need a sit-in. It was so embarrassing for them to be caught not telling the truth.'[10]

His second triumph was being elected as student rector. In Scottish universities, the rector is obliged by university statute to represent the voice of students. But usually a celebrity figure from the media, the stage or politics was elected, who did not take the position too seriously. For example in 1968, Malcolm Muggeridge, the writer and broadcaster, who had been elected as rector, denounced, like a later-day John Knox, student immorality from the pulpit of St Giles' Cathedral and promptly resigned. Brown argued that a student rector would be more closely in touch with student views. Cautiously, he backed a friend, a geography student called Jonathan Wills, to be the first student candidate. But, after winning the election, Wills served only a year before resigning. Brown was widely supported as his successor, even receiving the backing of the president of the Tory club. Gordon's campaign against Sir Fred Catherwood, former industrial adviser to the Labour Cabinet Minister, and Deputy Leader George Brown had plenty of razzmatazz, with T-shirts inscribed 'Gordon for me' and posters featuring mini-skirted girls called 'Brown's Sugars', after 'Brown Sugar' by the Rolling Stones from the 1971 album *Sticky Fingers*,[11] and he won by a big margin, with more than 60 per cent of the vote.

In contrast to most of his predecessors, Brown characteristically took the rectorship extremely seriously, energetically pursuing student issues and trying to open up the university to the wider community. To the horror of its Establishment members, Brown used his chairmanship of the University Court to take over the agenda of its meetings, as well as issuing press releases in its name. When one such release was torn up by the university authorities, he denounced the action in *The Student* as political censorship of the lowest and most dreadful sort. In April 1973, the university authorities decided to move against Brown – two members of the Court, who were among Scotland's most senior judges, proposed a rule change to end the rector's right to chair Court meetings. They also tried to exclude Allan Drummond, who Brown had appointed as one of his assessors, on the grounds that he had been involved in an occupation of his college.

Brown's response was intelligently measured. Instead of trying to lead a sit-in or occupation, so fashionable amongst students at the time, he took the judges to court and won. In the Court of Session, Lord Keith ruled that the rector had correctly interpreted the university's constitution – he had the right to choose his own assessor who could not be arbitrarily excluded. When Principal Swann tried to get the support of the university's Chancellor, the Duke of Edinburgh, for an appeal to the Privy Council, the duke's view was that the rector had the right to chair the Court. It was rumoured that Gordon Brown's girlfriend at the time, Princess Margarita of Romania, an Edinburgh student who was Prince Philip's goddaughter, had successfully lobbied him.

At Edinburgh, Gordon Brown was a glamorous figure who, with his long hair and good looks, was very attractive to women. He threw a number of parties in his notoriously untidy flat. An invitation to his New Year party was especially sought after. His most long-standing girlfriend, Princess Margarita of Romania, a dark-haired beauty, was the eldest daughter of the exiled King Michael and related to Britain's royal family. She was studying sociology and politics at Edinburgh and, like Gordon, was involved in student politics, especially the movement to elect a student rector. Their relationship lasted for five years. 'It was a very solid and romantic story', Margarita subsequently told *Harpers and Queen*. 'I never stopped loving him, but one day it didn't seem right any more. It was politics, politics, politics, and I needed nurturing.'[12] This was to be a pattern in Gordon's relationships until he married Sarah Macaulay in 2000. He was attracted to as well as attractive to women and, over the years, had a number of long-term relationships but, such was his obsession with politics that, in the end, he was unwilling to commit himself until he was nearly fifty.

With the settlement of this dispute with the University Court and the departure of Swann in September 1973 to become chairman of the governors of the BBC, it was time to compromise. Brown persuaded his opponents on the Court to bring in more junior academic staff and to give students a seat as of right. In return, he accepted a change of rule that students would no longer be allowed to stand for rector. Imaginatively, Brown also set up a commission to consider ways of involving the university in the community, including the admission of more mature and part-time students and stronger links between the university and local schools.

In retrospect, Brown felt the amount of time he spent on student politics was wasted and regretted the enemies he made in the university establishment. He commented, 'It was quite a revelation to me to see how politics was less about ideals and more about manoeuvres.'[13] Yet, albeit on a small canvas, he learnt something about politics – the presentation of speeches, how to write articles and press releases and the mechanics of mobilising support and coalitions, all of which were to prove useful to him when, following the end of his turn of office in the summer of 1975, he turned to politics proper.

It was almost inevitable that Brown should join the Labour Party. Above all, there was the influence of his father. It was not that the Reverend Brown was a committed member of the Labour Party though he certainly voted Labour in 1945 and on other occasions as well. It was more the impact of his example and his sustained interest in community affairs. As an eight-year-old, Gordon and his elder brother, John, were allowed to stay up late to listen to the results of the 1959 election when, to his parents' sadness, Gaitskell and the Labour Party were defeated. A few years later, when staying with his parents on his cousin's farm in Perthshire, he was a fascinated observer of the Kinross and West Perthshire by-election at which Sir Alec Douglas-Home, the Tory successor as Prime Minister to Harold Macmillan, was returned to the House of Commons, after having renounced his peerage. Following Sir Alec from village to village, the twelve-year-old Gordon heard the Tory politician repeat the same speech time after time. When asked whether he would be buying a house in the constituency, the former earl replied he would not as he had too many houses already. The young Gordon was suitably shocked by his response.

At university, despite his disappointment with the Wilson government, Brown joined the Labour Party and was elected chairman of the Labour Club. In the 1970 general election, which Labour lost, Gordon and his friends went to help a former Edinburgh student activist and then Workers' Educational Association (WEA) lecturer, the able Robin Cook, in his unsuccessful bid to win Edinburgh North. And, in the two general elections of 1974, Brown acted as subagent for Cook (later to be Brown's Cabinet colleague as Foreign Secretary) in his successful campaign to become Labour MP for Edinburgh Central. But Brown had his own ambitions and, over the next decade, concentrated on building up his reputation as a rising politician.

Overall, the history of the 1970s' Wilson and Callaghan governments was dominated by economic crises but, in Scotland, the main issue was devolution and, as one political commentator wrote, away from Westminster Brown became devolution's leading advocate.[14] At the October 1974 election, eleven Scottish National Party MPs were elected. The Scottish Secretary, Willie Ross, supported by most of the other Scottish Labour MPs, was utterly opposed to nationalism and to an elected assembly. But younger Labour activists, led by Brown, believed there was a strong case for a devolved Scottish Parliament. In a last blast as student rector, the twenty-four-year-old Brown edited a series of essays entitled *The Red Paper on Scotland*. His introduction, 'The Socialist Challenge', was well researched though very much a modishly leftist tract, arguing for a massive extension of nationalisation, a planned economy and a move towards workers' control. In somewhat obscure language, he called for 'a coherent strategy with rhythm and modality to each reform to cancel the logic of capitalism and a programme of immediate aims which leads out of one social order into another'. Only here and there were there what later became Brownite themes – for example, he spoke of 'the gap between what people are and what they may have it in themselves to become'. And, throughout the essays, as well as in Brown's introduction, there was support for devolution.[15]

In 1976, Brown was elected to the executive of the Scottish Labour

Party. Then, in 1978, aged only twenty-seven, he was chosen to chair the Scottish party's Devolution Committee, working closely with John Smith, the minister responsible for the legislation. The journalist, Neal Ascherson, called him 'the outstanding Scot of his generation'. Here is Gordon as recalled by friends at the time:

> a prodigious worker, attending meetings three nights a week and devoting all his weekends to political activity . . . [H]e carried around plastic bags stuffed with newspaper cuttings and statistical papers on issues close to his heart. Faced with an awkward question, he would fish about in the pile of documents and triumphantly pull out facts and figures to prove his point.[16]

Already, he was something of an obsessive, committed above all to Labour politics and Scottish devolution.

Brown worked tirelessly for a 'yes' vote in the referendum campaign, addressing thirty meetings in its final seven days. But the government was unpopular and the Labour Party itself divided, with Robin Cook, whom Brown had worked so hard to get into Parliament, a prominent opponent of devolution. It was to be many years before the rift between Brown and Cook, which opened up then, was to be healed. On 2 March 1979, the 'yes' camp won a narrow victory but it fell a long way short of the requirement of the devolution legislation that 40 per cent of all those entitled to vote had to vote 'yes' in order for an assembly to be set up in Edinburgh. The SNP withdrew their support for the minority Labour government and, on 29 March, on a confidence motion, the Callaghan administration was defeated by one vote.

Five weeks later, Mrs Thatcher won the ensuing general election. Brown stood as the Labour candidate for Edinburgh South, a Tory-held marginal, and was defeated by 2,460 votes. In May 1978, a more tempting prospect had been dangled before him when the MP for Hamilton died, thus creating a by-election in a Labour stronghold. Gordon's parents were living in the town, as Reverend Brown had moved to St John's Church there. Seven local branches invited Brown to stand for nomination but he felt he had an obligation to the Edinburgh South Party. There was the additional factor, which Brown must also have taken into account, that the strongest union in the area, the General and Municipal Workers, was backing a union official, George Robertson, who had recently been chairman of the Scottish Labour Party and was later to become Defence Secretary in Blair's government and Secretary General of NATO. Deciding that discretion was the better part of valour, Brown pulled out. Given there was no certainty that he would have won the nomination, it was probably the right decision. All the same, it was an opportunity which he turned down.

Brown had to wait four more years until the 1983 general election to become an MP. For employment, he turned to the media. In 1980, Brown, who had been a part-time lecturer at Glasgow College of Technology (to his disappointment he had failed to obtain a full-time post at Edinburgh University), joined Scottish Television as a programme producer, first covering politics then consumer issues. In the television age, it was an appropriate training for a future MP and Cabinet minister. If nothing else, it taught him about sound bites. He also completed his thesis, entitled *The Labour Party and Political Change in Scotland, 1918–29*. It was 532 pages long and described Labour's struggle to establish itself as the alternative to the Conservatives in Scotland.

Arguably, it was a good time for a promising young politician to be out of Parliament as the Labour Party descended into civil war and some of the most prominent right-wing Labour MPs broke away to form the Social Democratic Party (SDP), leaving the political field to Mrs Thatcher. Though communists were well entrenched in the unions, the hard left in its Bennite or Trotskyite form was weaker in Scotland than in England. The prevailing orthodoxy was Tribunite centre left – very much in tune with Brown's position at the time. On the Scottish Executive, Gordon Brown spoke up for the Foot–Healey leadership against attacks by George Galloway, Benn's chief henchman, and reminded him of the obvious point: '[W]e need to win the support of the voters. Anything which prevents this and which puts the relationship between the party and the trade unions in jeopardy is not only needless but harmful.'[17] Without aligning himself with the Scottish Labour Right and MPs such as John Smith, Donald Dewar and George Robertson, Brown was revealing himself as a pragmatic loyalist, with contacts across the Scottish Labour Party. Brought up by his father as an egalitarian, he was in politics not to be a romantic rebel, like his hero James Maxton, but, by winning power both for himself and his party, to make a real difference.

His reward came at the eleventh hour when, on 16 May 1983, he won the Labour nomination for the newly created 'safe' seat of Dunfermline East in the heart of the former Fife coalfields, near his home town of Kirkcaldy. He owed his victory not so much to his undoubted eloquence but, above all, to the crucial support of the Transport and General Workers, whose boss in Scotland, Hugh Wyper, was a communist. On the 9 June, Brown romped home in Dunfermline East with 51.5 per cent of the votes. But Mrs Thatcher won a crushing general election victory. One of his friends reported finding the new MP sitting in front of the TV at one o'clock in the morning, utterly dejected: 'He had just achieved something he'd worked on for a decade, but victory had turned to ashes as he watched Thatcher's rout of Michael Foot's Labour Party.'[18]

3

PROVENANCE
AND UPBRINGING

Peter Mandelson

Unlike Tony Blair or even Gordon Brown, Peter Mandelson could genuinely claim to be born into the Labour Party. His grandfather was Herbert Morrison, Lord President of the Council, Leader of the House of Commons and Foreign Secretary, London's local government supremo and one of the giants of the Attlee government. His mother, Mary, Morrison's only child, was a party member though, like many children with political fathers, the experience put her off politics for life. His father, Tony (as he was always called), was more active, with friends on the Left of the party, including their neighbour in Hampstead Garden Suburb, Harold Wilson. He would often attend Labour Party conferences as an observer. In October 1964, his father, with Peter and his elder brother, Miles, watched Harold and Mary Wilson leaving Hampstead Garden Suburb for Downing Street after Labour's general election victory. The following year, the Mandelsons were invited to Number Ten as the Prime Minister's guests to watch the Trooping of the Colour.

Herbert Morrison only occasionally visited his daughter and her family. His first marriage to Mary's mother, Margaret, had been unhappy and, after her death in 1953 four months before Peter's birth, Morrison married Edith, a vivacious Lancastrian who played golf and showed no interest in his family by his first marriage. Peter, who enjoyed his famous grandfather's visits, had memories of the elder statesman 'steaming up in his little Morris car, bow tie, grey hair . . . to lunch . . . [He] always tucked his napkin into his collar'.[1] The young Mandelson was once upset when Morrison, dropping in on his daughter, failed to stay until Peter got back from school, especially when his mother said, 'I don't expect we shall ever see him again.'[2] She was right. Morrison died in hospital of a cerebral haemorrhage on 6 March 1965. To their dismay, the first the Mandelsons heard of his death was on the ITN news.

Peter was closer to his mother than his father. His elder brother said that they were in tune with each other on both an emotional and intellectual level. They were also physically demonstrative towards each other. Peter described her as 'quiet, elegant, gracious, softly spoken but with tremendous steel'.[3] He called her 'duchess'. Apparently, she was the one with the moral authority in the home. Peter quipped that she taught them manners while his father taught them how to break the rules.

Peter's father, the good-looking and debonair Tony Mandelson, was far more extrovert than Mary. To his colleagues at the *Jewish Chronicle*, 'Mandy' (as he, like his son, was called) was an operator and a showman, who always wore a carnation in his buttonhole. At home, Peter's school friends were much taken with his amusing father, especially appreciating the bottle of wine on the dinner table. In the war, he had ended up as a major in the 1st Royal Dragoons, claiming to be the first allied soldier to enter Denmark. He was proud to be one of the few Jewish members of the Cavalry Club. As sometimes happens in relationships between son and father, Peter, as he grew up, was often irritated by Tony Mandelson's jokey manner and, later, by what he felt was his father's self-indulgent left-wing views.

Peter was brought up in a comfortable middle-class home. As he told the actor, Stephen Fry:

> All the things I had I want others to have. I had caring parents, a strong start, discipline instilled, a nice roof over my head. I didn't want for books or encouragement or somewhere to do my homework, friends, leisure time or travel. I want others to have this.[4]

In the 1960s, the Mandelson family took holidays abroad. Peter's father bought stylish, quite expensive cars such as a Sunbeam Rapier Coupe and an Alfa Romeo Giulia, and, when they reached eighteen, bought cars for his sons – in Peter's case, a second-hand Morris 1100. The Mandelsons were well off. In addition to his salary, Tony Mandelson had inherited money from his father, Norman Mandelson, who had also worked for the *Jewish Chronicle*. With his inheritance, he bought the Hampstead Garden Suburb house and helped finance the family's lifestyle. However, he also carefully invested the rest.

Peter's family remember him as a humorous, self-confident little boy, 'the opposite', according to his brother, 'of a shrinking violet'.[5] Apparently, he was always focused and, even as a small boy, very much in control. His mother described him to *Punch* as a boy who organised his friends and was likely to be successful: 'He knew what he wanted to do and did it.'[6]

Significantly, the Mandelsons did not send their two children to private schools though they probably could have afforded to do so. As members of the Labour Party, they chose state schools. Their two boys first went to Hampstead Garden Suburb Primary and then to Hendon County Grammar School, both excellent schools.

Peter was almost instantly a success at Hendon. After his second term, his form master said that he had shown initiative and sense of responsibility and had made an excellent form captain. Academically, he did well at English and history. By the end of the fourth year, the headmaster was wondering whether he would get the high grades necessary for an application to Oxford or Cambridge. He was not a sports star though, when he was fifteen, he made a very efficient manager of the school athletics team. Outside school, he was an enthusiastic Scout, becoming a troop leader.

He did not get involved in politics until his O-level year, when he formed a friendship with Steve Howell, whose mother was a keen Labour Party member. Howell described Peter as 'much more mature than other people in the year. I remember he used to spend time chatting with teachers on almost equal terms.'[7] Howell also noted another Mandelson characteristic – he liked gossiping about other people. He knew all the names of Labour MPs, some of whom he had met with his parents. Once, in 1969, he had an argument with his geography teacher about Wilson's abandonment of *In Place of Strife*, Barbara Castle's proposed legislation on union reform. Peter was impressed by the teacher's hostility to the climb-down and, as he left the classroom, he had an uncomfortable feeling that the Labour government had 'blown it', an early sign of his political antennae.

On 6 March 1970, with Steve Howell and Keran Abse (daughter of the playwright Dannie Abse and niece of the Labour MP, Leo Abse) Mandelson set up the Hendon Young Socialists: Peter was chairman, Steve secretary and Keran social secretary. It was the first time he had formed part of a close-knit trio. Chairman Mandelson told the meeting of twenty-seven YS members: 'We must be a group of action, action in that having discussed, we must make our feelings heard and felt.' Peter took it all very seriously. In their YS magazine, an editorial from Mandelson told his readers (presumably the other YS members): 'Our principal aim is to follow clause four [the commitment to common owner-ship which he helped to replace twenty-five years later] but if we are func-tioning with no purpose, to no aim, then it is hardly worth functioning at all. We might as well pack up and go home. Think on it.'[8]

Hendon County was a selective grammar school and Peter and his YS friends, acting in support of the Labour government's Department of Education circular calling for the abolition of selection, campaigned for a proposal to merge Hendon County with a nearby secondary modern. The plan was implemented a year later. Mandelson and Howell also took part in a revolt to end the prefect system and abolish school uniform for all six formers. The school authorities gave way and the prefect system was replaced by a rota of duties to be shared among all the six formers. Mandelson initially had misgivings about the revolt but went along with the majority of rebels.

Then at the beginning of 1971, Mandelson, Howell and Abse became disillusioned with the Young Socialists and joined the Young Communist League. Their move may partly have been dictated by political events such as the defeat of Labour in the 1970 election and the long-running American involvement in Vietnam. But, in Peter's case, it may also have been adolescent striking of attitudes, with the desire to have no enemies on the Left. By the time Mandelson left school, he had tired of selling the *Morning Star* and, as he left for a gap year in Tanzania, he asked his mother to tear up his membership card – it could have been either of the Young Communist League or even of the party itself. His brief flirtation with communism was over. It had done him no harm. His career at Hendon had been a success – his A-level grades were good enough to earn him acceptance at St Catherine's College, Oxford, to read Politics, Philosophy and Economics (PPE) and he had also ended up by becoming chairman of the school council or head boy.

For his gap year, Trevor Huddleston, Bishop of Stepney (to whom he had enterprisingly written asking for help and advice), arranged for him to work with the diocesans missions in rural Tanzania. In East Africa, he planted gum trees, constructed chicken cages and drove for the local Rural Aid Centre. He even acted as a medical aide to a missionary surgeon, operating a large cylinder of ether and sometimes even reading out sections of Bailey and Love's *Book of Surgery* to the surgeon as he operated.

In long letters home to his parents and his school friends, he recounted his experiences and also discussed his political and even religious views. He told Steve Howell that the deeply committed Christians with whom he was working 'are all genuinely much happier than anyone we know, having an incredible gift for life and are actually very moral and "good" people.'[9] But he wrote to Trevor Huddleston that he was not yet convinced by Christianity. He was impressed by the so-called 'Tanzanian socialism', inspired by the Tanzanian leader, Julius Nyerere, then thought of as the conscience of Black Africa. He could see that this kind of socialism was not applicable to an advanced society like Britain's but was not clear what was required in his own country. Revolution could lead to more misery. Yet could the Labour Party in Parliament, he asked himself, put right the injustices and unnecessary poverty which marred British society?

Mandelson went up to Oxford in October in 1973. In his own eyes, he felt that he was not particularly successful at university: 'You can either be a success socially, in the Union Society or academically and I fell between three stools.'[10] In fact, he got a respectable second, despite failing his Politics prelims, and the master of St Catherine's, the historian Alan Bullock, with whom Peter became friendly, thought that, if he had worked harder, he could have got a first. He was also president of the Junior Common Room at St Catherine's College, a post which taught him something about negotiation. It was after a student sit-in in the senior common room that he negotiated a package with Bullock which gave undergraduates more influence in the running of the college.

Mandelson was not involved in either the Oxford Union which he found too socially exclusive or the Labour Club which he felt was peopled by 'hacks, obsessed with running slates and stuffing ballot papers'.[11] His friends, mostly second-year students at St Catherine's who included Dick Newby (now a Liberal Democrat peer) and David Cockroft (who became an international trade union official) persuaded him to join Young European Left (YEL), a small pro-European group, and the United Nations Students' Association. Partly as a consequence, Peter's political stance became increasingly pro-European and moderate Labour. He had been pro-Zionist when he came up to Oxford but a trip to the Middle East in the summer vacation of 1974 (financed by a Cadbury grant) convinced him of the case for an independent Palestinian state on the West Bank and Gaza. He confided to one of his friends his ambition for a political career, hopefully ending up as Foreign Secretary, as his grandfather had been.

At Oxford, Mandelson may not have been a social 'star' but he certainly had a busy social life. His friends included a number of women, including Venetia Porter, daughter of Robert Porter, chief economist at the Ministry of Overseas Development, and Jenny Jeger, a YEL student at Hull University and niece of the Labour MP, Lena Jeger. In his third year, together with another friend, he shared a house with Venetia Porter. She said of him at that time, 'You definitely had the sense that he was somebody quite powerful. You know what it's like at university – you gravitate towards those people who seem to be somebody, who are interesting, who you want to be with.'[12]

As with all his female friends, Mandelson's relationship with Venetia was platonic. Though he did not deliberately conceal his sexual preference at Oxford, he did not flaunt it either. Dick Newby, his fellow student at St Catherine's, apparently never knew that he was gay while, according to her contemporaries, Jenny Jeger fell so much in love with Peter that she (though not Peter) considered marriage. In a less liberal age than now, coming to terms with his sexuality was always going to be difficult for Peter and his friends, both personally and politically.

In 1977, Mandelson got his first full-time job working in the Economic Department of the TUC under David Lea (now Lord Lea) and with his friend from Oxford, David Cockroft, as a colleague. Alan Bullock, who was one of his referees and was then chairing the committee on industrial democracy set up by the Labour government, obviously had a hand in his appointment. This post in the most important department of the TUC, at a time when the trade unions were a real power in the land, both industrial and politically, was very much a feather in Mandelson's cap. Yet his future at the TUC was soon under threat.

Mandelson's involvement in YEL at Oxford had led to him being appointed first vice chairman and then chairman of the British Youth Council (BYC), a mainly government funded umbrella organisation of various youth groups, which included the National Union of Students, the Young Conservatives, the Girl Guides and the Young Communist League. His chairmanship of the BYC brought him into contact with the leadership of the National Union of Students, including a former president, Charles Clarke (later to be a Labour Cabinet minister), and David Aaronovitch (then a Communist Party member, now a leading journalist). Aaronovitch described being exposed to the force of Mandelson's charm: 'You have this man who seems to be quite an old man in organisational terms . . . who at the same time is immensely funny, attentive, malicious, witty, always has a funny story to tell everyone, and is always slightly disconcerting because there is a kind of probing.'[13]

Through his chairmanship of the BYC, Peter met Labour Cabinet ministers. One of the BYC's sponsoring departments was the Department of Education and Science, whose Secretary of State was Shirley Williams. Clever, charming and charismatic and with a deep husky voice, in the 1970s she was the darling of the Labour moderates and talked about as a future Labour Prime Minister. Like many others, Mandelson fell under her spell.[14]

He was also invited to 10 Downing Street to meet the Prime Minister, James Callaghan, to discuss a BYC report called 'Youth Unemployment: Cause and Cures'. The report had been produced by a group of which Mandelson was research secretary; he was also the report's main author. In later life, he would often say that it was the best thing he ever did. In terms of policy formation, it was certainly superior to anything produced by either Brown or Blair at that time. It was hard hitting, constructive and imaginative. As befitted a time of economic crisis and growing unemployment, it recommended measures to expand the manufacturing, extractive and construction industries. Perhaps its most significant proposals were those on training and skills, including an ambitious guarantee of vocational training for the first two years of employment and grants for all school leavers. Callaghan, alerted by his political secretary, Tom McNally (now leader of the Liberal Democrats in the Lords), was interested in talking to its authors. Mandelson fully grasped the political opportunity which the invitation to meet the Prime Minister presented and was determined to accept.

The idea that junior backroom staff should go to 10 Downing Street to discuss employment issues with James Callaghan was anathema to TUC bureaucrats who were themselves (with the exception of the general secretary) unable even to speak at meetings of the TUC Economic Committee of top trade union leaders. The general secretary, Len Murray, was prepared to agree (but only as an exception) that two members of the Economic Department should meet the Prime Minister. The meeting took place and, far from curtailing his activities on the BYC and a related youth unemployment pressure group, Youth Aid, on whose governing body he also sat, it stimulated Mandelson to increase his public role and his links with Number Ten. In February 1978, he wrote to the Prime Minister, criticising the education service for not doing more for non-academic sixteen–nineteen-year-olds and, three months later, he send a letter to Tom McNally, proposing a committee of inquiry into youth issues. Self-confidently, he told McNally that the Prime Minister 'will want to be seen caring about vandalism and hooliganism' and concluded, somewhat presumptuously, 'You should know that the BYC is – or rather I am – playing with the idea of asking the PM to receive a young people's delegation at No. Ten.'[15]

By now, Mandelson had realised that the conflict between his two positions could only be resolved by giving up one of them. In June, he told his immediate boss in the economic department that he intended to leave the TUC and seek another year as BYC chairman because 'there is a great need at present for political continuity in the leadership of the BYC and I am personally identified with and committed to the developments we are pushing forward in the BYC'; and, in August, he gave in his notice to Len Murray, though regretted having to leave the TUC.[16] This intriguing episode illustrates two underlying themes in Mandelson's career: the first is the tension between the role of the backroom adviser, which he was so often to play in the future, and that of public advocate or representative, to which he also continued to be attracted; the second is the self-confidence which he was already displaying and which was to be such a feature of the Mandelson style of politics.

If Peter Mandelson was expecting his chairmanship of the BYC to provide the key to his future, he was to be disappointed. He carried out his duties with energy and flair. These included leading a BYC delegation to the World Youth Festival in Cuba, managing to unite the group behind a liberal democratic stance, as well as carrying a lone Union Jack amid the banners with communist or anti-imperialist slogans at the opening ceremony, and learning how to brief the press. But the fall of the Labour government in March 1979 and the subsequent civil war between Left and Right inside the Labour Party and the SDP breakaway created a new situation in which Mandelson, unlike Blair or Brown, was to be fully involved.

In 1979, he moved into a flat at Vanbrugh Court in Lambeth. His grandfather, Herbert Morrison, had been born in the borough at 240 Ferndale Road, Brixton, and, according to Charles Clarke, photographs and cartoons of the London Labour leader decorated the walls of his flat.[17] Later that year, there was a council vacancy in the Stockwell ward where the local Labour Party was relatively mainstream. The constituency party was dominated by an alliance between Trotskyites and Bennites, while the leader of the council was 'Red Ted' Knight, who had been a member of the Trotskyite Workers Revolutionary Party and espoused a policy of raising both spending and rates, irrespective of the circumstances and even if it brought the council into open conflict with the Conservative government. Mandelson was put up as candidate by the Stockwell ward and won the by-election.

He spent twenty-nine months on the council experiencing at first hand the behaviour of the hard Left. According to his allies, he bravely stood his ground in the Labour group, though his open rebellion against the Labour whip was infrequent – if he had revolted more often, he would have been expelled from the group. However, he increasingly attacked Knight in the press. For example, when, after the Brixton riots in April 1981, Knight called for the police to withdraw from Brixton, Mandelson commented that, '[g]iven the choice between having the Labour party and Ted Knight in the borough or the police, 99 per cent of the population would vote for the police'.[18]

His appointment in the autumn of 1980 as researcher to Albert Booth, the modest and unassuming shadow Transport Secretary who was a close ally of Michael Foot, brought Mandelson to the centre of Labour politics, albeit at a very junior level. He had tried to secure a similar post with the shadow Education Secretary Neil Kinnock (which went to Charles Clarke) but was content to work with Booth and his team, which included John Prescott, a rising trade union MP, and Geoffrey Robinson, a former businessman and MP for Coventry North West. The two big political events inside the Labour Party were the narrow defeat of Healey by Foot in the leadership election of 10 November 1980 following Callaghan's resignation and the even narrower victory of Healey over Benn for the deputy leadership on 27 September 1981. The first resulted in the SDP breakaway, led by Jenkins, Williams, Owen and Rodgers; the second, by stopping Benn in his tracks, effectively limited the size of the breakaway. Arguably by beating Benn, however narrowly, Healey saved the Labour Party.[19]

Mandelson became involved in the struggle for the deputy leadership through his contacts with the Hattersley office. Working on the shadow Cabinet corridor, he had got to know both David Hill, the experienced aide to Roy Hattersley, and Hattersley (then shadow Home Secretary and later Deputy Leader of the Labour Party) himself. Through them, he joined the Labour Solidarity campaign, the Centre-Right group set up by Roy Hattersley and Peter Shore to combat the Bennites and fight off the challenge of the SDP. At Mandelson's invitation, Hattersley addressed a Solidarity meeting in Brixton town hall, saying that it was an honour to speak 'in the presence of Herbert Morrison's grandson'.[20] At the crucial Brighton Conference in 1981, Mandelson stood at the back of the conference hall with George Robertson and other members of Labour's Right, as Healey's victory by an eyebrow – or four fifths of one per cent – was announced.

Was Mandelson ever tempted to join the SDP? One of his closest party friends in Lambeth, Roger Liddle, had left Labour for the SDP (though he later returned to become adviser to Tony Blair at Number Ten and to Mandelson himself), while the ever-beguiling Shirley Williams had flatteringly made it clear that she was keeping a place warm for him. Healey's deputy leadership victory was crucial. If Healey had lost the deputy leadership, Peter might have then considered joining the SDP or even giving up politics altogether.

This is not to say that he saw the Healey victory as a great break-through. It was merely the bare minimum required for the survival of the party. Roger Liddle described Mandelson's attitude as 'loyal but pessimistic'.[21] Another of his friends, Paul Ormerod, who stayed with Labour, recounted walking with Mandelson into the empty Commons Chamber (Parliament was in recess) and Peter saying, 'It's a great pity neither of us will be able to sit on these benches.'[22] It was in a despondent mood that he left Westminster in early 1982 for a job in the media, working for London Weekend Television (LWT). So, while Blair and Brown were holding their safe seats for Labour at the 1983 general election, Mandelson was merely covering for LWT the three-way fight for the crucial southern marginals which Mrs Thatcher won so crushingly. For the moment, he was out of the game. But he had already acquired considerable self-confidence and a knowledge of politics at the centre which was greater than that of Blair or Brown.

PART 2

ON THE RISE

4

KINNOCK'S YOUNG MEN

It was a depleted and depressed parliamentary Labour Party which assembled at Westminster after Mrs Thatcher's 1983 electoral triumph. The Conservatives now had a massive majority of 144 while Labour had been driven back to its bedrock support in its heartlands of the North of England (where Tony Blair's Sedgefield constituency was situated), Scotland (where Gordon Brown's Dunfermline East constituency was) and Wales (where Neil Kinnock had his constituency of Islwyn). The affluent, skilled and house-owning working class had deserted the party in droves. Labour had become the party of declining Britain, with only 27.6 per cent of the vote, its lowest share of the poll since 1918, and only 209 MPs. Admittedly, in terms of seats, Labour was still well ahead of the Alliance parties (the Liberals and the Social Democrats) which, because of the workings of the first-past-the-post system, had won only twenty-three but, in votes, the Alliance was breathing down Labour's neck, trailing by only 680,000. The question was could the Labour Party ever recover?[1]

The two new MPs, Brown and Blair, were quickly involved in a Labour leadership election, as Michael Foot almost immediately announced that he was standing down. Neil Kinnock, the eloquent left-wing shadow Education Secretary from Wales whose abstention in the 1981 deputy leadership election had helped Healey to beat Benn, was the overwhelming favourite though the shadow Home Secretary and former Cabinet minister, Roy Hattersley, had significant support amongst MPs. Brown confirmed his already considerable reputation and his left-of-centre credentials by being the only member of the new intake to be invited to join Kinnock's leadership Campaign Committee. Blair, like an undergraduate in freshers' week, went to all the leadership candidates' campaign meetings – Kinnock, Hattersley, Shore and Heffer. In the end, backing the winner, he voted for Kinnock as leader though he also voted for Hattersley as deputy leader – the so-called dream ticket which won over two thirds of Labour's electoral college at the Brighton Conference on 2 October and which was to guide the affairs of the Labour Party over the next nine years.

One of the first things a new MP has to do is get an office or at least a desk. Initially, Tony Blair was allocated an office with Dave Nellist MP – a highly inappropriate coupling as Nellist was a militant Trotskyite. After a few weeks, he arranged to team up with another young MP, Gordon Brown, in a small windowless room off the main committee room of the House of Commons – little more than a cupboard with two desks. Characteristically, Gordon's space overflowed with papers and dog-eared books; Tony's may have been neater but there was hardly room to turn. In such cramped and unglamorous surroundings began one of the most celebrated partnerships in British political history.

At this stage, Brown was very much the senior partner. As chairman of the Scottish Labour Party, he was already a leader of the party in Scotland. He was the author and editor of several published books. And, as a former TV reporter and editor, he knew his way around the media. His maiden speech on 27 July was well researched, well delivered, passionate and witty. He intervened in a debate on social security, quoting lavishly from unemployment and supplementary benefit statistics. In a tactic which he was often to use in future speeches and press releases, he claimed to have access to unpublished figures which, in this case, showed the real extent of unemployment and of poverty in his constituency of Dunfermline East.

Ignoring the convention that 'maidens' should be uncontroversial, Brown attacked the social security minister, Dr Rhodes Boyson, for once saying that there were plenty of jobs around for the unemployed as window cleaners, quipping:

> When the Prime Minister talked regularly during the election about ladders of opportunity, I had not realised that the next Conservative government would have something quite so specific in mind . . . Perhaps the exhortation 'up your ladder' will become as intellectually compelling as a solution to Conservatives as 'on your bike' [a reference to a remark made by the former Employment Secretary Norman Tebbit] was in the previous parliament.[2]

The next speaker in the debate, Alan Haselhurst, Tory MP for Saffron Walden, congratulated Brown on his 'force and fluency, and the wit he introduced into a powerful political speech'.[3] Gordon Brown had arrived at Westminster with a bang.

Blair's maiden speech, made a few weeks before on 6 July, during the Finance Bill, made less of a stir. Even so, it was an accomplished speech. Like Brown, he highlighted the plight of the unemployed, especially in his constituency. But, where Brown sought to make an impact with the sheer weight of statistics, Blair relied more on language. He said that, without work, his constituents 'not only suffer the indignity of enforced idleness – they wonder how they can afford to get married, to start a family, and to have access to all the benefits of society that they should be able to take for granted'. There was also a striking peroration in which he discussed his political beliefs:

I am a socialist not through reading a textbook that has caught my intellectual fancy, nor through unthinking tradition, but because I believe that, at its best, socialism corresponds most closely to an existence that is both rational and moral. It stands for co-operation, not confrontation, for fellowship, not fear. It stands for equality, not because it wants people to be the same but because only through equality in our economic circumstances can our individuality develop properly. British democracy rests ultimately on the shared perception by all the people that they participate in the benefits of the common weal.[4]

Later in his career, Blair would not have referred at all to the word 'socialism' or to 'equality' without heavy qualification. But already there was the emphasis on values, especially cooperation and fellowship, which he had learnt at Oxford and which were to inform his approach throughout his political life. And, in the last sentence, there was perhaps a hint of the 'one nation', 'big tent' thinking which was to become such a feature of New Labour under Blair.

Throughout the rest of the year and into the next, the two young men (the two youngest in the Parliamentary Labour Party) discussed the plight of the party and their political futures across their crowded room. Though their maiden speeches had been impeccably 'loyalist', both men believed that Labour had to change. Blair was convinced that the party's stance on nationalisation, defence and Europe was wrongheaded and unpopular. To friendly journalists, he proclaimed, 'This party has about eighteen months left.'[5] It was a dramatic and curiously self-confident statement for such a new MP. Though equally dismissive of Labour's 1983 manifesto (which the Labour shadow Cabinet member, Gerald Kaufman, had famously called 'the longest suicide note in history'), Brown was both more cautious and more experienced in the ways of the party. He proceeded to teach Blair about Labour politics and about how to become a rising opposition politician.

Blair was happy to be the junior partner. He learnt from Brown how to draft a press release, how to handle radio and television and how to write speeches that would appeal to a mass audience. According to Blair's friend, Charles Falconer, Blair was 'mammothly dazzled by Brown's power. I don't think he ever thought at that stage that he would be leader of the party. People always regarded Brown as the obvious man.'[6]

Even if Brown was the dominant figure in the relationship, it was a genuine friendship. Gordon may have had the knowledge, the experience and the historical perspective but Tony brought something to the partnership as well. He knew people in London outside politics whom Brown had never met. He also had charm and freshness. Together they were a formidable team. At Westminster, at an exceptional low point for Labour, Brown and Blair began to be talked about.

In the corridors of Westminster, Blair was already making his presence felt. He would intervene effectively at Prime Ministers Questions, once cheekily telling Mrs Thatcher, who had just banned employees at GCHQ (the government's communications centre) from belonging to unions, that 'the British people prefer democrats to autocrats'.[7] He made a highly polished and fluent speech at the TUC conference at a lunchtime meeting organised by the Fabian Society, using his legal training to deliver an informative account of Tory trade union legislation. At the same time, Brown was continually getting his name in newspaper headlines, as he cleverly exploited leaks of government documents. He could often be seen hurrying to meetings, usually carrying a pile of papers under his arm.

John Smith, whom Kinnock had appointed shadow Employment Secretary, chose Brown and Blair to serve on a Commons Standing Committee set up to examine, in detail, the Conservative government's latest trade union bill which, amongst other things, contained a requirement on unions to hold ballots before strikes. Smith had already worked with Brown in Scotland on devolution in the 1970s and had also met Blair through his close friend, Derry Irvine, who was Tony's mentor. The two members were assiduous in their attacks on the bill, even if sometimes they used arguments that they would find hard to justify later, including Blair's crude assertion that it was unacceptable for a government to interfere in the internal affairs of a union, even on strike ballots. The junior member of the government's employment front bench, languid Alan Clark, a better diarist than he was a minister, wrote:

> Labour has a very tough team. Little John Smith, rotund, bespectacled Edinburgh lawyer. Been around for ages . . . And two bright boys called Brown and Blair . . . They were bobbing up all over the place, asking impossible, spastic questions of detail – most of them, as far as I could make out, to do with the fucking *rule book*.[8]

It was only a matter of time before the two 'bright boys' were promoted to the opposition front bench. Somewhat surprisingly, in November 1984, Blair was the first to get a position. He owed his preferment as a shadow Treasury spokesman to the shadow Chancellor Roy Hattersley, who had been impressed by his ability and by his good manners when he went to speak for Blair at the Beaconsfield by-election – Blair wrote to thank him for coming. Hattersley found the new recruit fluent and industrious, with the lawyer's capacity to master complex City issues.

At about the time of Blair's promotion, Brown had been informally offered a front bench position as a Scottish spokesman. He said later that he felt 'it was better for me to stay on the backbenches and do more there'.[9] A more likely explanation was that, as an ambitious politician, he did not want to be tied up in Scotland. A better offer and a more suitable reward for his hard work came in November 1985 when Kinnock appointed him spokesman for Trade and Industry, with special responsibility for regional policy. John Smith, the new shadow Secretary for Trade and Industry, wanted an energetic deputy to help him run Labour's so-called 'Jobs and Industry' campaign. The two men toured the country presenting each region with a plan to revive the local economy and create more jobs. Invitations went out not only to party members but also to businessmen and Chambers of Commerce. Brown proved to be a capable campaigner and, for the first time, was able to raise his profile outside Scotland.

In September 1985, Peter Mandelson was selected as Labour's Director of Communications. Mandelson owed his appointment, which was to have such an impact not only on the Labour Party but also on the lives of Brown and Blair, to the support of both Kinnock and Hattersley. Kinnock's efforts to lead a Labour recovery had been stalled by the disastrous miners' strike of 1984–85, which has been rightly characterised as 'lions led by donkeys'. But, after the defeat of the miners, he turned again to the task of making the party electable.

At the 1985 party conference at Bournemouth, he made arguably the best speech of his life, a brave and eloquent attack on the Militant-led Liverpool Council for its reckless opposition to the Tory government, which put new heart into Labour MPs, including Brown and Blair. A few weeks earlier, the Labour Party had advertised for a new Director of Campaigns and Communications, with the remit of modernising the party's publicity effort. Mandelson, who was already on the lookout for a way back into Labour politics, was determined to put in for the job. His friend, Charles Clarke, now Neil Kinnock's Chief of Staff, had first tipped him off about the opportunity but it was Hattersley who gathered support for him.

In late September, Betty Boothroyd, who was then a member of the National Executive and later became Speaker of the Commons, rang me to inquire about Mandelson's credentials. He had been a member of Solidarity and had helped Hattersley in his leadership campaign. More to point, I also told her that he would make a capable and imaginative Director of Communications. At the crucial meeting she voted for Mandelson. However, the key vote was obviously Kinnock's. He was persuaded partly by Hattersley but mostly by Mandelson's media credentials.

At his interview, Mandelson performed brilliantly.[10] He told the National Executive that the chances of a Labour recovery were good, as the polling evidence suggested that voters preferred the Swedish model of social democracy to the American free market of Reagan and Thatcher. But Labour's message had to be simply explained 'in memorable phrases and policies' and its leadership projected 'as an able and united team'. And the party needed to extend its press and broadcasting contacts. When asked by Joan Maynard, a hard-Left MP known as 'Stalin's nanny', how he would have dealt with the miners' strike, he skilfully replied that he would have used it as an illustration of a divided Britain, a neutral answer that satisfied both Left and Right. Kinnock's greatest worry was about the colour of Mandelson's socks. He told Hattersley, 'You don't come to fucking interviews wearing pale blue socks.' Despite the socks, he got the job by the narrow margin of fourteen votes to ten.

The promise revealed in Mandelson's interview was more than fulfilled by his performance as Director of Communications. Arguably, over the years of the Kinnock leadership, he became one of the most important people in the party – certainly more important than most members of the shadow Cabinet. Though he quickly realised that Brown and Blair were highly talented (which was why he used them on television during the 1987 election), his priorities were to build up Kinnock's leadership and improve Labour's disastrous image. It was essential, Mandelson argued, to start reconnecting the party with the voting public, especially on health, social services, housing benefits, law and order and making people secure in their homes and in the streets: 'We have to present an image of the party . . . that chimes in with what people want to think.'[11] Working with sympathetic advertising and marketing people – whom he and a clever young advertising consultant called Philip Gould brought together in the so-called Shadow Communications Agency – he proceeded to transform Labour's communications strategy and methods.

Later, Mandelson called the period of the run-up to the 1987 election, when the party began to change how it appeared, the time of the 'Red Rose'. The use of the rose by the party instead of more traditional symbols such as the red flag was favoured by Neil Kinnock who had already quietly abandoned the flag in favour of the rose for the 1984

European elections. Now, the red rose became Labour's 'logo', an essential part of its campaigns, including the 'Freedom and Fairness' and 'Investing in People' policy launches of 1986 when, for the first time since 1981, the party went ahead of the Conservatives in the polls. But, as Mandelson himself admitted, the Labour Party's change was more a triumph of image over substance. Its unpopular policies on public ownership, tax and spend and, above all, on unilateral nuclear disarmament remained in place while Labour still retained an unenviable reputation for extremism and being in hock to the unions.

In 1987, thanks to both Mandelson and Kinnock, Labour fought an energetic, glitzy election, utilising modern media techniques. In the opinion polls, it impressively outscored the Tories on the so-called 'people's agenda' of unemployment, education and health.[12] But the polls also indicated that defence alone cost the party over one million votes while voters thought that the Tories were more likely to deliver higher living standards than Labour by a margin of two to one. The effect of Labour's campaign was to win one and a half million more votes than in 1983 but the Tories, with 42.3 per cent of the vote, still won a massive majority of 101 seats.

As relatively junior spokesmen, Brown and Blair had played only a minor part in Labour's campaign. Brown had launched the party's blueprints for the regions and had been in demand on regional television. At a news conference, chaired by the shadow Home Secretary Gerald Kaufman, Blair unwisely suggested that Mrs Thatcher's plans to increase private rented housing were the product of 'an unchecked and unbalanced mind', which, as Michael Brunson of ITN pointed out, was open to the interpretation that she was mad. Though Kaufman intervened to say that Blair was only attacking the ethos of Thatcherism, his comment was widely reported as a sign of Labour's desperation.[13] Both Blair and Brown increased their majorities but this was little compensation for Labour's third successive defeat, although neither of them expected Labour to win. In fact, Labour's 1987 defeat opened up the road to the top for these outstandingly able and ambitious men, bearing out the dictum that it is often better to enter Parliament at the nadir of one's party fortunes than as part of a triumphant landslide.[14]

Following the election, with Nick Brown, the MP for Newcastle East, acting as their organiser, both Brown and Blair succeeded in getting on the soft-Left 'Tribune slate' of recommended candidates for the shadow Cabinet elections. As a natural supporter of the Parliamentary Labour Party (PLP) Centre-Left, Brown had joined Tribune immediately on being elected to Parliament. Blair, who had been a Solidarity member in 1982 before he had got a seat, was more circumspect but, in 1985, he too decided to join Tribune, calculating that Tribune membership provided the quickest route to the top. By that time, Tribune was no longer the left-wing pressure group it had once been but included half all Labour MPs. Being on the Tribune slate gave Brown and Blair a better chance of getting into the shadow Cabinet. Helped by a Scottish group substantially increased by the election, it was Brown who was elected to the shadow Cabinet at his first attempt, coming eleventh with eighty-eight votes. Blair came seventeenth with seventy-one votes, just outside the fifteen-strong shadow Cabinet.

My diary entry for 1 August 1987 records a meeting with my Durham neighbour, Tony Blair, just after the shadow Cabinet election.[15] 'He comes across as fluent, intelligent and sincere – not at all the normal party politician. And he has a most attractive personality.' The diary then reports my remarks to him: 'Look Tony, I don't think we can win with Neil. You and Gordon Brown are the men of the future. I am unlikely to stand again for the shadow Cabinet [I was one of four Solidarity-backed members defeated in the July shadow Cabinet elections][16] and I shall do what I can to get you on to it as soon as possible.' The significant point about this entry was not my offer to help, which, at the best, could only be useful on the margin, but that already, only four years after their election to parliament, a senior member of the PLP was talking about two young MPs as future leaders of the party – and not only Brown but Blair as well.

From 1988 onwards, the record of Brown and Blair as opposition spokesmen was outstanding. Brown, who was appointed shadow Chief Secretary, had to step in when his boss, John Smith, the shadow Chancellor, who had succeeded Roy Hattersley after the election, suffered a serious heart attack. In reply to Chancellor Nigel Lawson's autumn statement, Brown had a genuine parliamentary triumph – 'a scintillating performance'.[17] He not only proved himself to be a master of the detailed public spending figures but cleverly argued that, because of higher inflation, there would be a real deterioration in public benefits and services and that, through neglect of investment and the persistence of high interest rates, the British economy would be 'ill-equipped and ill-prepared for the challenges of the 1990s'.[18] His fellow MPs were so impressed that he won first place in the 1988 shadow Cabinet elections, almost doubling his total the previous year and coming ahead of the shadow Chancellor, still convalescing in Edinburgh. In the 1989 elections, he retained first place and was promoted to shadow Trade and Industry Secretary, replacing the Euro-sceptic Bryan Gould. When Brown came to my constituency a few months later, I noted that he was certainly leadership material '[i]f he doesn't burn himself out too soon'.[19] His impassioned speech enthused many actvists.

Tony Blair was voted on to the shadow Cabinet for the first time in 1988. Blair was appointed deputy to the then shadow Trade and Industry Secretary, Bryan Gould, and was given responsibility for City matters. This was a post normally given to an up-and-coming politician and, if they proved themselves, it was an obvious launching pad. When the investment group Barlow Clowes crashed, wiping out the savings of many pensioners, he quickly made his mark by cleverly exposing the failure of government regulation.

But it was his next two positions, both in the shadow Cabinet, that confirmed Blair as a genuine contender for the leadership. In 1988–89, Kinnock appointed him shadow Energy Secretary to lead the opposition to electricity privatisation. His tactics during the committee stage when the privatisation bill was debated in detail were highly intelligent. Instead of wasting hours often late at night in ritual trench warfare, he concentrated on the key issues and arranged for them to be debated in prime time. As a result, both Labour's arguments and the duels between the youthful Tony Blair and the ageing Conservative Secretary of State, Cecil Parkinson, got full media publicity, very much to the advantage of Blair.

On the back of his success as shadow Energy Secretary, Blair moved up to fourth in the 1989 shadow Cabinet elections. His reward was a promotion to shadow Employment Secretary. It was his performance in this role, especially over the closed-shop issue, that provided the real break-through in Blair's rise to the top of the Labour Party. His opportunity came quickly. A month after his appointment, in a debate on 29 November, Blair was speaking warmly in favour of the latest draft of the Social Charter which had just been published by the European Commission. This gave positive rights to employees. However, he was ambushed by a former Tory minister, who pointed out that the Social Charter not only guaranteed the right to join a trades union but also the right not to join. Did the Labour Party support the right not to join a union? Blair was forced to obfuscate.[20]

The truth was that, as the Tory MP had shrewdly spotted, there was a conflict between Labour's support for the Social Charter (which later became the Social Chapter of the Maastricht Treaty) and the backing of the unions for the closed shop – the arrangement whereby all employees in a plant or a firm were forced to join a union. Blair, who had read the Charter, was quite clear which had to go.

After the debate, he firmly told Kinnock and Hattersley that the Labour Party had speedily to reverse its policy of support of the closed shop. Working in close cooperation with Peter Mandelson, he saw most of the top trades union leaders over the next week and informed them what he intended to do. But, although they understood that it was a shift that had to be made, few of them were prepared to say so in public. However, with considerable courage, Blair went ahead regardless. Arguably, this was a key moment in Blair's rise to the top of the Labour Party.

At a news conference on 6 December, he announced that he accepted the Social Charter in its entirety and, on Sunday 17 December, he issued a seven-page statement to his constituency in which he said that, in order to secure the right to join a union, which he attacked the government for failing to guarantee, the Labour Party was now prepared to accept the right not to join. When Norman Fowler, the Conservative Employment Secretary brought forward a Bill to abolish the closed shop, he found that his shadow's boldness had enabled Labour to escape from the dilemma on which he had hoped to impale it. Instead Blair was able to tease the Tories: '[T]here they were all togged up in their party best, and they put their hands into the magician's hat hopping to pull out a nice white, bright, sprightly, lively rabbit, but instead find that they are holding a very dead fox.'[21]

Though Mandelson had been one of the stars of the 1987 general election, he had been deeply depressed by the result and by the realisation of how much further Labour would have to change, especially in terms of policy, if it was ever to win again. After the election, he seriously considered leaving his job as Labour's Director of Communications and went as far as to apply for a BBC post as corporate affairs director. But the job went to a Tory, Howell James, who was better qualified to defend the licence fee with a Conservative government in power.

However, Mandelson was soon involved in the battle for reforming the Labour Party. He wrote to Charles Clarke, Kinnock's Chief of Staff: 'Modernising policy is key to our next election image, particularly in economic, wealth creation, taxation, work – we should make a virtue of change, be as forthright and open as . . . possible.'[22] Thus began a revision process under Kinnock which led to the abandonment of a number of policies, including unilateral disarmament and old-style nationalisation. Despite this progress, Mandelson remained dissatisfied with the pace of change.

During the 1987 election, he had worked closely with Bryan Gould, Labour's election co-ordinator but, afterwards, he saw the younger Brown and Blair as more authentic and effective modernisers. Writing in December 1988, he listed the successes of the opposition front bench. At the top of the list was Gordon Brown scoring over Lawson and Tony Blair taking the initiative on electricity. He saw his own role as increasingly revolving round 'the strong future leadership of Gordon Brown and Tony Blair and the political nourishment and companionship I get from this group'.[23] He admired their political gifts and shared their view that, unless the party changed far more than it had so far, it might be out of office for a generation. This was a key moment in the birth of New Labour for which Mandelson deserved a great deal of credit.

While remaining loyal to Kinnock, Mandelson saw it as his business to get the two men into the newspapers and on television and radio as much as possible and generally to help promote them whenever and wherever he could – to the understandable annoyance of other shadow Cabinet members. The three men became virtually inseparable, seeing each other and talking to each other several times a day. Brown and Blair deferred to Mandelson on presentational matters and, in turn, they both gave him inspiration and friendship. At this stage, Mandelson was closer to Brown and spent more time with him, especially in the evenings after Blair, a devoted father, had gone home to his growing family – sons Euan and Nicholas and daughter Kathryn – in Islington. He, like Blair, regarded Brown as the senior partner.

Mandelson's own ambitions were aroused by his involvement with the two other modernisers. He realised that, if he was to be part of what he called 'the successor generation', he would have to win a parliamentary seat – an ambition which was encouraged by his two friends. With the support of the regional secretary of the GMB trade union, Tom Burlison, who was on the National Executive of the Labour Party, he set his sights on Hartlepool, the neighbouring constituency to Tony Blair's where the local MP, Ted Leadbitter, had decided to retire.

With the backing of the GMB, which had five branches in the town,

Mandelson soon had a substantial lead in the union section. At that time, before the introduction of one member, one vote (OMOV), parliamentary selections were organised on the basis of 40 per cent for affiliated union members and 60 per cent for individuals. So, although Mandelson had a head start, he had still to win over individual delegates. With his customary attention to detail, he launched a meticulous local campaign and, despite scurrilous rumours about his sexuality circulated by the wife of one of the other candidates, his charm and glamour as one of Labour's national stars brought him success.

For the selection conference in December 1989, he carefully crafted a speech to appeal to all the delegates – the tribute to Ted Leadbitter, the mention of his famous grandfather's experience as an MP and his own as a local councillor, the many glowing references to Hartlepool and the commitment to live in the town. It was an indication of the close relationship between Mandelson and Brown that Brown had generously drafted for him a characteristically Brownite peroration:

> When I see pensioners, many of whom here in Hartlepool have to choose between heating and eating, when I see children who because of cuts in child benefit are ill clad and undernourished, when I see teenagers in this great town with no job, no training place, no cash and no hope . . . when I see all those unmet needs on the one hand and unused resources on the other then that is the socialist challenge.[24]

Mandelson easily won the nomination with over 63 per cent of the votes cast.

Publicly Neil Kinnock welcomed Mandelson's triumph: 'Peter, as ever, will be a great asset to the Labour Party and most certainly he will be a fine representative for the people of Hartlepool.'[25] In private, the Labour leader did not believe that it was possible for him to continue as Director of Communications in an election period now that he had become a parliamentary candidate and, on the Friday of the 1990 party conference,

Mandelson, despite all he had achieved for the party, was forced to step down as Director of Communications. But, although he had lost his party post, he quickly picked up temporary employment as a consultant and a columnist for the *People*. Above all, he had a safe seat at Hartlepool which he was assiduously nursing in expectation of a general election.

Labour went into the 1992 election thinking it had a chance of winning. The economy was depressed, the Tories had been in power for a long time and public opinion polls put Labour ahead. However, as in 1987, there was a muddle over tax and spend, with Labour committed to abolishing the upper limit on National Insurance to pay for its plans to increase pensions and tax credit. The abolition of the upper limit on National Insurance may have been sensible economically but politically it would have meant sharp increases in taxes for those earning over £22,000 which enabled the Tories to claim that the shadow Chancellor, John Smith, was clobbering the middle classes. Without consulting Smith, Kinnock, whose opinion poll ratings were not only behind Major's but behind Smith's as well, told journalists that Labour would phase in the abolition of the upper limit. A semi-public row followed. As part of Smith's economic team, Brown and Blair tried unsuccessfully to persuade the shadow Chancellor to shift position but, when he refused, remained loyal in public.

Apart from the tax issue, Labour's campaign was relatively gaffe free though Mandelson's perspective at its centre was badly missed. Kinnock, however, gave a number of weak performances on TV, while Blair and Brown, who were both pessimistic about a Labour victory, were not on the box as much as they thought they ought to be. On election day, the exit polls put the Tories only narrowly ahead but, when the super-marginal Essex seat of Basildon was comfortably held by the Tories, Kinnock knew he had lost. One diarist commented, 'To his great credit he [Kinnock] had made Labour a decent party to which to belong, but twice failed to win the election for us.'[26] He speedily resigned as leader. But defeat not only ends careers, it also helps to make them. New opportunities were about to open up for Brown and Blair.

5

JOHN SMITH'S BRIEF REIGN

The 1992 election result was Labour's fourth successive defeat and, in many ways, the most disappointing of the lot. Despite Kinnock's brave efforts to change the party, it still finished 7 percentage points behind the Conservatives – only 35 per cent to the Tories' 42 per cent – and John Major had an overall majority of twenty-one. The results in the southern part of the country were especially disheartening. The party was only able to win three seats out of a hundred and nine in the south-east, by far the most populous of the UK regions. Labour supporters asked themselves, 'Must Labour always lose?'

In 1992, in time for the party conference, I wrote a pamphlet, published by the Fabian Society, entitled 'Southern Discomfort'.[1] It was based on the results of qualitative research among floating voters in southern marginal seats. It showed that many 'swing' voters, apart from their distrust of Kinnock, also believed that a Labour government would mismanage the economy, increase taxes and deliver the country into the hands of the unions. More generally, they felt that Labour, seen as a class-based party rooted in the past, had nothing to offer upwardly mobile families. I argued that, if Labour was ever to win again, big changes would be needed, including rewriting Clause 4 of the party constitution, introducing one person, one vote in party decision making and making Labour the party of genuine opportunity for all. 'Southern Discomfort' was widely quoted in the press and caused a stir in the party. It broadly reflected the thinking of the three leading modernisers – Blair, Brown and Mandelson.

On the morning after Labour's election defeat, Blair, who had expected Labour to lose, went on television to say that the party had failed to win not because it had changed too much but because it had not changed enough and that it had to modernise much further if it was to win the next time. He told the BBC that he regarded Labour's failure to win seats in the south-east of England and in London as highly significant – if the party was ever to win again, it needed the support of the middle classes. Blair's bold initiative came at a moment when most of Labour's leaders were in a depressed state. He was not only the first to give a credible explanation of the party's defeat, he was also displaying courage, decisiveness and a sense of timing – all crucial attributes of a leader.

Five weeks before the general election, Blair had told the political columnist and novelist, Robert Harris, that he expected Labour to lose the election and that Gordon Brown was likely to stand for the leadership, that he would run as deputy and that Mandelson would run the media campaign for them.[2] If Blair's remarks to Harris (whom he had only just met) revealed the extent of his ambitions, his idea of a moderniser's 'dream ticket' was always very much a long shot. As he knew very well, John Smith was an odds-on favourite to succeed Neil Kinnock (who everybody correctly expected to resign after defeat) and Gordon Brown had given his word to Smith that he would not challenge him for the leadership.

Over the weekend after Thursday's election, the modernisers held a series of meetings to decide on tactics. Brown came down from Scotland to talk to Blair and the first meeting took place at Blair's home at Trimdon in his Sedgefield constituency, where they were joined by Nick Brown, the MP for Newcastle East, who had helped to organise their campaigns for the shadow Cabinet. They met again at Nick Brown's home in his constituency and lastly at County Hall, Durham, where they were joined by the new MP for Hartlepool, Peter Mandelson.

Blair may well have tried to persuade Brown to run against their friend and mentor John Smith – indeed, it was later claimed by one of his allies that Blair felt that Brown had bottled out of a contest when he had his best chance.[3] But it was entirely understandable that, in the circumstances of 1992, Brown should have decided not to go for the leadership. Apart from the issue of loyalty to Smith, most of the cards were stacked against him. Smith was popular both with the party and the voters and he already had the support of two of the major unions, the T&G and the GMB. A defeat for Brown would not only have been a personal setback, it could also have weakened the modernisers' cause.

The real issue was the deputy leadership and whether Blair should run for it. In 1992, Blair was not a credible candidate for the leadership – a *Sunday Times* poll of 138 Labour MPs put Smith easily top with Brown a distant second and Blair not even mentioned. But, as deputy, he could bring, with his youth and middle-class connections, a crucial balance to the Smith leadership. On the Sunday, my diary records that I rang Tony Blair to urge him to stand as deputy. It noted that, 'Tony is definitely interested, but has to consult with his friend, Gordon Brown. I promise to ring John Smith on his behalf, which I do.'[4] On the telephone, Smith was non-committal. He had probably already decided to choose Margaret Beckett, a woman representing a Midland seat and supported by the T&G. What was most interesting about the exchange with Blair was that he felt he had to consult Brown.

In fact, the modernising trio never agreed on Blair putting his hat in the ring. Nick Brown, with his number-crunching hat on, made the point that, under the existing electoral system of union block votes and without one member, one vote, Blair, whose success in changing Labour's position on the closed shop had upset a number of trade union leaders, would find it difficult to win. There was a further, if unspoken, consideration – and that was the impact of a Blair candidature on Brown.

Smith had already ruled Brown out as his deputy on the grounds that two Scots in leadership positions would be unacceptable to the voters. But, if Blair became deputy, Brown feared that Blair would leap ahead of him in the race for the succession to John Smith. Significantly Mandelson had prepared a memorandum putting the case for Brown as deputy:

> Smith and Brown together offer a combination of experienced authority and lively imagination to carry Labour forward . . . They are the party's best brains, leading a team of front bench talent who will be in step with the party and in tune with the country.[5]

At that stage, Mandelson was clearly putting Brown first, though, by the end of the weekend, he had come round to the idea that, if Brown could not run for either the leadership or the deputy leadership, then they should put Blair forward as the modernising candidate for the latter option. However, this idea was vetoed by Gordon Brown. On Tuesday, it became clear that Smith had chosen Beckett as his deputy and, by the following day, Blair, like Brown, announced his support for the Smith–Beckett ticket.

Blair may have claimed that, in 1992, Brown did not have the 'bottle' to stand as leader but the same charge could also be levelled against him as regards the deputy leadership. Roy Hattersley, who resigned as deputy leader at the same time (on the Monday) as Kinnock announced his resignation as leader, had advised Blair not to stand because he believed that Blair, more than Brown, was Smith's natural successor and being deputy now would not help him become leader later. However, others, especially his wife, Cherie, thought that Blair should have stood, even if it meant straining or even undermining his relationship with Brown. It may be that, on balance, Blair was right to defer to Brown and decide not to stand in 1992, especially if it would have involved running without the support of either Smith or Brown. However, his frustrating experience in the few days after the 1992 defeat had the effect of making him all the more determined to put himself forward if and when the opportunity occurred in the future, whatever his friend Gordon Brown might say. In this sense, what happened in 1992 was crucial to Blair's rise to the leadership.

The modernisers made a contribution to the Smith–Beckett campaign. Brown and Blair wrote parts of Smith's 8,000-word manifesto, while Mandelson was asked by Robin Cook, Smith's campaign manager, to help with the media. Mandelson wrote a note for his meeting with Cook in which he set out Smith's attributes as follows: 'Cabinet experience, authority, knowledge, electoral appeal, stabilising, unifying, most feared by the Tories.' His weaknesses, according to Mandelson, were: 'Right man for last election, not next, no ideas, undynamic, uncomfortable in role.'[6] The last point was quickly proved wrong. Although his campaign got off to a slow start, Smith trounced his only rival, the anti-European, Bryan Gould, by winning 90 per cent of the vote, including all but fourteen of the constituencies. In the ballot for deputy, Beckett got over 50 per cent of the vote, with Prescott coming a respectable second and Gould a poor third.

In his twenty-two months as leader, John Smith established his authority over his party, his command over the Commons and the respect and trust of the British electors. Following the collapse in September 1992 of the Conservative government's economic policy when the pound was driven out of the European Exchange Rate Mechanism (ERM), Smith cleverly exploited the government's humiliation, even though he had backed British membership of the ERM. He also managed to expose the divisions in the Tory ranks over the Maastricht Treaty Bill, without reneging on the principle of support for the Bill. Putting his leadership at risk, he overcame strong union opposition to one member, one vote. By the time of his death, his reassuring and self-confident performance had put Labour on the road to victory at the next election.

Yet, for the three modernisers, Smith's brief reign as leader was a frustrating period. Smith was cautious about party modernisation because, for understandably tactical reasons, he wanted the media to concentrate on the government's difficulties, not on Labour's. According to Mandelson, Smith felt threatened, even upstaged, by Brown and Blair: 'There was only one quality he valued which was unity and they threatened unity by going on about modernising.'[7]

In January 1993, Brown and Blair went to Washington to get tips from the advisers of Bill Clinton, the Democrat newly elected as United States President. While they were away, Smith called Mandelson in. Apparently, he told the third member of the modernising trio (partly as a message to the other two) that it would be helpful if he could be allowed to get on with winning the next election: 'All this Clintonisation business, it's just upsetting everyone. Stop boat-rocking with all this talk of change and modernisation. It will just divide the party. If we remain united we'll win.'[8]

However, in their criticism of Smith's attitude to modernisation (especially strong in Blair's case), the modernising trio underestimated Smith's achievement in getting his proposals for one member, one vote through the 1993 Labour Party conference, despite being opposed by two of the biggest unions, the T&G and the GMB. The conference opened with Smith facing defeat. He was prepared to resign if he was defeated though he would have insisted on a second ballot, making it into a confidence vote on his leadership. To underline that he meant what he said, he pointed out to the General Secretary of the GMB, John Edmonds, that he could always make a good living outside politics as a QC if he was forced out.[9]

In the crucial conference debate, Smith turned not to the modernisers or even to Margaret Beckett (who had seemed lukewarm in her support in a TV interview earlier in the week) but to the more traditionalist figure of John Prescott to wind up. In my diary, I described his speech as being 'incoherently eloquent', much of it being a diatribe against the modernisers, though his peroration, urging conference to back a leader who had put his head on the block, was genuinely moving.[10] In fact, Smith owed his narrow victory not so much to Prescott as to a last-minute decision by the

Manufacturing, Science and Finance Union (MSF) to abstain. Unlike Blair, Brown and Mandelson, Smith saw his conference success over one member, one vote as about as far as he was prepared to go in modernising the party. If his approach appeared too conservative to the modernisers, the acceptance of the key principle of one member, one vote both for the selection of parliamentary candidates and the election of leaders took power away from trade union leaders and gave it to individuals. In doing so, it helped Blair win the leadership in 1994 and made Labour more electable.

Under Smith, the modernising trio may have felt somewhat isolated, especially in comparison with their more favoured position in the Kinnock period. This was most obviously the case for Mandelson whose assistant Derek Draper cheekily called this time 'the wilderness years'. Smith gave Mandelson one by-election to run but it was in a hopeless seat for Labour. The truth was that Smith did not trust him or his way of handling the media. As the Labour leader told *Woman's Own* magazine, 'I don't like the black art of public relations that's taken over politics. We're talking about the government of the country – not the entertainment industry.'[11]

Yet being out of favour at the centre was no bad thing for Peter Mandelson. It meant that he was forced to concentrate on building up his relationship with his Hartlepool constituency and learning the ropes as a backbencher. During the week he intervened in Commons debates. He played a particularly active role in the debates over the long-running Maastricht Treaty Bill. As a committed pro-European, he was one of a group on the Labour side who spoke up in support of the bill, risking hostile interventions from Euro-sceptics on both sides of the House, as well as listening to interminable filibustering speeches. At weekends, he would return with pleasure to Hartlepool, holding regular surgeries and involving himself in constituency issues. Although he remained in close contact with Brown and Blair, helping them with their tactics and publicity, he was beginning to make his own independent way as a talented member of Parliament.

Smith had recognised Gordon Brown's outstanding ability and pre-eminence in the party by making him shadow Chancellor. In 1992, for the third successive year, Brown had topped the poll in the shadow Cabinet elections and was therefore in a strong position to see off an old rival and Smith's campaign manager, Robin Cook, who also had his eye on the shadow chancellorship. For the first time, Brown was also elected to the National Executive, coming third, and Blair was also successful in seventh place.

Brown was determined to use his new post as shadow Chancellor to establish Labour as a party that voters could trust on tax and spending. That meant ditching the economic policy on which Labour had fought the last election and enforcing a strict control of spending commitments on the shadow Cabinet. He was right to take a hard line on the economy but he was unwise to treat his colleagues in a high-handed and insensitive way. In addition, Brown's support of the ERM and his opposition to UK devaluation within it exposed him to party criticism when the pound was forced out of the ERM. However, his stance enabled him subsequently to attack the Tories as the party of devaluation. In the debate on the UK's rejection from the ERM, he concluded his speech with these words:

> Ministers who continue to hold responsibilities now cannot command respect. They may hold office for five years, but even after five months they have lost all authority to govern. They have failed the country and they will never be trusted again.[12]

As Brown predicted, the ERM debate was a turning point in the public's attitude to the Tories and the shadow Chancellor had put himself and his party in a strong position to exploit the new situation.

Some of Brown's closest friends argued that his tough attitude on economic policy in 1992–94, which he adopted for the sake of the party, lost him the leadership. Yet, if he had taken a softer line to curry favour with his critics, he would rightly have been criticised for not doing his job properly – and that would have damaged him more in the longer term. A more valid criticism is that, during this period, his TV appearances became somewhat monotonous and predictable. But the main reason Brown did not become leader in 1994 was not so much because of the inadequacy of his own television performances but because of the flair and presentational brilliance of his friend and close colleague, Tony Blair.

Before accepting the position of shadow Home Secretary, Blair consulted Roy Hattersley, who had given him his first post on the front bench and who was the retiring shadow Home Secretary. Hattersley said:

> It's a rotten job in government. It's a pretty good job in opposition . . . in government you're waiting for somebody to break out of prison every day. In opposition you're hoping that somebody will break out of prison so you can complain about it.[13]

Blair's approach was more ambitious. Since the liberalising reforms of the Labour Home Secretary, Roy Jenkins, in the 1960s, Conservative critics had sought to portray the party as 'soft on crime' and out of touch with public opinion – an attack which the behaviour of a few MPs and some extreme left-wing Labour councils seemed to validate. By skilful positioning, Blair sought to combine a liberal attitude on issues such as abortion, gay rights, racial equality and the death penalty with a tough approach to crime and family responsibility, a strategy which he was to pursue in government.

In a Radio 4 interview on 10 January 1993, Blair said, 'I think it's important that we are tough on crime and tough on the causes of crime too.' Ironically, it was Gordon Brown who had suggested to Blair that he should adopt this formula. On their trip to the United States a few days before, Paul Begala, Clinton's strategist and speech-writer, had explained how the Clinton wing of the Democratic party had sought to come to terms with social change by putting responsibility back at the centre of Democrat thinking. This chimed with the community philosophy that

Blair had picked up at Oxford and helped provide a moral background to his new, populist stance on crime. In March 1993, he wrote in the *Sun*, 'It's a bargain – we give opportunity, we demand responsibility. There is no excuse for crime. None.'[14]

The horrific murder of the two-year-old, James Bulger, by two ten-year-olds on Merseyside provided an occasion for Blair's social moralism. In his Wellingborough speech (19 February 1993), he said:

> The news bulletins of the last week have been like hammer blows struck against the sleeping conscience of the country urging us to wake up and look unflinchingly at what we see . . . If we do not learn and then teach the value of what is right and what is wrong, then the result is simply moral chaos which engulfs us all.[15]

In other speeches, he stressed the importance of 'strong families' though he also pointed out, in contrast to Mrs Thatcher, that a strong society was needed to support strong families. Foreshadowing his 'third-way' approach, he argued, 'If the old left tended to ignore the importance of the family, the new right ignores the conditions in which family life can most easily prosper.'[16]

Blair's stance on crime and the fresh language in which it was expressed caught the attention of the media across the political spectrum. Smith may have warned him after the Bulger speech to 'stop hogging the lime-light'[17] but the truth was that the shadow Home Secretary, with remarkable flair and eloquence, had managed to seize an issue which had been a Tory preserve and make it a Labour one. 'We are the party of law and order,' he proclaimed at the 1993 party conference. In a remarkable two years, he emerged as a possible successor to John Smith and a potential Prime Minister.

Brown and Blair, with Mandelson acting as their media spokesman, were still friends and allies. They sat together in shadow Cabinet passing notes and swapping jokes. At Westminster, they shared ideas and discussed problems. To outsiders, the trio of Brown, Blair and Mandelson seemed an amazingly close-knit unit – as indeed they were. Robin Cook said, 'I was conscious during 1992–94 of a cave with three people in it, Brown, Blair and Mandelson. They plotted and briefed endlessly.'[18] Yet, as both Brown and Blair grew more eminent, they acquired separate entourages and camp followers. Symbolically, perhaps, their offices were now in different parts of the Palace of Westminster, Brown's in Millbank, Blair's in Parliament Street. Brown's team had been strengthened by the employment of: Ed Balls, the clever *Financial Times* leader writer, to advise him on economics; Charlie Whelan, the rumbustious, public-school educated, trade union press officer recruited by Mandelson to improve Brown's media relations; and the calm and reliable Sue Nye, who had worked for Neil Kinnock and was a friend of Mandelson, to bring some order to his office. Blair's team was smaller but equally gifted. Anji Hunter, his friend from his school days, who had acted as his political assistant from 1987 to 1991, returned in 1992 to help organise his political life while Tim Allan acted as his researcher and speech-writer. Blair also had some influential informal advisers such as Alastair Campbell, former political editor of the *Daily Mirror* and later Blair's press secretary, and Philip Gould, who had helped organise Kinnock's Shadow Communications Agency (SCA).

The rise of Tony Blair did not go unnoticed in the press. On the morning after John Smith's election as leader in July 1992, the *Sunday Times* Colour Magazine had run a flattering profile of Tony Blair under the headline 'Labour's Leader in Waiting'. Two days later, the *Evening Standard* published an article entitled 'The Coming War Between Gordon Brown and Tony Blair'[19] which presciently predicted that, like Crosland and Jenkins in the 1960s and 1970s, the ambitions of Labour's two young pretenders were bound to lead to rivalry and conflict. On 27 September 1993, Philip Stephens of the *Financial Times* noted that political commentators increasingly referred to Blair as the party's foremost moderniser or the next Labour leader.

But, until the early morning of 12 May 1994, there was not a vacancy for the Labour leadership. Despite the discontent of the modernisers, John Smith was very much in control of his party. The previous Thursday, Labour had won 42 per cent of the votes cast in the local government elections and was looking forward to a successful European election. Smith was confident that he would lead the Labour Party to victory at the next general election. Smith's sudden death of a heart attack was a shock even to his political opponents.

In the Commons the Prime Minister, John Major, praised Smith as 'one of the outstanding parliamentarians of modern politics – a fair-minded but tough fighter for what he believed in'. Paddy Ashdown, leader of the Liberal Party, said, 'We have lost today one of the foremost parliamentary talents of our time, a powerful advocate of the politics of progress in Britain, and a thoroughly decent and deeply gifted man.' The modernisers sometimes felt that Smith was a barrier to modernisation. But he had brought the party together and, at the time of his death, it was ready, far more than in 1992, for the modernisers.

6

THE BLAIR–BROWN DEAL

Blair first heard the news of John Smith's death just after 9 a.m. while he was on his way from Aberdeen Airport to fulfil a Euro-election engagement in the Granite City, after taking a call from David Hill, Labour's chief press officer. Brown, who had already spoken to Murray Elder, his school friend and Smith's Chief of Staff, rang Blair from London to confirm that the Labour leader was dead. In an interview in the *Independent* two months later, Blair described his reactions:

> It was a cataclysmic event because I was in a state of shock and grief, obviously, over John, who I was very close to and to whom I owed a lot. And then – I mean, you know, whatever anyone says – within moments of these things happening, the world just moves on.[1]

Brown is said to have been contacted by a close personal friend who asked if he had heard the news. 'Yes,' said Brown. 'What are you doing?' she asked. 'I'm thinking, I'm thinking,' he replied.[2]

Over the next few days, two things became clear. Firstly, in contrast to 1992 when he deferred to Brown over the deputy leadership, Blair was going to run for the leadership, whatever Brown thought and whether he ran or not. Secondly, the movement of opinion inside the Labour Party, throughout the media and amongst the general public was such that Blair immediately became hot favourite. The only real question was whether Brown would also decide to run.

On his return to London, Tony Blair was met at Heathrow by his wife. Cherie had been very disappointed that her husband had not put himself forward in 1992 and was determined that he should run. This time Blair did not need convincing. His determination was bolstered by his reception at Westminster. Fellow shadow Cabinet member, Mo Mowlam, and three former members of Kinnock's staff – Adam Ingram, an MP who had been Kinnock's Parliamentary Private Secretary, Charles Clarke, who had been his chief of staff, and Lord Eatwell, who had been his economic adviser – were waiting in Blair's office to offer their help. Jack Straw, shadow Education Secretary and an important bell-weather figure who was to run Blair's campaign, came out of his office opposite to pledge his aid. Peter Kilfoyle, an opposition whip from Liverpool, reported that backing for Blair amongst Labour MPs was overwhelming. Robin Cook, who was himself considering standing, said that, by 4 p.m. on that day, the Tea Room, where Labour MPs snacked, had decided that the Parliamentary Labour Party vote would go to Blair.[3] Blair, only too well aware of the need for restraint, quietly thanked MPs who came to his office or telephoned in pledging their support.

Like much of Westminster, I had spent Thursday in shock at the death of John Smith, who had been a friend for thirty years. However, on the Friday morning, I rang Tony Blair to tell him that he should run. As I noted in my diary, 'I am left in no doubt that he is preparing to do just that.' However, my diary entry went on:

> There is the problem of Gordon Brown. It would be counterproductive
> if both Tony and Gordon stood . . . Tony is much more attractive to the

electors and so much more likely to lead us to victory. Still, it will mean Gordon, who is both exceptionally able and ambitious, giving up what may be his only shot at the leadership.[4]

It was clear that Blair was trying to persuade Brown not to stand because he asked me to speak to two of Brown's senior Scottish supporters, Donald Dewar, John Smith's closest friend in politics and the shadow Social Secretary, and George Robertson, the European spokesman. Both were well aware of Blair's overwhelming appeal to the voters but said it was important that, if Brown was going to withdraw from the contest, he should be allowed time to consider his position.

Blair and Brown had met on Thursday evening in the house of Blair's brother Bill. Brown had spent much of the day writing obituaries. In a moving one for the *Daily Mirror* he had extolled John Smith's virtues, including his fearless sense of duty, putting service to others first, and his politics which 'were shaped more by Kirk and community than ideological theories'. As one commentator noted, he might have been writing his own manifesto.[5] When Blair told Brown he was under strong pressure to run, Brown made clear that he had every intention of standing himself. He also reminded Blair that they had an informal pact not to run against each other and that, when they had talked about it in 1992, they had agreed that Brown, as the senior partner, had first claim. Blair replied that things had now moved on and he was seen as the clear favourite. In other words, there was a stand-off. Over the next nineteen days, there were many further meetings and frequent telephone conversations between the two men to try to resolve the issue.

In reality, most of the pressure was on Brown. Brown might have had support from some trade unions and possibly in the constituency section of the party's electoral college. But the media and public opinion polls carried the powerful message that, of the two, Blair was far more likely to win the election for Labour. On the afternoon of

Smith's death, the well-known political commentator, Sarah Baxter, had written an article in the London *Evening Standard* in which she said, 'There is only one political successor to John Smith who is streets ahead of all the other candidates. He is Tony Blair.' The next day, the rest of the press, including not only *The Times* and the *Financial Times* but also the *Daily Mail* and the *Sun*, followed suit. The *Daily Mail* proclaimed: 'Blair is the man the Conservatives most fear – a man of rare ability . . . and he has an unblemished reputation for honesty and integrity.' And the *Sun* admitted: 'Blair has the looks, style and message that could appeal to many disenchanted Tory voters.' On Sunday, a MORI poll in the *Sunday Times* confirmed that Blair was the public's choice with 32 per cent support. Brown trailed behind John Prescott and Margaret Beckett with only 9 per cent. Most Labour MPs were desperate for a winner and Blair, with his appeal to wavering and non-committed voters especially in the south, was the obvious choice.

Brown's campaign advisers, headed by Nick Brown and supported by his brothers, Andrew and John, were urging him to stand. Nick Brown believed that his namesake had significant support in all sections of the electoral college and could make a formidable challenge. However, at the same time, Gordon Brown was also receiving some more unwelcome advice. On 18 May, the political consultant, Philip Gould, adviser to both Brown and Blair, told Brown that Blair had a much better chance of winning because he not only met the mood of the nation, he exemplified it. Gould told James Naughtie: 'He [Blair] would create for Labour and for Britain a sense of change, of a new beginning, which Gordon could not do.'[6] Two days before, Brown had also received a carefully written note from his friend Mandelson in which Peter argued that Blair was the front runner and that, if Brown now stood, it would be highly damaging not only to the modernising cause and the party but to Brown's standing in the country. He concluded by saying that:

drift is harming you . . . You have either to escalate rapidly (and to be effective I think I would need to become clearly partisan with the press in your favour) or you need to implement a strategy to exit with enhanced position, strength and respect. Will you let me know your wishes?'[7]

According to Mandelson, before it was sent, the letter was seen by Donald Dewar, Brown's senior Cabinet supporter, who apparently did not object to its contents.

In the Brown camp, Mandelson's intervention was considered to be treachery. They already thought, almost certainly unjustly, that Mandelson was working for Blair and briefing the press against Brown. The truth was that Mandelson continued to admire both of his two friends immensely and the prospect of having to choose between them placed him in an almost impossible dilemma. One of his closest friends, Roger Liddle, said that, while his relationship with Blair was easier, 'the great figure, the leadership figure was Gordon'. On the Saturday night after Smith's death, at a birthday party for his wife, Caroline, Liddle had an agonised conversation with Mandelson about the leadership – Liddle was seeking to persuade him to back Blair but Mandelson seemed to think he could still persuade Blair not to run. From the moment he heard of Smith's death, he had tried to be impartial between Blair and Brown. When, on the day of Smith's death, he met Blair in a deserted Commons division lobby – the Commons had adjourned as a mark of respect to Smith – he was distinctly cautious, while admitting that Blair was entitled to consider himself a possible candidate. Earlier, when he had met Brown in his flat, while acknowledging his friend's pre-eminent role, he had insisted that the trio would need to discuss what happened next together.

His soundings with MPs and the media over Friday and Saturday made it clear to him that Blair was very much in the lead. Even then, he told journalists that they should not write off Brown's chances. His only possible mistake was agreeing to an interview on *The Week in Politics* to discuss the leadership in which he said that the question facing the party was:

who will play best at the box office, who will not simply appeal to the traditional supporters and customers of the Labour Party, but will bring in those extra, additional votes that we need in order to win convincingly at the next election?

In listing possible candidates, he put them in the following order: 'Tony Blair, for example or Gordon Brown or Robin Cook or John Prescott.' To the Brown camp, by now very much on the defensive, this appeared to be an appeal to the party to vote for Blair.

At John Smith's funeral on 20 May in Edinburgh, attended by 1,500 people, Blair and Brown, both looking strained, sat a few pews away from each other, with 'Tony Blair standing a little apart from other shadow Cabinet Ministers as if he already knows that the mantle has fallen on him'.[8] But Brown had not yet given up. Two days after the Smith funeral, he delivered a big speech to the Welsh Labour Party. It was a fine oratorical performance, pitched to appeal to party activists and with an almost biblical peroration:

For everything there is a season, and a time to every purpose . . . For us now more than ever before, this is the time to unite. Because we have travelled too far, too many miles together, for us now to lose sight of our destination. Together we have climbed too high for us not to achieve the summit. And it is near.[9]

The message was unclear. Was this the start of a Brown campaign, as some newspapers suggested, or was it signalling the end? Or was it, rather, Brown keeping his options open and saying, 'I'm a still a major figure'?

However, a series of BBC opinion polls over the following weekend suggested that Brown had made little impact. Blair had a clear lead in all sections of the electoral college while a Gallup survey of Labour Party members for *On the Record* put Blair on 47 per cent, Prescott on 15 per cent and Brown on 11 per cent. The unkindest cut of all was a poll of Scots Labour MPs published in the *Scotsman* on 27 May. Fifteen MPs said they would back Brown if he stood. Only six said they would back Blair but six others said that, although they felt a personal obligation to Brown, they hoped he would stand down so that they could back Blair, who was most likely to win the general election for Labour. Brown's brother, John, later said, 'Gordon said to me that was the finish. It was the key issue in coming to a conclusion, that poll in *The Scotsman*.'[10]

In one of his few comments on the 1994 leadership election, Brown told his biographer, Paul Routledge:

> The newspapers, with a few notable exceptions, did not back me – not least because I was out of fashion. I was never part of the London scene anyway. But that did not in my view mean much, once the campaign started among ordinary Labour party members and indeed backbench MPs.[11]

His campaign manager Nick Brown continued to argue that Gordon Brown, if he had remained in the contest, would have had the support needed to win. But he had to say that in order to preserve his friend's position in the media and in any discussion with Blair.

In truth, Brown's path to the leadership was blocked. As the opinion polls had shown, Blair had the 'modernising' vote virtually sewn up. If Brown was going to mount a challenge to Blair, then it would have to be as a traditionalist candidate. He would have had to attack his friend, Tony Blair, from the Left and appeal to all the conservative instincts of the party; Peter Mandelson called them 'the forces of darkness'.[12] As Brown was well aware, such a candidature might have fatally undermined the prospects for modernisation but without any guarantee that it would have been successful. On 28 May, Margaret Beckett hinted that she was preparing to stand. This was likely to mean that she would get the nomination of the big unions the like the T&G and GMB, making it almost impossible for Brown to assemble a winning coalition. Meanwhile John Prescott was waiting in the wings. It was quite possible that Brown faced not just defeat but humiliation. He came reluctantly to the conclusion that the best course was to seek a deal with Blair.

Allegedly, the deal was that Brown would allow Blair a clear run for the leadership of the party in return for which Blair would stand down at some unspecified time in the future and he would then back Brown to become the next Labour Party leader. These terms were popularly believed to have been agreed over a meal that Brown and Blair shared at the Granita restaurant in Islington but, as the political biographer John Campbell put it, 'Like an international summit meeting, the Granita dinner was only the formalisation of an agreement tortuously negotiated over the previous days.'[13] Gordon Brown had already signalled on BBC Radio on Bank Holiday Monday, 30 May, that he was pulling out:

> I will make my decision, as I believe my colleagues will make their decision, on what is necessary for Labour to win the next election. I don't think anybody's personal interest should come before what is the greatest public endeavour that the Labour Party is engaged in – that is, to return a government to power that is interested in creating the economic efficiency and social justice that this country needs.[14]

That evening, Brown called his campaign managers together. He and his 'fixer', Nick Brown, his childhood friend, Murray Elder, and his new public relations adviser, Charlie Whelan all met at Joe Allen's, a restaurant in Covent Garden. Nick Brown and Whelan continued to try to persuade him to run but Gordon told his campaign team that he was going to make an agreement with Blair on the best terms he could get. This was the real moment of concession.

On the face of it, a candidate who is withdrawing from a contest –

A long-haired Gordon Brown wins the election for student Rector at Edinburgh University in 1971. He was called 'the outstanding Scot of his generation'.

The young Blair fights the Beaconsfield by-election for Labour in 1982. He lost his deposit but his charm and good manners impressed party leaders.

A long-haired and bearded Peter Mandelson as Vice Chairman of the British Youth Council in 1977. A friend described him as 'immensely funny, attentive, malicious, witty'.

The Blair–Brown partnership – when John Smith died, Brown expected Blair to back him for the party leadership but, after the two men had apparently struck a deal, Brown stood down in favour of Blair, who had more support, and in return he was given the chancellorship.

Mandelson masterminded Labour's triumphant 1997 campaign and here he is photographed with Fitz the bulldog, who was used in an election broadcast to demonstrate the party's patriotic credentials.

Tony Blair, with his wife Cherie and their family, voting in his Sedgefield constituency at the 1997 election. Though he could hardly dare to believe it, Labour was heading for a landslide victory.

Tony Blair waves to his supporters outside 10 Downing Street after his party's historic victory. He said, 'We have been elected as New Labour and we will govern as New Labour.' Nobody, including Blair, quite knew what he meant.

A youthful Tony Blair outpaces other European leaders at the Intergovernmental Conference in Amsterdam. The Foreign Office Permanent Secretary commented, 'Blair enjoyed Amsterdam. He found he was good at European negotiations and had a real flair for them.'

OPPOSITE
Bottom left: Super Chancellor Brown raises his dispatch box to the media before delivering his second budget to the commons in March 1998. In his first two years as chancellor, he introduced a number of innovative measures, including transferring control over interest rates to the Bank of England.

Bottom right: Mandelson looks pleased to be carrying two dispatch boxes. After a short period as Minister without Portfolio, Blair promoted him to the Cabinet as Secretary of State for Trade and Industry from which he was forced to resign for failing to reveal a loan from a fellow minister.

Blair's first Cabinet – it was the most inexperienced administration since the first Labour govern-ment in 1924 and most of the big decisions were taken by Blair and Brown.

Blair and Mandelson in Northern Ireland after Blair brought his closest ally back into the Cabinet as Secretary of State for Northern Ireland, a move described as 'the fastest rehabilitation from disgrace in modern political history'.

An emotional Mandelson and a sad Blair photographed on the frontbench after Mandelson had been forced to resign over the Hinduja passport affair. The Hammond inquiry subsequently completely exonerated Mandelson.

Relations between Blair and Brown were frosty during the 2001 election campaign, which Labour won in a landslide. At the victory party, the two men barely exchanged a word.

In June 2003, Gordon Brown tells the Commons that the UK has failed the five tests for joining the euro. It is a defeat for Blair who wanted to keep the issue open.

Prominent Labour supporters enthusiastically applaud Blair's keynote speech at the 2003 party conference while Brown's hands look as though they are clasped in sullen disapproval.

even if his advisers tell him he could have won – has few cards in his hand. However, Blair was desperately anxious to have Brown on his side. Both Blair and Mandelson, who was now advising Blair, knew what a dangerous enemy Brown could be if he felt slighted. They also greatly respected his ability. In addition, in Blair's case, there was an element of guilt. There had been a pact in 1992 in which he, Blair, had agreed to let the senior partner, Brown, have first shot at the leadership, a pact which, because things had moved on, was no longer operative. Now Blair was determined to tie Brown in by offering him a deal which he could not refuse.

Nobody knows exactly what was discussed at the Granita restaurant on the evening of 31 May as there were no minute takers. Ed Balls accompanied Brown to help him find the then fashionable restaurant in Islington (now defunct) but left soon after. Brown and Blair were recognised by a journalist who was dining there with her husband but, as the two men were sitting in the back, they were able to get on with their discussion in private. To begin with, Brown was concerned about securing positions for his supporters in the shadow team and in any future government and believed that he had a promise from Blair that he would be consulted on key ministerial and party appointments.

The most important immediate issue, however, was the role which Brown himself would play in government. Mandelson had rightly warned Blair that Brown would ask for what amounted to an unprecedented 'super' chancellorship, with control not only over economic policy but large areas of social policy as well. Blair was prepared to concede to Brown's demands, so eager was he to have him on board. The next day (1 June) at his house in Hartlepool, Peter Mandelson finalised a briefing note for the media which amplified this agreement. It read:

> Both [Blair and Brown] recognise the importance of the partnership they
> have built up and of the Smith legacy of unifying the Party and making
> use of all its talents. In his Wales and Luton speeches, Gordon has spelled

out the fairness agenda – social justice, employment opportunities and skills – which he believes should be the centrepiece of Labour's programme and Tony is in full agreement with this and that the Party's economic and social policies should be further developed on this basis.

Apparently, Brown made an amendment to the text – in place of 'Tony is in full agreement with this', he wrote 'Tony has guaranteed this will be pursued'. Blair twice refused on the grounds that it would be wrong to limit his room for manoeuvre as a future Prime Minister. But Brown leaked his version of the agreement to Peter Riddell, the highly respected *Times* columnist, who wrote in his column of June 2:

> The word yesterday was that messrs Blair and Brown would operate as a partnership, with the latter the driving force on the economic side. Mr Blair, it is said, has guaranteed Mr Brown that the latter's 'fairness' agenda, broadening employment opportunities and improving training and skills will be the centrepiece of Labour's economic and social programme.[15]

Thus the Granita agreement, in both its Brown and Blair versions, enshrined the extraordinary powers of the super chancellorship which Brown would inherit if Labour won the general election. As Mandelson had foreseen, it amounted to an unprecedented partnership, almost to a 'dual premiership', giving Brown control over much of domestic policy. In opposition, such a deal may not have seemed so important. In government, Blair would come bitterly to regret the extent of the concession he had made to Brown, whether out of guilt or fear or a mixture of both.

There was a further issue which was also discussed – and that was the question of succession. The Brown camp claimed that it was Blair who raised the succession issue, not Brown. According to one version, Blair promised to stand down as leader and back Brown after ten years. The Blair camp denied making any such precise commitment. Indeed, it is not a commitment that is really in the power of anyone, not even a Prime

Minister, to make. What could have happened was that Blair, with his exceptional political antennae, instinctively understood that Brown needed to be given hope. A colleague once said about Blair, 'One of Tony's weaknesses is that whatever has just happened he always wants you to leave the room feeling happy.'[16] He could well have said, 'Look, Gordon, I am not going to be leader for ever – and, when I stand down, I will back you to succeed me.' In his February 2010 television interview with Piers Morgan, Brown seemed to confirm this version. However, in practice, he behaved as though he expected Blair to step down sometime during his second term. For the time being, it did not matter that there were different interpretations of what was said about the succession though, obviously after Labour's second election victory, it became very important indeed.

At 3 p.m. the next day, 1 June, after a Mandelson initiative allowed news about the deal to be leaked, Brown issued a press release which, in the manner of such press releases – especially those issued by Brown – said:

> I now believe that speculation and confusion about my position should be swiftly brought to an end so that we can concentrate on victory in the European Election campaign. When nominations open on June 10, I will encourage Tony Blair to stand and, if he should, I will give him my full support to become not only the Labour Party's next leader but the next Prime Minister of our country.

The two men then somewhat artificially staged a walk around New Palace Yard, the courtyard below Big Ben, for the TV cameras. I noted in my diary:

> It reminds me of that 1976 German Social Democrat (SDP) election poster of Schmidt and Brandt, when the SDP was trying to show that, despite their differences, they could still work together. It will, indeed, be vital for Tony and Gordon to continue to cooperate. It will need Gordon to swallow his pride and Tony to be extremely tactful.[17]

I also wrote to Gordon Brown to congratulate him on his statesmanship in standing aside, adding that to become Chancellor of the Exchequer was itself a formidable achievement and that his turn for the top job might come. A few days later, I met Brown in the Commons and, in the course of the conversation, Gordon admitted that, if he had entered the contest, he would probably have been defeated.

After Brown's announcement, Blair's election campaign was plain sailing. Unlike his two rivals, John Prescott and Margaret Beckett, who announced their candidature at Westminster, Blair appropriately launched his campaign where his career had started – in his Sedgefield constituency. When the result was announced at the University of London's Institute of Education Centre on 21 July, he had won an overwhelming victory in all sections of the electoral college including the trade unions. His own flair and ambition, the victory of one person, one vote in the electoral college and, above all, Labour's desperation for election victory had brought the forty-one-year-old Tony Blair to the leadership.

Later, at his celebration party at Church House, Blair thanked his supporters, including a mysterious 'Bobby' for his help. This was a coded Kennedy-esque reference to Mandelson who, behind the scenes, had been advising Blair on his campaign. Blair had thought it necessary to disguise Mandelson's participation because a number of his campaign team, including Mo Mowlam and Peter Kilfoyle, had threatened to resign if he was involved because they thought he would deter some political Blair supporters. Such was Mandelson's reputation as an arch media manipulator and 'fixer' that some, even in the Labour Party, called him 'the Prince of Darkness'.

The sudden death of John Smith and the events which followed, culminating in the Granita Pact and the election of Tony Blair as leader of the Labour Party, fundamentally shifted the relationships within the modernising trio. In a way, the loser from Blair's election as leader was Mandelson. The Brown camp wrongly blamed him for Blair's popularity in the media and in the public opinion polls and believed, again probably wrongly, that he had played a treacherous role both in supporting Blair behind Brown's back and in advising Brown to withdraw from the contest. Brown's relations with Mandelson did not recover until, as Prime Minister, he made him Secretary of State for Business in 2008. As a result, Mandelson, who had previously looked up to Brown as the senior partner in the modernising trio, was thrown into the arms of Blair, who tended to use him as an intimate consultant and adviser, a kind of super courtier, rather than allowing him to develop an independent career of his own – though, in 1998, he brought him into the Cabinet as Secretary of State for Industry.

Obviously the key change was in the position of Tony Blair. In 1992, when Kinnock resigned, Brown was still the senior partner. Two years later, Blair leapfrogged him to become leader of the Labour Party. This was – and remained – a bitter blow for Brown who still believed he was better qualified to be Prime Minister. There is a persuasive argument that it would have been better for all concerned if Brown had stood for the leadership as it would have produced a definite result – almost certainly a Blair victory over Brown. But, at the time, Blair felt that the danger of an open conflict between the two modernising standard bearers would weaken the modernising cause. There was also the possibility, however remote, that it would have let in a more traditional candidate.

In the days following the death of John Smith on 12 May up to 1 June when Brown pulled out of the leadership race, Blair and Brown had a series of meetings in an attempt to work out a modus vivendi which would give Brown an exceptional role in both opposition and government – as well as hope for the succession – while, crucially, ensuring Blair had a clear run at the leadership. For some years, the deal, by providing the basis for the continuing partnership between Blair and Brown, worked to the benefit not only of the two men but also of the Labour Party. But its ambiguities and the fact that the partnership was now governed more by mutual self-interest than by their former close friendship meant that it was inherently unstable and open to challenge.

7

THE TRIUMPH OF
NEW LABOUR

The new Labour leader inherited a strong legacy from John Smith. Under his emollient, inclusive leadership the party was more united than it had been for thirty years. It had a big lead in the public opinion polls and had performed extremely well in both the local and European elections. Far more than in 1992, the party was ready for Tony Blair and the modernisers. Blair was also fortunate to be facing a Tory party still demoralised by 'Black Wednesday', when sterling was driven out of the European Exchange Rate Mechanism, deeply divided over Europe and increasingly out of touch with the electorate. However, Blair was convinced that, if Labour was to establish political dominance, hopefully stretching beyond just one election victory, then, like Mrs Thatcher in the 1980s, it would have to win the battle of ideas and values.

In June 1994, at the start of his campaign for the leadership, he wrote a short memorandum, outlining his main themes, which was later incorporated into his campaign manifesto. He stressed that he came to the party through beliefs not background and that values were at the heart of his policies. He also wanted a bold new agenda for the party which would redefine what being left of centre was now about. Socialism, he said, was 'not a set of rigid economic prescriptions but a set of values', based on a belief in society and community. Drawing on what he had learnt from Thomson and Macmurray at Oxford and from his northern constituency, he argued that individuals prospered best within a strong and cohesive society, 'where opportunity and obligation go hand in hand'.[1] Although Blair saw the need for new policy directions, especially on welfare, the economy, the constitution and Europe, his major contribution – and his special skill – was in providing a new framework or narrative within which he could reinvigorate and reposition his party.

Before Blair went on holiday on 27 July, he was told about the response of a focus group of waverers in Slough, a key marginal (this was part of the research for the third Fabian pamphlet in the 'Southern Discomfort' series). Though they liked what they had seen of him, there was still much to do to reassure their vital swing votes. Blair showed interest in the case for a revision of Clause 4 as a symbol of change.[2] On holiday in France, he met Alastair Campbell, whom he was trying to persuade to become his press secretary, and told him that he was thinking seriously of having a review of the constitution and scrapping Clause 4. Apparently it was Blair's boldness on Clause 4 which persuaded Campbell to join Blair's office.[3] Over the summer, Blair also spoke to Brown and Mandelson about the abolition of Clause 4.[4] At a meeting of modernisers at Chewton Glen, a hotel and country club in the Hampshire countryside, Blair told Philip Gould, 'Conference must build New Labour. It is time we gave the party some electric shock treatment.'[5] However, despite these bold words, until a few days before conference, he was still undecided whether to risk announcing a review of the constitution in his keynote address.

Very few people in the party believed in the existing Clause 4 any longer. It had been written by Sidney Webb over seventy years before and committed the Labour Party 'to secure for the workers by hand or by brain

the full fruits of their industry . . . upon the basis of the common ownership of the means of production, distribution and exchange'. However,
Blair's immediate predecessors as leaders, Smith and Kinnock, did not
believe a revision was worth the trouble it could create. Thirty-five years
before, Hugh Gaitskell's ill-planned attempt to change the clause had
failed, defeated by the conservatism of the unions and the Left. His
successor, Harold Wilson, commented cynically, 'We were being asked
to take Genesis out of the Bible. You don't have to be a fundamentalist
to say that Genesis is part of the bible.'[6] Now, in the post-Soviet era when
the command economy was confined to a few countries like North Korea,
the case for a massive extension of public ownership was almost univer-
sally acknowledged to be anachronistic. Allowing the existing Clause 4
to stand not only tied the party to an outdated economic doctrine but
was also an impediment to explaining what it now stood for. Screwing
up his courage, Blair decided that revising Clause 4 would provide the
ideal opportunity to demonstrate that, under his leadership, Labour really
had changed.

Delegates to the 1994 party conference at Blackpool were greeted by
a new slogan – 'New Labour, New Britain' – against a pale green background. It was a statement of intent, rather than an accomplished fact.
However, in his first conference speech, Blair showed himself to be an
uncompromising moderniser. In words which would have been booed a
few years before, he said:

A belief in society, working together, solidarity, cooperation, partnership
– These are our words . . . It is not the socialism of Marx or state control.
It is a straightforward view of society: in the understanding that the individual does best in a strong and decent community of people, with principles
and standards and common aims and values . . . Our task is to apply those
values to the modern world. It will change the traditional dividing lines
between right and left. And it calls for a new politics – without dogma
and without swapping our prejudices for theirs.[7]

This was a bold attempt to move away from old-fashioned socialism towards a more modern approach, based on principles and values.

At the end of the speech – the last three pages of which had not been issued to the press – Blair, without specifically mentioning Clause 4, called for a clear and up-to-date statement of its objects and objectives to be debated by the party and, if agreed, to become part of the constitution. The speech was given a standing ovation. George Robertson summed up what happened next: 'As the applause died, you could hear the sound of pennies dropping all round the hall.'[8] At a Fabian meeting that evening, I said, 'I have been outflanked by my leader.' I had not been expecting Blair to go so far in his first speech to conference. Robin Cook, who was addressing the same meeting, struck a sceptical note about the whole exercise.[9] A few hours before making his speech, Blair had briefed Cook about his intentions. Cook's response was: 'You may well win but, by the time the blood is cleared from the carpet, I doubt you will think it was a fight worth having.'[10]

Despite the applause for Blair's speech, two days later, a resolution reaffirming Clause 4 was narrowly carried – a reminder that the new Labour leader did indeed have a fight on his hands. Crucially, his deputy, John Prescott, had been persuaded to support the change but, during the winter, a majority of MEPs and some powerful trade union leaders came out against revision, while the *Tribune* newspaper published a survey of constituencies which appeared, erroneously, to suggest that a majority were against. The former deputy leader, Roy Hattersley, who was emerging as a critic of Blair, poured cold water on the idea of change: 'I have learned, during the forty years since Clement Attlee was Prime Minister, that the party does best when it is at peace with itself.'[11] Blair, realising that his leadership was on the line, decided to take personal charge of the Clause 4 campaign.

Calling together key members of his staff and party officials including Tom Sawyer, the party's new General Secretary, he cleared his diary and, with John Prescott, launched the 'New Labour, New

Britain' roadshow. Over the next three months, he held two or three meetings a week, visiting twenty-two towns and cities. Margaret McDonagh, one of Blair's leading campaigners and later to become General Secretary of the party, said about Blair: 'At the beginning he wasn't so sure of himself but he rapidly found his measure and came over as funny and clever, and also passionate'.[12] Party members across the country saw the Labour leader at his most persuasive, shirt-sleeved best. The Tony Blair who had captivated his Sedgefield constituency party – and, in doing so, built up one of the highest memberships in the country – now did the same nationwide. In turn, he was impressed by the party. As he told the *Guardian*, 'The Labour Party is much nicer than it looks.'[13]

On 29 April 1995 at the Methodist Central Hall, Westminster, where the original Clause 4 was adopted in 1918, a new Clause 4 was approved by 65 per cent of the total vote. And 90 per cent of the constituencies supported the new clause. Significantly, the two big unions who were opposed, the T&G and Unison, had failed, unlike the constituencies, to ballot their members. It was a personal triumph for Blair, who had taken a big risk. By demonstrating so clearly his ability to modernise the Labour Party, his victory over Clause 4 provided a crucial launching pad for Labour's rise to power.

Blair's new Clause 4 made no mention of nationalisation and little of policies, although it accepted 'the enterprise of the market and the rigours of competition'. In Blairite fashion, it was expressed primarily in terms of values, declaring that:

> by the strength of our common endeavour we achieve more than we achieve alone, so as to create for each of us the means to realise our true potential and for all of us a community in which power, wealth and opportunity are in the hands of the many not the few, and where the rights we enjoy reflect the duties we owe, and where we live together, freely, in a spirit of solidarity, tolerance and respect.

Critics argued that the new clause was so general that it could be supported by a wide swathe of progressive opinion, even perhaps by some Tories. But that was precisely the point. Blair was determined that the party should be in a position to attract new support, well beyond its core vote. As he explained his 'big tent' philosophy to *She* magazine in March 1995, 'Socialism . . . is not about class, or trade unions, or capitalism versus socialism. It is about a belief in working together to get things done.'[14] The adoption of a unifying, 'one nation' message was a key turning point for New Labour.

From the revision of Clause 4 in April 1995 to the general election of May 1997, Blair, with a characteristic mixture of radicalism and caution, prepared the party for the general election. The Tories were in such disarray that, in the summer of 1995, their leader, John Major, decided to resign in order to seek the endorsement of his parliamentary party in a fresh leadership election. Major won but a third of his party did not vote for him. Even so, the Labour leader never became complacent. Roy Jenkins described Blair's behaviour thus: 'Tony is like a man who is carrying a precious vase across a crowded and slippery ballroom. He is desperate above all that the vase should not fall and be smashed.'[15] In this task, Blair was assisted not only by the two other leading modernisers but also by a fourth figure, Alastair Campbell, Blair's new press secretary. Campbell was not only a skilled tabloid journalist but an extremely powerful personality who, until his resignation in 2003, spent more waking hours with the Labour leader than even Brown and Mandelson. In the story of New Labour, Campbell is entitled to be ranked as a kind of 'Fourth Musketeer', a trusted confidant who was always on hand to give Blair the bluntest of advice. Blair's office was also joined by a chief of staff, the cool and efficient former diplomat, Jonathan Powell, and by a highly intelligent head of policy, David Miliband, who later became Foreign Secretary in Brown's government. Together with his personal aide, Anji Hunter, and Sally Morgan, who was responsible for relations with the party, they made a formidable team.

As a symbol of his special position in Blair's shadow Cabinet, Brown also had his own group of advisers. The key members were his economic adviser, the clever former *Financial Times* journalist, Ed Balls, his press spokesman, Charlie Whelan, (recruited by Mandelson) and Sue Nye, his personal assistant. They were joined by the millionaire Labour MP, Geoffrey Robinson, whose well-appointed Grosvenor House Hotel flat provided a highly convenient meeting place where Brown's so-called 'Hotel Group' could discuss political strategy and devise economic policies not only to help win the general election but also to guide a Labour government once the election was won. The windfall tax on privatised utilities and the plan to give independence to the Bank of England were both designed in Robinson's flat.

Brown had been badly bruised by his failure to win the leadership in 1994. Robert Peston, who wrote a highly favourable account of Brown's chancellorship (published in 2005) and was given full access to Brown and his entourage, said that, after 1994, a change came over his personality. According to Peston, he became more sombre, less relaxed and more introspective. He had been deeply hurt by what he saw, arguably mistakenly, as a betrayal by his oldest and closest political friend and psychologically took a long time to recover.

However, the partnership between the two men survived. Even if there was no longer the trust – at least on Brown's side – that there had been before, they still needed each other. Brown stayed up late helping Blair with his victory speech in July 1994. In the autumn, Blair ignored calls for Brown to be replaced as shadow Chancellor by Cook who had come top in the shadow Cabinet elections. If Brown did not play a prominent part in the campaign to change Clause 4, he was always on hand to give advice on tactics. Blair needed Brown's help on economic policy and, to realise his own plans, Brown needed the support of Blair in the shadow Cabinet and, of course, required Blair to win the general election. The two men were bound together by hoops of steel – and would continue to be.

If the Blair–Brown relationship was essential to achieving a Labour election victory and to an effective post-election government, Blair also continued to rely on his other leading political strategist, Peter Mandelson. The trouble was that relations between Brown and Mandelson were at an all-time low. Brown had not forgiven Mandelson for what he considered to be Mandelson's treachery in preferring Blair to Brown after John Smith's death. Just how strongly Brown felt was brought home to Mandelson at the Chewton Glen modernisers' meeting in September 1994. Brown and Mandelson had stayed up for a nightcap after Blair had gone to bed. Brown had then argued that, if he and Mandelson were in agreement, Blair would always take their advice. Mandelson said that his loyalty to Brown was not in question but that he was not prepared to join in an alliance 'to outmanoeuvre Tony'. Brown, in a foretaste of future disharmony, replied, 'Choose for yourself.'[16]

Mandelson dated his break with Brown not so much to the events leading up to the 1994 leadership election but to this later conversation. If Brown appeared to be shocked at how complete Mandelson's switch of loyalty had been, it seemed to Mandelson that Brown was finding it difficult to adjust to the new reality – that there could only be one leader. Much to his annoyance, Blair had to devote time to managing the relationship between Brown and Mandelson. He would ask members of his staff, 'Why, oh why, can't my two best people get on with each other?'[17] Blair was determined that both men should play a prominent role in Labour's election campaign. There was a prolonged argument between Brown and Mandelson over who should do what which was only decided in October 1995. In addition to his duties as junior civil service spokesman, Mandelson was appointed chairman of the crucial general election planning group, situated at Millbank, which was to report to the overall strategy committee, itself chaired by Brown.

But this sensible solution to the organisation of the campaign did little to improve what had now become a dysfunctional relationship between the two men. At meetings, Brown often refused to speak directly to

Mandelson, addressing his remarks to Blair, while Mandelson would make acid and contemptuous asides. There were also issues of substance between the two men – for example, over the Chancellor's plan to end child benefit for the parents of sixteen- to eighteen-year-olds and whether to support a new top rate of tax. However, these differences could have been resolved much more easily if their relationship had been better.

On 9 May 1996, there was a sudden explosion when Mandelson stormed out of a meeting and then flew off to a conference in Prague, writing a letter to Blair on the way and resigning as election manager. What made matters worse was that two days later there was a report in *The Times* saying that Blair was having to make considerable efforts to heal the chronic split between Brown and Mandelson. Blair was furious. He wrote a reply to Mandelson in which he said that, while it could be difficult to work with Brown, there were faults on both sides. He was certainly not prepared to tolerate walkouts or stories in *The Times*. 'We are not players in some Greek tragedy,' Blair chided Mandelson. He went on:

> Have you any conception of how despairing it is for me when the two people that have been closest to me for more than a decade, and who in their different ways are the most brilliant minds of their generation will not lay aside personal animosity and help me win?[18]

As Mandelson fully understood, if it came to a choice between Brown and him, Blair would always go for Brown. But Blair did not see why he had to choose between them. He summoned both men to his office and pleaded with them to work together. Blair's biographer remarked that the incident on 9 May was a reminder of quite how 'emotional, volatile and egotistical politicians can be'.[19] It was also an example of how the trio's decade-long friendship had become, as far as Brown and Mandelson were concerned, one of fierce competition and rivalry – 'Like scorpions in a bottle' was the way a mutual friend described it.[20] The only one who came well out of the drama was Blair who, by deploying his remarkable diplomatic skills, managed to keep the trio together.

As the election drew near, Blair's campaign team summed up New Labour's approach – 'reassure (the party really had changed), remind (about the Tory record) and reward (with what Labour could offer).'[21] With hindsight, it could be argued New Labour's caution was excessive – as shown by its meagre policy commitments. The party was good at saying what it was against. It was much less good at saying what it was for.

It is clearly inappropriate to compare 1997 with the Labour victory of 1945. In 1945 Labour won on an ambitious programme which, to a considerable extent, had already been agreed across the parties. What happened was that the voters turned to Bevin, Morrison and Attlee rather than Churchill to implement the social gains provided by the wartime coalition government. A better comparison is with Harold Wilson in 1964. Wilson's commitment to replace 'the closed, exclusive society by an open society in which all have an opportunity to work and serve' and 'to streamline our institutions, modernise our methods of government, bring the entire nation into a working partnership with the state' could have been made by Blair, while the New Labour slogan of 'New Labour, New Britain' was a straight crib from Wilson's election campaign.

However, one difference between the Wilson and Blair campaigns was that, in 1964, Wilson made a series of detailed speeches about policy issues. Blair's conference and other speeches were often highly eloquent performances with some memorable sentences and phrases. They were good at setting out New Labour's values, agenda and positioning but they were short on policy detail. It was partly in answer to that criticism that the party came up with the idea of a pledge card, giving specific and achievable commitments – smaller classes for five-, six- and seven-year-olds, paid for by abolishing the assisted places scheme; fast-track punishment for persistent young offenders; cutting NHS waiting lists by an extra 100,000 patients by releasing £100 million saved from NHS red tape; getting 250,000 under-twenty-five-year-olds into work, using money from a windfall levy on the privatised utilities; tough rules for government spending and borrowing; low inflation and interest rates.

For the media and politicians, these pledges may have seemed small beer but, for voters, they were very persuasive. Labour's campaign 'guru', Philip Gould, commented, 'The pledges worked better than anything else I have ever tested in politics . . . They worked because they connected immediately to people's lives; because they were relatively small; because they were costed.'[22] And these symbolic policy pledges were linked to a popular new Labour leader, whose photograph was on the other side of the pledge card.

Blair and Brown were wary of making any larger commitments because they were determined to avoid the trap Labour had fallen into during the 1992 election, when expensive promises on pensions and child benefit had laid the party open to Tory attacks on Labour's tax proposals to pay for them – the so-called 'Labour Tax Bombshell'. On 20 January 1997 in a much-publicised speech, the shadow Chancellor, Gordon Brown, underlined Labour's cautious approach by making it clear that an incoming Labour government would neither increase the basic rate of income tax nor put up the top rate. In a move which would cause difficulties for the future, he also pledged not to spend more than the Tory government had already set aside for the first two years of the next government. Even the *Daily Mail* was impressed by the prudence of the shadow Chancellor:

> Gordon Brown's speech was as significant an exorcism as we have witnessed in the post-war history of British politics. Impressively, the shadow Chancellor set about laying to rest the gibbering ghosts of tax and spend that have bedevilled his party's prospects for a generation. What can no longer be denied is that, on the Tories' favourite background of tax, he is proving an ever-more formidable adversary.[23]

Brown was making his own powerful contribution to a Labour victory. Blair took a number of other initiatives to strengthen Labour's electoral chances. One of the most intriguing was his contacts between 1994 and 1997 with the Liberal Democrats. Blair's leadership was almost immediately welcomed by three out of the four founders of the SDP – Roy Jenkins, Shirley Williams and Bill Rodgers. Blair formed an especially warm relationship with Jenkins. Jenkins told the Liberal leader, Paddy Ashdown, 'I think Tony treats me as a sort of father-figure in politics. He comes to me a lot for advice, particularly about how to construct a government.'[24]

For Blair, with Mandelson's strong support, cooperation or even coalition with the Liberal Democrats provided a way into government if Labour failed to win an overall majority. Even if Labour won a majority, he was attracted to the prospect of having Liberals in the government. It would, he believed, help him to keep the Left under control. In the longer term, there was the possibility, strongly espoused by Jenkins, of bringing together the progressive left-of-centre forces. However, there were a number of formidable obstacles to coalition with the Liberals. The majority of the shadow Cabinet, led by Brown and Prescott, were hostile while Blair himself was not convinced of the case for proportional representation which was the Liberal's basic demand if they were to enter government. Labour's landslide victory effectively killed off the idea of a Lib–Lab government though, after the election, Blair set up a joint Cabinet Consultation Committee and the Commission on Electoral Reform under Jenkins. However, the close relationship did make a difference to the electoral result. The number of seats won by both Labour and the Liberals was increased by tactical voting, a process which was encouraged by the good relations between Labour and the Liberals, especially Ashdown's abandonment of the policy of equidistance between the two major parties.

At a different level, Blair's flirtation with Mrs Thatcher showed how far the Labour leader was prepared to go to disarm his opponents. While John Major quarrelled with the former Prime Minister, Blair flattered her, saying, 'She was a thoroughly determined person and that is an admirable quality.'[25] The pay-off came when Mrs Thatcher told a dinner meeting at the Reform Club in London, 'Tony Blair is a man who won't let Britain down.'[26]

However, the most blatant example of 'supping with the devil' was Blair's wooing of the media magnate, Rupert Murdoch. In July 1995, with Alastair Campbell and Anji Hunter, Blair flew all the way to Australia as Murdoch's guest to address the News Corp 'Leadership Conference' in Hayman Island, the Murdoch papers' private resort. Accepting that, in the 1980s, Thatcher and Reagan had got some things right, including a greater emphasis on enterprise, Blair argued that the modern left of centre was best able to combine security and change. He confronted Murdoch's Euro-sceptic views, saying that Britain, even under the Tories, would be driven into closer European integration. Blair's boldness was rewarded when, at the start of the election, the *Sun*, which had so cruelly attacked Kinnock in 1992, came out for Blair. 'Give change a chance' was its welcome slogan – though the Labour government was to discover that there was a price to pay for the *Sun*'s support.

Equally important was Blair's policy of reaching out to business. While the trade unions were firmly told that they should expect 'fairness not favours', the Labour leader sought the backing of well-known business figures, such as Alan Sugar and Richard Branson, in order to demonstrate that New Labour was pro-business.

On 17 March 1997, John Major, after putting off polling day as long as possible, finally called an election for May. He had been hoping that improving economic conditions would turn the opinion polls in his favour. But Labour's average lead in the polls at the start of the election was 22 per cent. He also gambled on a long six-week campaign in which the Conservatives would have time to put Tony Blair's New Labour Party under pressure. In the event, it was Tory weaknesses which were exposed. The first two weeks were wasted on cases of Conservative 'sleaze' while the party's divisions over Europe and the single currency were only too obvious throughout the later part of the campaign. However, it is probable that, even if the Tories had fought a good campaign, they would have been heavily defeated. As John Major admitted in his autobiography, 'Quite simply, they [the voters] had fallen out of love with us.'[27]

In New Labour, they also faced a formidable political force. Tony Blair, the popular young leader, scarcely put a foot wrong throughout the campaign. Gordon Brown, working from the Millbank media centre, chaired both the strategy meetings and the morning press conferences very effectively. Peter Mandelson ran the highly professional team at Millbank, with its rebuttal unit, key seats section and a video recording centre. John Prescott toured the key marginals. The modernisers were able to present the party as having learnt from its past mistakes and now being capable of providing a credible alternative government. As Peter Mandelson and Roger Liddle wrote in their book, *The Blair Revolution*, New Labour's strategy was 'to move forward from where Margaret Thatcher left off, rather than to dismantle every single thing she did'.[28] Hence, Labour's acceptance of the role of the market in the new Clause 4, Blair's refusal to repeal the Conservatives' trade union legislation and Brown's prudent attitude to tax and spend. With his emphasis on 'education, education, education', Blair had sketched out a fresh educational agenda ('we will increase the share of national income spent on education'). He also had something to say about health (an improved NHS), social cohesion (with the emphasis on law and order), political and constitutional reform (above all devolution to Scotland and Wales) and a more constructive and co-operative attitude on Europe. But, apart from the five pledges, he was careful not to make any spending commitments which would lay the party open to a Tory onslaught over tax. Indeed, so confident did Labour become on the tax issue that they felt able to attack the Conservatives for introducing twenty-two tax rises since 1992.

On the issue which dominated the election, Europe, Blair played a defensive game though he did not change Labour's policy on the single currency of keeping the option of joining open, subject to a referendum, in the next Parliament. However, his 'mood music', especially when writing for a *Sun* audience, was increasingly Euro-sceptic, while a Labour party political broadcast unashamedly featured a bulldog. Despite the big polls leads (except for one rogue poll which cut the Labour lead to 5 per cent), Blair was running 'scared' – so much so that he made the quite unfounded accusation that the Tories were about to abolish the state pension.

However, as election day approached, Labour politicians began to scent victory though, remembering 1992, they refrained from triumphalism. At 10 p.m. on 1 May, the exit polls predicted a massive swing to Labour. The results confirmed the exit polls. At 12.14 a.m., Labour celebrated its first gain – Edgbaston was won for the first time on a 10 per cent swing. Labour gains then followed thick and fast. By 3.10 a.m., Labour had won an overall majority and finished with 418 seats, some in the most surprising places, such as Hastings, Hove and Wimbledon, and an overall majority of 178. Labour had won by a landslide, making impressive inroads in all social groups – for example, Labour outscored the Conservatives among professional and white-collar employees and among house owners, as well as those aged under thirty.[29]

After his count, Tony Blair, with his wife, flew down to London from his constituency to join a dawn victory rally at the Royal Festival Hall. At 12.30 p.m., he saw the Queen at Buckingham Palace and then entered Downing Street to the cheers of Labour staff and their families, waving Union Jacks. Peter Mandelson commented on Labour's victory, 'There was no reason left not to trust Labour . . . we had removed the target. Without New Labour, the Conservatives could have won again.'[30] This was a pardonable exaggeration. John Smith would have beaten the Tories. But, by running as the 'safe' alternative, New Labour made it more certain. The question now was what would the modernisers do with the power they had so decisively won.

PART 3

IN POWER

8

LEARNING THE ROPES

On entering 10 Downing Street on the day after the 1997 election, Tony Blair said, 'We have been elected as New Labour and we will govern as New Labour.' What did he mean? Speaking in the debate on the Queen's speech of the new Parliament, the new Prime Minister gave a minimalist explanation: 'The British people do not have false expectations. They simply want a government with clear leadership.'[1] After so long out of power, the modernisers wanted to show that, above all, Labour was capable of providing competent, fair and honest government. They also wanted to win a second term. Hence their stress on economic stability, improving public services, especially education and health, and tackling crime and anti-social behaviour. And hence Blair's continued emphasis on the 'big tent' approach.

What was remarkable about Blair's new team was its inexperience. None of the top ministers had held office. Of the Cabinet, only four had been ministers before. The only minister with Cabinet experience was the Attorney General John Morris, who was outside Blair's Cabinet. Arguably, it was the most inexperienced administration since the first

Labour government in 1924 though the then Labour Prime Minister, Ramsay MacDonald, at least had the assistance of two ministers who had previously been in a Cabinet. New Labour had to learn the ropes.

It was immediately apparent that the dominant personalities in the Cabinet were Blair and Brown. In opposition, they had been used to running things in partnership. The respected commentator, Peter Riddell, remarked, 'Their style was bilateral, not collective... Their normal method of operation was by pre-emption, selective briefing and bouncing colleagues.'[2] In government, they saw no reason to change their approach. Initially, at least, Cabinets were no more than reporting sessions. The real decisions were taken by Blair and Brown, usually in consultation with the relevant departmental minister.

The government's first decision, announced on 6 May 1997 and arguably the most important economic one taken in Labour's first term, was the transfer of operational control over interest rates from the Treasury to the Bank of England (see next chapter). This bold move created a more predictable and transparent framework for economic decision making, entrenched low inflation and low interest rates and helped underwrite the economic and monetary stability which characterised most of New Labour's period in power and was a major factor in its electoral success.

There are two notable features about the decision on bank independence. First, this was a Brown policy, devised by Brown and his advisers in the years before the 1997 election. Brown had, of course, consulted Blair and Blair had agreed in principle but, in line with his understanding with his colleague and perhaps also with his lack of interest in economics, was content to leave the implementation to Brown. Second, the decision was taken by Brown and Blair alone. It had not been openly endorsed in Labour's election manifesto, which said only 'we will reform the Bank of England to ensure that decision-making on monetary policy is more effective, open, accountable and free from short-term political manipulation'. It was not even discussed in Cabinet. When the Cabinet Secretary pointed this out to Blair, the Prime Minister cheerfully and characteristically replied, 'We'll ring around.'

To strengthen his power at the centre of government, Blair brought his main advisers from opposition into 10 Downing Street. Jonathan Powell became his efficient chief of staff, with a special dispensation to give orders to civil servants. He also had responsibility for Northern Ireland. Alastair Campbell, as head of communications, was also given similar special powers. In the world of twenty-four-hour communications and almost permanent campaigning, Campbell was bound to play a vital role in Blair's Downing Street. He was not only chief of the Government Information Service and, in January 1998, of the newly created Strategic Communications Unit, responsible for planning presentation and co-ordinating announcements by departments on a weekly 'grid', he was also the Prime Minister's official spokesman, giving twice-daily briefings to the parliamentary press lobby. In addition, he acted as Blair's ubiquitous adviser. On a number of headline issues in the first term – the response to Diana's death, the Good Friday Agreement, the Kosovo war and the fuel protest of 2000 – he gave Blair invaluable advice, often going beyond presentation. His crucial importance to Blair was underlined by the fact that he had the right to attend all meetings at Number Ten, including meetings with individual ministers. The Tories had a point when they called him 'the twenty-third member of the cabinet'.[3]

Other key advisers included David Miliband, later Brown's Foreign Secretary, who became head of the Policy Unit, Anji Hunter, who was given the title of Special Assistant to the Prime Minister, in which part she continued to act as Blair's personal eyes and ears, especially amongst the southern middle classes, and Sally Morgan who remained responsible for relations with the party. During the first term, the number of politically appointed advisers at 10 Downing Street trebled to twenty-four.[4] Not surprisingly this was criticised by the civil service but it was understandable that a party that had been out of office for so long felt it needed sympathetic advice.

Mandelson, who was, with Brown, one of Blair's two most important political strategists, was made Minister without Portfolio. Meeting Blair on election day, he had told the Labour leader that he wanted a proper job to do, preferably Minister for Europe at the Foreign Office. Blair, who wished to have Mandelson by his side in Downing Street, replied that, as Minister of Europe, Peter would find himself uncomfortably situated between Blair and the new Foreign Secretary, Robin Cook. He did, however, promise Mandelson that he would bring him into the Cabinet after six months.

What did the job of Minister without Portfolio entail? Somewhat grandly, Mandelson told Blair that he wanted to focus on the broad strategy of government, 'embedding' New Labour principles, acting as the Prime Minister's representative across departments and sometimes performing the role of 'frontman', explaining what the government was doing. At a meeting with the Cabinet Secretary, Sir Robin Butler, it was agreed that, as Michael Heseltine had done for the Conservative government, Mandelson would chair the so-called 'presentation' meeting of advisers and key spokesman at 8.30 or 9 a.m. each weekday. He would also join the weekly political strategy meetings of Blair, Brown, Alastair Campbell and Jonathan Powell. He would meet the Cabinet Secretary for an hour each week – a meeting which both enjoyed – and, even though he was not a member of the Cabinet, he would sit on eleven out of nineteen Cabinet Committees, as well as having privileged access to Number Ten papers. His biographer wrote, 'It was power all right, though almost entirely the refracted power of a new Prime Minister with an immense majority.'[5] The point was that, like Brown and, in his own way, Alastair Campbell, Mandelson commanded the Prime Minister's ear. 'Being Peter' was giving considered, disinterested and trusted advice to Tony Blair. To a journalist, he described his job as being 'not a big wheel' so much as 'an oiler of wheels'.[6] This was being unduly modest. Mandelson was now a power in the land.

He was also given other, more specific responsibilities. Although, following the Labour landslide, Blair did not bring any Liberal Democrats into his government, he continued to keep their key figures in play – above all, their leader, Paddy Ashdown, and their elder statesman, Roy Jenkins.

In opposition, Mandelson had been closely involved in the talks with the Liberal Democrats. In government, he continued the role of chief liaison officer – for example, he was present at a dinner at Number Ten on 21 October 1997 when Blair discussed with Ashdown and Jenkins the idea of bringing two Liberal Democrats into the Cabinet. But, despite Blair's warm words, nothing came of it. The proposals of the Jenkins Commission on the voting system,[7] which came out for the so-called 'Alternative Vote Plus' (the alternative vote for single member constituencies, with a top-up to provide an element of proportionality), were also kicked into the long grass. Blair, with Mandelson's support, may have had ambitions to bring Labour and the Liberals closer together but he did not feel he could risk the hostility of his party to such a move, particularly when, after the election, he did not need Liberal support in Parliament.

Mandelson's job had also acquired a European dimension. As Blair's special emissary, he visited the capitals of other EU members to assure the UK's partners of the new Prime Minister's strong pro-European views, while explaining that, because of the need to win a referendum as promised in Labour's election manifesto, Britain was unlikely to join the single currency in the first wave in 1999. The question now facing the new Labour government was whether also to rule out joining for the whole Parliament. Gordon Brown, who, in opposition, had arguably been more enthusiastic about European Economic and Monetary Union (EMU) than Blair, now changed his mind. In October, he gave an interview to *The Times*, the headline of which said, 'Brown rules out single currency in the lifetime of this parliament'.

Brown's unexpected and clumsy intervention, which infuriated pro-EMU MPs and business supporters alike and annoyed Blair, also shocked Mandelson (see next chapter for a fuller account of this episode). After a week of meetings and conversations between, amongst others, Mandelson, Blair, Brown and Cook, the Chancellor, careful to keep euro decision making in his hands, announced to the House of Commons that Britain would not be joining EMU until after a further general election, other than as a result of a 'fundamental or unforeseen change in economic circumstances'. He added that, if the single currency worked and the economic case was 'clear and unambiguous', the government believed that Britain should be part of it.[8] Though the outcome was disappointing to pro-Europeans, Mandelson could take some comfort from the fact that Brown's statement ruling out joining in the 1997 Parliament had left a little 'wriggle room' and that EMU had been accepted in principle. In personal terms, the Minister without Portfolio had also shown himself to be a formidable champion of the European cause.

Mandelson's third major responsibility was for the ill-fated Millennium Dome at Greenwich. This was a high-risk venture, the brainchild of Michael Heseltine, Deputy Prime Minister in the previous Tory government. However, Tony Blair, backed by Peter Mandelson, unwisely decided to proceed with the project. In June 1997, John Prescott, also a supporter, forced it through a sceptical Cabinet in Blair's absence and Mandelson was given the job of seeing it through. The Dome at least gave him something 'solid' to get his teeth into. It could be said, as John Lloyd wrote in the *New Statesman*, he was 'born to it'.[9] His grandfather, Herbert Morrison, had, after all, been the instigator and chief organiser of the celebrated 1951 Festival of Britain. Mandelson became a 'Dome' enthusiast, exaggeratedly praising it to journalists as 'the global focus for the new millennium', 'consumerism and community in equal measure' and 'a great shared national experience'.[10]

Unfortunately for Mandelson and the New Labour government, the Millennium Dome was far less successful than the Festival of Britain. Though the Dome itself, designed by Richard Rogers, was a fine building, the exhibition lacked an overall theme and the number of visitors was only half the projected twelve million. The total cost was over £900 million – 80 per cent of this was funded by the National Lottery and the Dome's critics thought this would have been better spent on other things. In his speech to the 2000 Labour Party conference, Blair admitted, 'If I had my time again, I would have listened to those who said that government shouldn't try to run big visitor attractions.'[11]

In 1997, Mandelson stood unsuccessfully for Labour's National Executive against Ken Livingstone, the left-wing MP for Brent East and later Mayor of London. He was eager to establish an identity independent of the Prime Minister and thought that his prominent role during the general election would help him win. While Blair was on holiday, Mandelson fought a high-profile and media-oriented campaign, forgetting that his target audience was not the national electorate but the Labour Party membership. His defeat with 68,023 votes to Livingstone's 83,669 was a personal setback. If he had been advising others, he would not have made the same mistake. More seriously, his flamboyant campaigning tactics annoyed the Prime Minister, causing a temporary coolness in their relationship.

The New Labour government got off to a flying start. Although Blair had played down talk of a Roosevelt-style 'first hundred days', there was a feeling of excitement, even euphoria, at the change of government, especially one elected with such a huge majority. 'Things can only get better' was the theme tune of Labour's 1997 election campaign and, in contrast with the lacklustre outgoing government, the new government certainly appeared to be extremely active. The announcement of Bank of England independence on 6 May was followed next day by a meeting of the new parliamentary party at Church House. Rejecting Attlee's Attorney General's unfortunate dictum in 1946 that 'we are the masters now', Blair proclaimed, 'The people are the masters, we are the people's servants.'[12]

On 16 May Blair flew to Northern Ireland to show his commitment to the peace talks, mainly between Sinn Fein and the Ulster Unionists, which had stalled in the final months of the Major government. On 29 May, on his way from a NATO summit in Paris that Blair had also attended, President Clinton, accompanied by his wife Hillary, came to London and was welcomed by Tony Blair's new Cabinet. On 16 June, in contrast to the previous Tory government, Blair impressed his European colleagues at the Intergovernmental Conference in Amsterdam by agreeing to more co-operation over defence and foreign policy and some increase in majority voting while, at the same time, reserving the positions which were important to the UK, such as taxation and border controls. Sir John Kerr, then Permanent Under-Secretary at Foreign Office, commented: 'Blair enjoyed Amsterdam. He found he was good at European negotiations, and had a real flair for them.'[13]

But it was not his success on the continent of Europe which made the biggest impact on public opinion. It was his inspired handling of the crisis that arose for the monarchy following the death in Paris of Diana, Princess of Wales, with her boyfriend, Dodi Fayed, in a car accident in the early hours of 31 August. His eloquence and skill marked him out not only as an exceptionally able and intuitive communicator but also as a political leader with a real ability to rise to the level of events. His few, simple words spoken outside Trimdon Church in his constituency, ended in a sentence which movingly summed up for many people what they felt about Diana: 'She was the people's princess and that is how she will stay, how she will remain in our hearts and our memories forever.'[14] He then persuaded a reluctant Queen to make a television broadcast, to fly the flag at half mast over Buckingham Palace and to hold a public funeral for Diana at Westminster Abbey. It was a superb performance which saved the monarchy from a growing backlash and pushed Blair's approval ratings up to over 90 per cent, making him, for the moment, the most popular Prime Minister since polling began.

However, Blair's honeymoon with the press, if not with the general public, came to an abrupt end over the so-called Ecclestone affair. Bernie Ecclestone, who ran Formula One Motor Racing, had donated £1 million to the Labour Party. New Labour's acceptance of donations from businessmen was motivated both by its desire to become less dependent on trade union money and by its policy of promoting good relations with business. Problems arose when there were possible conflicts of interest, as in the Ecclestone case.

On 4 November, the government announced a plan to exempt Formula

One from its ban on sport sponsorship by tobacco companies. The press noticed that Ecclestone had a meeting with Blair at 10 Downing Street in mid October. Then, on 9 November, the Labour Party admitted that it had received money from Ecclestone but had decided to pay it back. In a television interview for BBC's *On the Record* at Chequers, the Prime Minister's country residence, Blair apologised for his handling of the affair but insisted that he had done nothing wrong. He declared, somewhat piously, 'I would never do anything either to harm the country or anything improper. I never have. I think most people who have dealt with me think I'm a pretty straight sort of guy.'[15] I noted in my diary, 'John Humphrys gives him a good going-over and Tony comes out of it better than he went in. But he won't be able to do such an interview again.'[16] Blair the moralist could not afford such carelessness. Like Caesar's wife, he had to be above suspicion.

Then on 10 December, Blair ran into serious trouble with his own MPs over the extraordinary episode of the cuts in single-parent benefits. Forty-seven Labour MPs voted against the government and more than thirty abstained. What was worse was that even the loyalists who voted in favour were not convinced by the government's arguments. In the division lobby, three government ministers came up to me and asked me to complain to the Prime Minister.[17] These views were passed on to Blair.

Later both Blair and Brown admitted that it was an entirely unnecessary 'cock-up'. An acceptable compromise would have been simultaneously to raise child benefit by enough to compensate lone parents for the loss of their premiums. Blair's biographer commented, 'Had Blair not been so eager to appease the "family values" lobby, he could have waited to eliminate the lone-parent premium by levelling up.'[18]

The Secretary of State for Social Security, Harriet Harman, got the blame and lost her job in the July 1998 reshuffle (see next chapter). Her deputy, Frank Field, appointed by Blair to 'think the unthinkable' about reforming the welfare state and who was locked in open political warfare with Harman, resigned at the same time because he was not offered her post. In reality, it was the fault of Blair who, partly to please the *Daily Mail* readership, had talked in vague terms about 'a fundamental reform of the welfare state' without working out what he meant and, above all, of Brown who wanted to make a public show of sticking to Tory public spending targets. Later the shrewd Alistair Darling, who took over from Harman, was able to bring in, without much fuss, a Welfare Reform Act, introducing compulsory interviews for lone parents and restricting entitlements to incapacity benefit to cut the swollen numbers. The Working Families Tax Credit, introduced by Gordon Brown in 1999 (see next chapter), was, however, an imaginative new way to help the working poor. As to the revolt of Labour MPs over lone-parent benefits, it was a reminder to both Blair and Brown that, despite the massive majority, Labour backbenchers could not be taken entirely for granted.

The background to the row over lone-parent benefits was that, for the first two years of the first term, the government operated within a self-imposed straightjacket. In opposition, Brown had insisted that the incoming Labour government would stick to Conservative spending plans for the next two years, which included cuts in lone-parent benefits. However, in his first Comprehensive Spending Review in July 1998 (see next chapter), the new Chancellor, while keeping within his spending limits, also announced what appeared to be large increases in education and health expenditure, financed by drawing on reserves. In annual terms, these were useful but modest additions. But, by a process of unacceptable triple accounting, the Chancellor, trying to have it both ways, inflated the increases over three years up to £40 million. This was a gross exaggeration of relatively small increases in education and health spending. In reality, budgets in all the spending departments continued to be tight, which may have impressed the financial markets but made things difficult for spending ministers and delayed Labour's plans for significant improvements in public services, especially in education and health, for at least two years.

It was in other areas that the new government made its mark. The Labour 1997 election manifesto contained a number of major commitments on constitutional matters, including a Scottish Parliament with tax-varying powers, a Welsh Assembly, a strategic authority for London and support for the peace process and devolution in Northern Ireland. Labour had 'form' on devolution. The Callaghan government in the 1970s had been brought down by the devolution issue but Blair was fortunate to inherit from John Smith a well-prepared home-rule programme which, with the big Labour majority, could now be far more easily implemented.

Blair's sensible contribution was to insist on referenda in both Scotland and Wales, with separate questions in Scotland on the principle and on tax-varying powers, both to prevent the devolution legislation being obstructed by a Tory-dominated House of Lords and to entrench the change. The Scottish referendum, in which Brown played a leading role, was won by large majorities, on a respectable turnout of more than 60 per cent. After elections in Scotland, Donald Dewar, Blair's intelligent and trusted Secretary of State for Scotland, became Scotland's first First Minister, leading a Lib–Lab administration elected by proportional representation. It remained to be seen whether, in the longer term, the Scots would continue to be satisfied by a devolved parliament or whether, as the Scottish National Party (SNP) hoped, they would, in the end, demand independence.

The 'yes' vote in Wales was carried by the narrowest of margins – 0.6 per cent – reflecting the greater divisions and doubts in that country. Both in Wales and in London, which voted in a referendum for a mayor and an assembly, Blair's sure touch deserted him. In Wales he tried, in the end unsuccessfully, to prevent the most popular Labour figure in the principality, Rhodri Morgan, from becoming First Secretary while, in London, both Blair and Brown were implacably opposed to the candidature of Ken Livingstone for mayor, failing to understand that the former hard leftist, who had been the bane of the Labour leadership in the 1980s, had turned himself into a charismatic populist. In May 2000, Livingstone ran as an Independent, comfortably winning the mayoral election and pushing the luckless Labour candidate, former Cabinet Minister Frank Dobson, into third place. Blair commented, 'Sometimes I think the experience in the Labour Party in the early eighties almost sort of scared me too much.'[19]

By contrast, Blair's handling of the negotiations leading up to the Good Friday Agreement, of April 1998, in Northern Ireland was exceptionally skilful. Building on the progress made under the previous Conservative Prime Minister, John Major, and making good use of the warmth and informality of his new Secretary of State for Northern Ireland, Mo Mowlam, he invested considerable political capital in the peace process. In October 1997, he met Gerry Adams, leader of Sinn Fein, the political wing of the terrorist organisation, the IRA. It was the first time that a British Prime Minister had met a Sinn Fein leader. He also developed close personal relations with David Trimble, leader of the Ulster Unionist Party. The United States Senator, George Mitchell, chairman of the peace talks, set Easter weekend 1998 as a deadline. On 7 April, Blair took a calculated gamble and flew into Belfast to join the negotiations, saying, 'A day like today, it's not a day for sound-bites really, we can leave those at home, but I feel the hand of history upon our shoulder, in respect of this.'[20]

There then followed days and nights of intense negotiations, in which Blair and the Irish Prime Minister, Bertie Ahern, were fully involved. President Clinton was also available at the end of a telephone. In the end, after a last-minute wobble by the Ulster Unionists over IRA decommissioning of weapons, which Blair settled by a personal letter of assurance, the agreement was finally signed around 5 p.m. on Friday 10 April 1998. This involved the setting up of a Northern Ireland Assembly giving all parties a share in office, a North–South ministerial council to assist cross-border relationships and a British–Irish Council, bringing together the two governments and the devolved institutions in Northern Ireland, Scotland and Wales. The agreement was then backed by 71 per cent in a Northern Ireland referendum, including even a majority of Unionists. Meanwhile, in the south, 94 per cent voted to renounce the Republic's claim, enshrined in its constitution, to sovereignty over the whole island. Although there was a long way still to go before peace could be fully secured and democratic institutions assured in Northern Ireland, the Good Friday Agreement was an outstanding, indeed genuinely historic, achievement of which Blair and the New Labour government were entitled to feel proud.

One of the most lasting legacies of the Blair premiership was the far-reaching programme of constitutional changes introduced in the government's first term. In addition to the devolution of power in Scotland, Wales, Northern Ireland and in the capital itself discussed above, there were also the incorporation of the European Convention of Human Rights into UK law, the Freedom of Information Act, changing the method of electing the European Parliament to a regional list of proportional representation and the removal of all but ninety-two hereditary peers from the House of Lords.

Yet, paradoxically, constitutional issues were never at the top of the Prime Minister's personal political agenda. In part, this was because he had inherited much of the programme from his predecessor. There was also a contrast between these largely pluralist and decentralising reforms and Blair's centralising style of leadership. He believed in strong government and was not much interested in the creation of checks and balances to restrict power.

He was never a great House of Commons man – as he admitted at his final Prime Minster Questions (PMQs) on 27 June 2007[21] – though, when necessary, he could make fine debating speeches. He certainly dominated the House, especially during his first term. Yet, he deliberately cut down the number of times he had to attend parliament, changing PMQs from twice-weekly, fifteen-minute sessions on Tuesday and Thursday afternoons to half an hour at noon on Wednesdays. He also voted infrequently. However, he was also the first Prime Minister to submit himself to questioning, in 2002, by the Parliamentary Liaison Committee, consisting of the chairmen of all the select committees, and, during his time in office, select committees were strengthened. But his eyes glazed over whenever select committees were discussed.[22]

One of the main priorities of the incoming Labour government was to end Britain's isolation in Europe. The new Prime Minister was arguably the most pro-European Prime Minister certainly since Edward Heath. He had voted 'yes' in the 1975 EU referendum, he took his holidays in France and Italy and his command of French was good enough to speak directly to MPs in the French National Assembly. His ambition was to reconcile the British to membership of the European Union and for the UK to play a cooperative part in its workings. At Aachen in the summer of 1999, Blair spoke of his 'bold aim . . . that over the next few years Britain resolves once and for all its ambivalence towards Europe. I want to end the uncertainty, the lack of confidence, the Europhobia.'[23]

The British government supported enlargement, a process which was brought to a formal conclusion in 2004 when the EU was expanded to twenty-five. The UK also helped initiate the Lisbon agenda of economic reform to make the EU more flexible and innovative. In December 1998, jointly with President Chirac, Blair launched a joint Anglo-French initiative on European defence. These were the actions of a government determined to play a leading role in the EU.

But the decision not to join the single currency in the first wave or soon after inevitably hampered Labour's efforts. On 30 June 1998, Tony Blair spoke as President of the European Council at the launch of the European Bank in Frankfurt. It was a fine speech, emphasising the Labour government's constructive attitude towards the European Union and making friendly noises about the euro. However, it was difficult to see how in the long term the UK could sustain the position of a leader in Europe while it remained outside the EU's biggest project.

Blair was also reluctant to make the case for Europe to the British people. He would make the occasional address though most of his best speeches were reserved for the Continent. Labour's campaign in the 1999 European elections was abysmal, without message or organisation. On a low turnout, Labour won only twenty-nine seats to the Tories' thirty-six. When I showed Blair Labour's national election material with the extraordinary slogan 'What did you ever get out of Europe?', he could only shake his head.[24] Later that year, Blair and an unwilling Brown joined Michael

Heseltine and Ken Clarke and the new Liberal leader, Charles Kennedy, at the launch of Britain in Europe, a cross-party organisation set up to explain the case for British membership of the EU and the benefits of joining the single currency. Yet the government's support for joining the euro was conditional while Blair and Brown were reluctant to do any serious campaigning, lest they aroused the hostility of the Murdoch press. In the end, despite Blair's constructive EU initiatives and warm words about the euro, he was not prepared to take any risks over Europe in case it jeopardised the prospects of winning a second term.

Roy Jenkins, somewhat unrealistically, told Blair that he should use his prestige as 'one of the victors of the Kosovo war to persuade the British of the merits of the single currency'.[25] He was right in believing that Kosovo was one of Blair's finest hours. In March 1999, he ordered British bombers to join NATO air strikes against Slobodan Milošević's regime in Serbia after Milošević had sent Serbian troops into Kosovo, provoking nearly half the mainly ethnic Albanian population of two million into flight or hiding. It was Europe's worst humanitarian crisis since the Second World War.

Adopting a Gladstonian posture, Blair told the House of Commons on 23 March, 'We must act to save thousands of innocent men, women and children from humanitarian catastrophe, from death, barbarism and ethnic cleansing by a brutal dictatorship. We have no alternative to act and act we will.'[26] Initially, he, like President Clinton, ruled out the use of ground troops but, when it became increasingly clear that the bombing campaign was proving ineffective, Blair became NATO's leading hawk. On the eve of NATO's fiftieth-anniversary summit meeting in Washington, he met a reluctant Clinton, much weakened by the Lewinsky affair, to try to persuade him to support the deployment of ground forces. The meeting was a stormy one and Clinton's annoyance with the British Prime Minister was increased by Blair's speech the following day in Chicago, justifying intervention.

In his Chicago address, Blair argued that 'the most pressing foreign policy problem we face is to identify the circumstance in which we should get actively involved on other people's conflicts'. He went on to say that '[a]cts of genocide can never be a purely internal matter' and set out five tests which needed to be satisfied before intervention. These included: the strength of the case; exhausting all diplomatic options; the military means available; preparing for the long term; and the national interests involved. On Kosovo, he said, with almost Thatcherite firmness, 'Success is the only exit strategy I am prepared to consider.'[27] Blair's moralism was strengthened by the visit he paid with his wife, Cherie, in May 1999, to a Kosovan refugee camp in Macedonia. He told the refugees that 'this is a battle for humanity, it is a just cause, it is a rightful cause'.

At the beginning of June 1999, Milošević, under pressure from the Russians and fearing that Clinton would send in American troops, backed down and began to withdraw Serbian forces. Blair had played the role of chief advocate but it was the United States and Russia who produced the shift in Milošević's tactics. He drew a number of lessons from the Kosovan conflict which were to be important in the future, especially over Iraq. First, that it was crucial to get and remain close to the US, especially to the US President.[28] Only the Americans had the troop numbers, the firepower and the logistical support to be able to intervene effectively. Any differences between the US and UK had to be argued out in private. Second, the Europeans could be uncertain allies. Though the French and Germans had supported the bombing, they were against the use of ground troops. This, he believed, reinforced the case both for closer European defence cooperation and for the UK acting as a bridge between the USA and Europe. Third, given the UN veto that unwilling countries, such as Russia, China and sometimes even France, could exercise, intervention had sometime to be based, as over Kosovo, on coalitions of the willing.

Blair came of age over Kosovo. He had gone out on a limb – so much so that the Cabinet Secretary, Sir Richard Wilson, warned him that he had placed himself in a very dangerous position. Yet, he had continued to insist on the need to help the Kosovans because he felt that it was a just 'cause'. He believed that the successful outcome to the conflict had proved his point. His new self-confidence was to be a major factor in the run-up to the Iraq war three years later.

By the end of 1999, the Labour government was riding high. The economy was doing well, with low inflation and steady growth though, on the social front, health and education spending, especially health, were weak areas. Blair had proved himself an impressive Prime Minister with the ability, especially over Northern Ireland, Kosovo and Princess Diana's death, to rise to the occasion. His party did not love him but it respected his vote-getting ability. He remained popular with the voters of Middle England who relied on him to look after their interests. To those who had known him as a young man, it was fascinating to watch him grow into a great communicator, equally at ease in Parliament, at party conference or on television. As Prime Minister, without developing any side or pomposity, he was acquiring real authority. Above all, he was a charismatic performer, able to dominate the political scene both at home and abroad.

9

SUPER CHANCELLOR

During the first term, Gordon Brown established himself as an exceptionally strong and powerful Chancellor of the Exchequer. At the same time, the partnership between Blair and Brown, on the whole, worked well. A close observer of the relationship perceptively wrote:

> The pulse that beats between Blair and Brown is their government's supply of nervous energy . . . [I]t was their bonded, concentrated power at the centre of their government that allowed an administration of more or less completely inexperienced ministers to manage their first term in a way that produced the second big majority.[1]

The story of the New Labour government was, in part, one of two rival camps; yet it was also one of partnership, arguably initially the most effective in British political history.

Brown's chancellorship began with a burst of creative energy. Clapped into the Treasury by enthusiastic civil servants, Brown immediately handed over to the Permanent Secretary, Sir Terence Burns, a carefully prepared letter for the Governor of the Bank of England, Edward George, setting out the details of the transfer of operational control over interest rates from the Treasury to the Bank. This bold initiative, announced on 6 May 1997, five days after the general election, was warmly welcomed by the City mainly because, as Robert Peston wrote, 'in some ways it was the natural culmination of a series of reforms implemented after the UK's humiliating exit from the European Exchange Rate Mechanism on September 16, 1992.'[2] Although the previous Conservative government had not gone as far as to introduce the reform – both Prime Minister John Major and Chancellor Kenneth Clarke were opposed though two previous Chancellors, Nigel Lawson and Norman Lamont, were in favour – it had introduced inflation targeting and the publication of the minutes of meetings between the Chancellor and the Governor over interest rates. At the same time, such bodies as the cross-party Commons Treasury Select Committee and the Liberal Party had come out for giving the Bank control over interest rate policy.

But it was Brown, with the support of Blair, who had the courage and the good sense to introduce the change immediately Labour came to power. He had been convinced both by his aide, Ed Balls, and by the Chairman of the US Federal Reserve, Alan Greenspan, that bank independence could bring price stability. There was also a powerful political argument. Previous Labour governments had almost invariably been beset by economic and financial crises. Giving up control of interest rates to the Bank as a deliberate act of policy was a brilliant way of helping the New Labour government acquire economic credibility.

Brown and his aides – above all, Ed Balls – had prepared a plan for bank independence which has stood the test of time. Key features included: the setting of the inflation target of 2.5 per cent by the Chancellor though, in practice, a Chancellor would be highly unlikely to raise the target; a 'symmetrical' inflation target, in the sense that inflation below 2.5 per cent was as much to be avoided as inflation above it; operational control over interest rates by a new Monetary Policy Committee, to include outside economic experts; and, for the first time, parliamentary scrutiny of monetary policy, especially by the Commons Treasury Select Committee.[3] The Brown model is now accepted by all the main political parties, including the Tories.

The Governor of the Bank, Edward George, was delighted by the news that his beloved Bank – he had been at the Bank for thirty-five years – was to control interest rates. But he was less pleased by Brown's other scheme of hiving off the Bank's banking supervisory functions to a new body, the Financial Services Authority (FSA), set up to regulate financial services, though he was temporarily appeased at a meeting with the Chancellor on 4 May by a promise of consultation – a promise which he conveyed to his staff – and a separate bill. However, Brown, informed by the Lord Chancellor that there would be room for only one Treasury bill in the first session of parliament, decided to bring forward the announcement of the setting up of the FSA and the transfer of banking supervision from the Bank and include it in the first bill. George, who believed that Brown had gone back on his promise of consultation, was furious and openly considered resignation, a step which would have been highly damaging to both the new government and the Chancellor.

As it was, Brown got a ticking-off from the Speaker, Betty Boothroyd, for his sudden announcement about the FSA, at the end of a speech, while the former Chancellor, Kenneth Clarke, complained that the government was in too much of a hurry, 'like eighteen-year-olds in the saloon bar trying every bottle on the shelves'.[4] On the principles of the issue, Brown had a strong case. Following the collapse of the Bank of Credit and Commerce International (BCCI) and the Barings crash, the Bank's recent track record on bank supervision could hardly be said to be impressive and, as Edward George later admitted, another crash could have undermined the new Monetary Policy Committee's reputation as the keeper of sound money. As so often, it was the Chancellor's handling of the personalities involved which was at fault. His relationship with the Governor of the Bank took some time to recover while Brown blamed his Permanent Secretary, Terence Burns, for his original suggestion of delay in stripping the Bank of its supervisory powers. In the case of Burns, it was the first of a series of spats with Brown and his team which led to the Permanent Secretary's resignation a year later.

The centrepiece of the Chancellor's first budget on 2 July was the so-called windfall tax which Brown and his leading advisers had painstakingly prepared in opposition. This one-off tax, levied in two tranches on the privatised utilities, raised £5.2 billion, £3.5 billion of which was used to fund the Welfare to Work programme to reduce long-term and youth unemployment. The remaining money was reserved for education – especially school buildings. Brown was also able to please his supporters by announcing that, though he was sticking, as he had promised in opposition, to Tory spending plans, he would release funds from the so-called contingency reserve for education (£1 billion) and health (£1.2 billion). His speech, introducing his first budget, was short (just about an hour), well delivered and warmly received by Labour backbenchers.[5] Brown was quickly establishing himself as an authoritative Chancellor.

One change in taxation announced in Brown's first budget was more controversial, especially in the City. This was the abolition of the tax credit on dividends paid to shareholders, which raised £5 billion for the Treasury. Later critics pointed to the negative impact of this on pension funds. But the government argued that £3 billion of the proceeds was to be used for a cut in corporation tax, which increased the value of companies and, therefore, the pension funds' assets, and that a rising stock market would more than compensate pension funds for their loss.[6]

Brown's second budget, introduced on 17 March 1998, combined a number of objectives. A top priority was to bring together the tax and benefit system to 'help people into work' and redistribute money to the working poor. Hence the announcement of the Working Families Tax Credit (WFTC), the purpose of which was to guarantee a minimum income for working families with children and to tackle the unemployment and poverty traps facing low-paid families. This reform was underpinned by raising the minimum starting rate for paying National Insurance and by the introduction of the National Minimum Wage. As with bank independence and the windfall tax, much of the preparation for the WFTC had taken place in opposition, with Brown working with another aide, Ed Miliband, brother of David, on ideas originally devised in the United States. Over the years ahead, Chancellor Brown developed these ideas further – so much so that a Treasury official called it a quiet revolution.

Yet, while Brown pursued more traditional Labour aims of reducing poverty and getting people back to work, he also reassured middle-class voters by not putting up taxes and the City by reducing public borrowing by £17 billion. The *Guardian* commented that the 'Chancellor offers relief to working poor without punishing middle England'. It was a skilful performance, which had been rehearsed beforehand at Chequers with the Prime Minister.

The publication of a new three-year Comprehensive Spending Review (CSR) on July 1998 completed the first phase and, in many ways, it was the most dynamic period of the Brown chancellorship. The CSR which set out the government's spending plans for the next three years had the merit of enabling departments to plan for the medium term. It also established two new fiscal rules: first, over the so-called economic cycle, the government would only borrow to invest; and, second, it would keep public debt at 'a stable and prudent level' – about 40 per cent of GDP. The CSR continued the government's cautious fiscal approach, allowing current spending to rise by only 2.25 per cent a year in line with the Treasury's estimate of trend growth.

However, as mentioned previously, at the same time, the Chancellor announced apparently very large increases in spending on education and health. In its report on the CSR, the Treasury Select Committee rumbled the Chancellor, ticking him off for 'triple accounting' and urging that, in future, totals should be expressed in terms of annual increases rather than as a misleading cumulative figure.[7] Robert Peston commented:

Brown and Balls were endeavouring to have their cake and eat it: they wanted to be generous in the eyes of the Labour Party and mean in the eyes of the City. Amazingly, they more or less got away with it.[8]

During the first two years of Labour's first term and, as the economy increasingly flourished, Brown visibly grew in stature and confidence. Apart from the bold and striking policy initiatives described above, he remade the Treasury in his own image. Especially after Burns left in 1998, a new generation of younger civil servants were promoted to key positions. Through a system of public service agreements on the performance targets individual departments introduced at the same time as the Comprehensive Spending Review, the Treasury extended its writ through Whitehall. Its sway, reflecting the Chancellor's policy interests, was especially strong on welfare and pensions, employment and industrial issues.

At the centre of the Brown empire, the Chancellor was surrounded, like Blair, by his own praetorian guard, most of whom had served with him in opposition. The key personality was Ed Balls whose influence both with the Chancellor and inside the Treasury was so great that he was often called the 'Deputy Chancellor'. All proposals had to go through him. Balls, brought up in Nottingham where he joined the Labour Party at an early age, learnt economics at Oxford and Harvard and then joined the *Financial Times*. He was clever, tough (though sometimes too inclined to throw his weight around), and able to hold his own with the best brains in the Treasury. Above all, he got on with Brown who could be extremely moody. In January 1998, he married Yvette Cooper, who had been elected as an MP in 1997, and, later, both Cooper and Balls served in Brown's Cabinet. Ed Miliband, who had joined Brown later than Balls, in 1995, seemed to be a gentler character but, even so, was also influential – later he too became a member of Brown's Cabinet. Sue Nye, wife of Gavyn Davies, then chief economist at Goldman Sachs, was Brown's highly competent 'gatekeeper' and office manager, keeping a grip on the Chancellor's movements and also maintaining relations with Anji Hunter, a close friend, at 10 Downing Street.

There were two other more controversial figures in Brown's entourage. The first was Geoffrey Robinson, the millionaire businessman and Labour MP, whose Grosvenor House flat had, in opposition, provided a haven for both Brown's policy preparations and leisure activities. While in opposition, Robinson had financed the research for Brown's taxation policies. He had also lent Blair his Tuscan villa in both 1996 and 1997, as well as making a donation to the running of the leader's office. In the summer of 1996, he had made a loan of £373,000 to Peter Mandelson to buy a house in Notting Hill Gate – at the time few people know about the loan and certainly not Blair. When Labour came to power, Robinson was made Paymaster General outside the Cabinet. Arguably, given that Blair was indebted to Robinson, he should not have made him a minister though there is no evidence that the thought ever occurred to him. In any case, the Chancellor wanted to have Robinson by his side as a self-confident 'can-do' fixer, dealing with such issues as the private finance initiative and taxation.

However, in November 1997, Chris Blackhurst of the *Independent on Sunday* revealed that Robinson was the beneficiary of a secret, offshore trust, set up to provide a tax-free 'home' for a bequest of millions of pounds to him by an older woman, Joska Bourgeois. Although this was not actually illegal, it was highly embarrassing for a New Labour minister to be benefiting from massive tax reliefs while, at the same time, launching Individual Savings Accounts (ISAs) which gave less generous tax breaks to investors than the schemes which they replaced. A reprimand by the House of Commons for failing to register his business interests and a DTI investigation into his business affairs, especially his links with Robert Maxwell, further weakened his position. By mid summer 1998, Blair had come to the conclusion that Robinson was 'severely damaged goods'.

Alastair Campbell called Charlie Whelan, Brown's media spokesman and spin doctor, the 'little oik'. This was a backhanded tribute to the often excessive nature of Whelan's efforts on behalf of the Chancellor. It was, however, highly debatable whether these helped the Labour government or even, in the long run, the Chancellor himself. Brown, despite his towering stature and his success as Chancellor, was oddly insecure. Sensitive to criticism, unforgiving of any perceived slights and unnecessarily obsessive about the possibility of any challenge to his informal position as the natural successor to Blair, he turned to Whelan and, at a higher level, to Balls for advice, assistance and counter-briefing.

Blair, who like Campbell thought Whelan was a menace, had not wanted Brown to take Whelan into government. The fiasco over the *Times* headline of 18 October that Labour would not join the single currency until after the next election was mostly blamed on the Chancellor's media spokesman. Two Liberal Democrat press officers observed Whelan leaving the bar of the Red Lion Pub in Westminster and shouting into his mobile, 'Yes, Gordon is ruling out British membership . . . It doesn't say it in the interview but Gordon is effectively ruling out joining in this parliament.'[9] Blair himself was forced to ring up Whelan on his mobile to find out what was happening. Mandelson urged Blair to sack Whelan for his unprofessional behaviour but Blair pointed out that Whelan, in briefing the press, was merely following Brown's instructions. Clearly, Blair did not want an open clash with Brown.

Then came the publication in January 1998 of Paul Routledge's book on Brown, written, according to the blurb, with Brown's 'full cooperation'.[10] Routledge was then political editor of the *Independent on Sunday* and a friend of Whelan. The book described Brown's political career so far and came to the conclusion that Brown was potentially the most radical of post-war Chancellors. But the press, above all the *Guardian*, which had got hold of an early copy of the book, concentrated on what the book had to say about the 1994 leadership election. It revealed that Brown had not yet got over his disappointment that Blair, and not he, had become the leader. Brown also still appeared to believe that Blair had let him down and that, if he, Brown, had run, he could have won. The truth was different. Yes, there had been an informal pact between Brown and Blair but that was back in 1992 and, by 1994, things had changed. The momentum was now behind Blair and not Brown. Indeed, as mentioned previously, Brown told me that he would not have won anyway. What was disturbing to Labour MPs was that, four years later, Brown and his followers should still have been harbouring old grudges.

If the Brown entourage had behaved foolishly in using the Routledge book to bring up the 1994 leadership election again, 10 Downing Street's response was almost equally unwise. When the story broke, Blair and Campbell were away in Japan which was perhaps a factor in what happened. Until now, Blair had put up with Brown's sometimes heavy-handed behaviour towards his colleagues and his, at times, blatant self-promotion. As one of his Cabinet colleagues said about Blair's efforts to manage his Chancellor: 'He mediates, he negotiates, he diffuses, he cajoles, he rails, he shouts, he hugs, he flatters.'[11] This time he felt that Brown had gone too far. His irritation may have been intensified by the idea being put around by the Brown camp that the Chancellor was the real power in the land, the chief executive to the Prime Minister's non-executive Chairman.[12] At any rate, 'a senior source inside Downing Street', someone who apparently had a good claim to know the mind of the Prime Minister, told Andrew Rawnsley, columnist on the *Observer*, that it was time for Brown to get a grip on his 'psychological flaws'.[13]

Brown was both outraged and deeply wounded. 'This damages me and you,' he told Blair. 'Why are you letting this go unpunished?'[14] Blair was apologetic about the way the row had escalated but pointed out that Brown had brought it on himself by encouraging Routledge's book. He also repeated his warnings about Whelan. Publicly, Blair praised his Chancellor: 'He is my Lloyd George. Gordon has the intellectual firepower of eighteen Ken Clarkes.'[15] He had forgotten that it was Lloyd George who had pushed out Asquith from the premiership.

It was indeed an unedifying spectacle with the government's two most powerful ministers allowing their 'spin machines' to brief against each other. At the time, it was thought that Mandelson was responsible for the 'psychological flaws' remark but Rawnsley refuted this. The Brown camp blamed Campbell though he has since denied being involved. Still, the spat was damaging to the government and led to talk in the press of a Blair–Brown split. It was certainly unwise of Brown to talk to Routledge about the 1994 leadership election. As my diary records: 'It suggests that he still nurses a grudge. Surely he ought to be satisfied with being a modernising, radical Chancellor.'[16]

There were two other events which disturbed the Brown–Blair relationship during 1998. The first was the July 1998 reshuffle. Blair grew to hate reshuffles and usually did not do them well. In his first attempt, he sacked Harriet Harman and Frank Field. He brought Peter Mandelson into the Cabinet as Secretary of State for Trade and Industry and made Jack Cunningham the so-called Cabinet 'enforcer'. Though Alistair Darling was promoted to Social Security Secretary, other supporters of Gordon Brown were sacked or, as in the case of the Chief Whip, Nick Brown, moved to other jobs (Nick Brown became Minister of Agriculture). Blair had also wanted to get rid of Geoffrey Robinson but Brown successfully pleaded that he should stay.

Apart from bringing Mandelson into the Cabinet and removing some dead wood, Blair wanted to show the political world that he was Prime Minister in reality as well as name – hence the move against the Brownites. But, as he told his advisers who were pressing him to be bolder, there was a balance to be struck:

> I'm just telling you there is a case to be cautious if it all ends up with GB offside . . . We have come this far together in part because of his nous and political skills and I want to keep them inside the operation . . . the PLP will see it [the reshuffle] as a bit of a hit on GB. I do not want them to see it as an all-out attack.[17]

The second incident was Mandelson's resignation over his undisclosed loan from Geoffrey Robinson just before Christmas 1998 (discussed more fully in the next chapter) which came only five months after his elevation to the Cabinet in the July reshuffle. As the source of the information seemed to be someone in the Brown camp and as, once again, it was a Paul Routledge book, this time on Mandelson, which provided the vehicle for bringing the information into the public arena, it was not surprising that many saw this as Brown's revenge on Mandelson. The two main losers as a result of the Mandelson resignation were Mandelson himself – obviously – and Blair but Brown also suffered collateral damage. Geoffrey Robinson was forced to resign at the same time, while Charlie Whelan went eleven days later. The *Times* columnist, Peter Riddell, said to me at the time that, in his view, Brown had also been a major loser, 'appearing vindictive and a bad team player, only out for himself'.[18]

At the end of January 1999, I had a meeting with Gordon Brown in his room in the Commons at which I referred to the events surrounding the Mandelson resignation and pointed out that what happened before Christmas was damaging to the Chancellor. 'It was damaging to us all,' Brown replied. I noted in my diary that the departure of Whelan may have been a blessing in disguise for Gordon: 'Hopefully he may have decided to stop being manipulative and rely on the fact that he is an excellent Chancellor to speak for itself.'[19]

In fact, with Whelan's and Mandelson's departures, the relationship between Blair and Brown improved. Brown was the highly successful Chancellor, building on the inheritance left to him by Kenneth Clarke and developing his own policy initiatives, above all bank independence. But Brown also needed Blair. He needed Blair to support him in Cabinet, particularly over restraints on public spending. And, if New Labour were to win a second term, Blair's charisma and popularity with Middle England were key ingredients. The partnership between Blair and Brown was essential to their success – and to their government's.

10

MANDELSON RESIGNS – AND RESIGNS AGAIN

The story of Peter Mandelson's two resignations from the Cabinet – the first on 23 December 1998 and the second on 24 January 2001 – was a mixture of tragedy and farce. Over his undeclared loan from Geoffrey Robinson, Mandelson was culpable so it was understandable, though perhaps not inevitable, that the Prime Minister should accept his first resignation. The second resignation, which related to the application for naturalisation by SP Hinduja, was entirely unjustified and reflected badly on Tony Blair's judgement. Mandelson's departure in 2001 from front-line British politics, until his unexpected recall by Brown in 2008, was a major blow to the Labour government. His five months as Trade and Industry Secretary and his longer period in office as Northern Ireland Secretary had shown that he was a first-rate Cabinet minister who could have gone further. Though (even after he left for Brussels in 2004 to become a European Commissioner) he remained ready to offer personal advice to Blair, he was no longer there to run election campaigns as he had done so successfully in 1997. Above all, his exceptional strategic input to New Labour was missing at a crucial time for the party.

Ironically, given the involvement of the Brown camp in Mandelson's first resignation, it was the Chancellor who told Mandelson that he was going to the DTI. Greeting Mandelson in his flat in Great Peter Street, Westminster, with a cold bottle of champagne, Brown said 'Congratulations, you've got one of the top jobs. It is a promotion you deserved and I've always wanted you to be in the Cabinet.'[1] Hopeful that at last the two men could patch up their differences, Blair had sent Mandelson to see Brown to discuss the appointment. In fact, over the previous six months, Mandelson and Brown had met on a number of occasions – the first time in January after the row over the Routledge book. At this first meeting, Brown had accepted the need for better working relationships between the three modernisers. He added that he would support Mandelson's promotion to the Cabinet though, at subsequent meetings, he made it clear that he was against the idea of Mandelson becoming the Cabinet 'enforcer' – a sort of beefed-up Minister without Portfolio – at the centre, preferring, he said, to see him minister at a more independent department such as the Department of Culture. Mandelson, who badly wanted to become a politician in his own right rather than the leader's 'little helper', tended to agree though he wanted a more important ministry than culture.

When Brown congratulated him on getting into the Cabinet, Mandelson replied truthfully if tactlessly that the Chancellor did not really want him at the DTI. Brushing this remark aside, Brown sensibly said that it was essential that the Treasury and the DTI worked together. Mandelson agreed and they parted amicably.

In the short time that the new Secretary of State for Trade and Industry held office, he proved himself a highly competent Cabinet minister. He handled the closure of Fujitsu in Tony Blair's constituency with skill. He negotiated a trade union legislation package which corrected the imbalance left by the outgoing Tory government, without upsetting the employers. He told the TUC in September:

We will never again contract out the governance of Britain to anyone, not to the TUC or its member unions any more than to big corporate interest. But we would much prefer modernised trade unions to be our active and committed partners along the way. The choice is yours – opposition or legitimate influence.[2]

He also negotiated a compromise with Brown over the future of the Mail Office – with more commercial freedom to reinvest and borrow – though not without a damaging row with the Chancellor and an eventual appeal, to the chagrin of Brown, to the Prime Minister. Whelan briefed that Mandelson had 'bottled out' of making tough decisions. So much for the new Brown–Mandelson rapprochement.

But perhaps his most important achievement was the Competitiveness White Paper which gave his department a new working philosophy. As the White Paper put it:

[T]he present government will not resort to the interventionist policies of the past. In the industrial policy-making of the 1960s and 1970s to be modern meant believing in planning. Now, meeting the demands of the knowledge-driven economy means markets working better.

Old-style state aids were out but there was still a role for targeted public investment, including help for high-technology business and regional investment. DTI officials were impressed.

However, there was a time bomb ticking which would destroy his career at the DTI – and that was the undeclared Robinson loan. In October, Mandelson had received unwelcome publicity when he was 'outed' on the BBC's *Newsnight* by the *Times* sketch writer, Matthew Parris, himself openly gay. For the next month, Mandelson vainly tried to prevent media discussion of his sexual identity. Though he had never denied his sexuality, he took the entirely legitimate view that it was his own affair. This was not only a matter of protecting his private life. He also wanted to try and safeguard the privacy of his Brazilian partner, Reinaldo Avila da Silva.

On 16 December, the day after the publication of his Competitiveness White Paper, his aide, Ben Wegg-Prosser, informed him that he had had a tip-off from a friendly journalist that a far more explosive fact about his life was about to be exposed in a second Routledge book – an unauthorised biography of Mandelson which would reveal the Robinson loan.

The background to the Robinson loan was as follows. In the summer of 1996, the year before the first Labour landslide, Robinson gave Mandelson a loan of £373,000 to buy a small house in Northumberland Place, Notting Hill, which he would otherwise not have been able to afford. Robinson, who, though part of the Brown entourage, saw himself as a go-between for Blair and Brown, apparently said to Mandelson, 'Look Peter, you'll be in the government and eventually you'll be in the Cabinet, you shouldn't have to worry about these things, you should have somewhere in London where you can be settled, where you can bring people around, and have a proper base.'[3] These beguiling words were music to Mandelson's ears. Although he could eventually expect something like half a million pounds from his mother and he might possibly get a decent advance from his memoirs, it would be in the future. The advantage of the Robinson loan was that it would enable him to live comfortably in a fashionable area straightaway.

Mandelson was going through an 'upwardly mobile' period of his life. As one of his friends remarked, 'Peter was on this extraordinary, violent rollercoaster. In the space of eighteen months, he had gone from a well-known figure in London to one of the most famous politicians in Europe.'[4] Beguiled by Carla Powell, the Italian wife of Charles Powell, Mrs Thatcher's former foreign affairs adviser and brother to Blair's chief of staff, Jonathan Powell, he went to grand dinner parties and receptions, including being the only Cabinet minister to be invited to Prince Charles' fiftieth birthday. Rupert Murdoch called him 'a star fucker' while Mandelson himself admitted that 'I came over a bit grand. I was trophy-like. I was caught up in a bit of a whirl.'[5]

Alastair Campbell had warned Mandelson that what Campbell called his 'lifestyle ambitions' could endanger his political career. It was surely unwise of him to have borrowed what was then a large sum of money, certainly in relation to his income, and especially from a fellow minister who belonged to the Brown camp. If another politician in similar circumstances had asked Mandelson for his advice, he would almost certainly have said, 'Don't do it.'

However, it was not so much the loan itself – ill advised though it was – that brought the Secretary of State for Trade and Industry down. It was more the failure to disclose it, combined with the ferocity of the media's reaction. Without specifically mentioning loans, the code of conduct for ministers, drawn up by Blair, said that ministers should avoid accepting any gift or hospitality which might compromise or seem to compromise their judgement or place them under an improper obligation. Ministers should also consult with their permanent secretaries about any conflicting interests. There was also the question of whether the loan should have been declared in the register of members' interests. And there was the issue, raised by the Tories, of whether Mandelson had mentioned the loan when he filled in his application for a Britannia Building Society mortgage.

Although Mandelson's Permanent Secretary at the DTI, Sir Michael Scholar, agreed that the Cabinet minister had properly removed himself from an inquiry by the DTI into Robinson's business activities, both he and the Cabinet Secretary, Richard Wilson, were also clear that Mandelson should have told the then Cabinet Secretary, Robin Butler, about the loan when he first became a minister and certainly told Scholar when he became Secretary of State of Trade and Industry. Above all, he should have told his friend and closest ally, the Prime Minister, Tony Blair, who, like Campbell, was furious at Mandelson's folly.

When the story finally broke in the *Guardian*, Mandelson did his best to defend himself but the tabloids, scenting blood, went for the kill. As Mandelson reported to Blair, over the telephone on the evening of 22 December, journalists, many of whom wanted to pay off old scores, were 'completely hysterical, out of control, and out for my blood'.[6] Ominously, Blair suggested that they should sleep on it.

The next morning's press were almost uniformly hostile, though the *Guardian* concluded that resignation would be a sentence out of proportion to the crime. Curiously, before speaking again to Blair, Mandelson telephoned Gordon Brown in Scotland, even though he believed that the information had been leaked by one of Brown's closest allies. At that time, Brown, perhaps with a guilty conscience, thought that Mandelson should make a handsome apology but not resign. However, Blair had already decided that his closest ally would have to go. He told him over the phone that, if he tried to stay, he would damage himself and the government. If he went, he might, after a suitable interval, return. As soon as they finished speaking, Campbell drafted the exchange of letters between the two. Later, the Blairs invited Mandelson and his partner, Reinaldo Avila da Silva, down to Chequers for the night. It was an execution, New Labour style.

Did Mandelson really have to resign? A conversation, on the day before he resigned which Blair had over the phone with his political adviser, Philip Gould, who was spending Christmas in Jamaica, illuminated the Prime Minister's thinking. When Gould argued that, by letting Mandelson go, he was damaging himself, Blair replied, 'Read the papers, Philip. Think again.'[7] It was a weakness that, for Blair, the media were judge and jury.

Mandelson had not been dishonest but he had broken the spirit, if not the letter, of the rules. Above all, he had behaved unwisely, laying himself open to attack by his many enemies in the media. In the circumstances, it was understandable that Blair should have decided to let him go though, in his letter to Mandelson, he said that 'in the future, you will achieve more, much more with us'.

At Chequers, Blair offered Mandelson some advice to help him rebuild his career – sell the house, mix more in Parliament, be a team player, reconnect with the party. A few months later, I had a long talk with the fallen minister, ostensibly about the Britain in Europe campaign but, in fact, mostly about his future. He remarked that one of his problems was that he was not a normal backbencher because his every word and action was open to scrutiny by the media. I suggested that he could do three things which might stand him in good stead in the future – make speeches about Europe, write articles about the reform of social democracy and be seen with and talk to the new generation of Labour MPs, many of whom owed their seats partly to him. Greater popularity with the party would make it easier for Blair to bring him back. He asked plaintively, 'Will Gordon ever make it up with me?' He explained that the Brownites made it 'difficult for me to return to government'.[8]

Mandelson took his rehabilitation seriously. He made speeches on Europe, addressed trade union meetings, went to other constituency parties – he was already an excellent constituency MP – and took part in House of Commons debates. In June, he sold his house, paid off the Robinson loan and the Britannia mortgage and bought a two-bedroom flat near Notting Hill Gate. That month, he was also acquitted by a House of Commons Select Committee inquiry of 'dishonest intent' in failing to disclose the Robinson loan. Then, suddenly, on 11 October 1999, Blair brought Mandelson back into the Cabinet as Northern Ireland Secretary, in a move described by one commentator as 'the fastest rehabilitation from disgrace in modern political history'.[9]

It was an excellent appointment. Mo Mowlam, the popular Northern Ireland Secretary, had lost the confidence of the Ulster Unionists who, instead of dealing with her, tended to go straight to 10 Downing Street. To regain some distance from detailed negotiations and make progress with the talks, Blair wanted his closest colleague in the Northern Ireland Office. Mandelson's political skill and hard work were important factors in the setting-up of a devolved power-sharing government – though it had to be suspended from 11 February to 30 May 2000 – and in a so-called confidence-building move by the IRA to allow independent inspection of its arms dumps, as a step towards decommissioning. Given Mandelson's success in Northern Ireland, it was all more reprehensible that Blair gave way in such an ill-considered and panicky fashion to media pressure and made him resign over the Hinduja passport affair.

The background to this was an inquiry that Mandelson and/or his private office made to the Home Office about the impact of government policy on the second naturalisation application by SP Hinduja in the summer of 1998 when Mandelson was Minister without Portfolio. In the run-up to the general election, a story appeared in the *Observer* of 21 January 2001 that attempted to link this inquiry with the £1 million donation made by the Hinduja brothers to the Millennium Dome. Ludicrously, Mandelson was forced by Blair to resign over what Sir Anthony Hammond, QC, in his official review of the affair, described as the 'intrinsically insignificant issue' of whether or not Mandelson had spoken on behalf of SP Hinduja directly to Mike O'Brien, the then Home Office Minister. Mike O'Brien was certain that there had been a brief conversation while Mandelson was equally certain that contact had been through their private offices. After discussion with Home Office ministers, including the Home Secretary, Jack Straw, and the Prime Minister's spokesman, Alastair Campbell, Mandelson reluctantly accepted that he had been mistaken and offered his resignation to Blair who accepted it.

Hammond's official review established not only that the issue of who spoke to whom was irrelevant – and that there was, in any case, no documentary evidence either way – but far more importantly, on the crucial question as to whether either Mandelson or O'Brien had behaved improperly and whether the SP Hinduja application had been handled correctly, both Mandelson and O'Brien were completely cleared. In other words, there was no case at all for Mandelson's resignation.

The whole affair had been incompetently handled. Instead of waiting for the official review to establish the facts, there had been conflicting briefings. Tony Blair had panicked and, egged on by Alastair Campbell, had accepted the media's agenda and deadlines. In the short term, he may have been given high marks for speed and ruthlessness. In the longer term, it was at the cost of losing not only one of his best ministers but also a top political strategist. Above all, it was a blatant injustice.

11

SECOND LANDSLIDE

Like a sportsman hunting trophies, Blair was desperate to win a second term. His Labour predecessors had a distinctly patchy track record. Following the 1945 landslide, the Attlee government barely scraped into power in 1950 and was defeated in 1951. Harold Wilson won four elections in the 1960s and 1970s but never managed to win two consecutive full terms. The narrow victory in 1964 was followed by a substantial victory in 1966 but Wilson lost to Heath in 1970. Wilson formed a minority administration in February 1974 and just won the October election that year, which enabled Labour to limp through to 1979, when Callaghan, Wilson's successor, was turned out by Mrs Thatcher. The modernisers wanted at least to secure two full terms for New Labour.

In the modernisers' view, the key to re-election was to show that Labour was fit to govern – hence the emphasis on running the economy well and on demonstrating overall competence. Blair was also intent on keeping together the coalition of support which had voted the party into power in 1997, balancing the needs of Labour's heartlands while continuing to appeal to Middle England. The New Labour strategy was highly successful. The party was ahead of the opposition in the opinion polls every month but one and it also held every seat it defended in by-elections.

At the same time, Blair sought to provide ideological justification for his electoral strategy and to help explain New Labour practice in government. During 1998, he published a Fabian pamphlet, entitled 'The Third Way: New Politics for the New Century', in which he argued for 'a Third Way', which moved decisively beyond an Old Left preoccupied by state control, high taxation and producer interests and a New Right treating public investment and often the very notions of 'society' and collective endeavour as evils to be undone.[1]

In February 1998, there was a four-hour 'Third Way' seminar with Blair and Clinton, at the White House, discussing such issues as how to combat 'inequality and insecurity in the labour market' and 'One Nation, building cohesive and inclusive societies, tackling social exclusion'. In September that year and in April 1999 there were further meetings, widened to include the Prime Ministers of Italy and the Netherlands and the President of Bulgaria. The election of Gerhard Schröder of the SPD in Germany in the autumn of 1998 led to a joint declaration with Blair in June 1999 in London, entitled 'Europe: The Third Way/Die Neue Mitte'. This was, perhaps, the high tide of international 'Third Way-ism'.

The idea of the Third Way was criticised in Britain by Roy Hattersley, the former Labour leader, and in France, by Lionel Jospin. Hattersley sarcastically welcomed a meeting at Number Ten 'for the very good reason that, since the Prime Minister believes in the Third Way, it is important for him to find out what it is'. The Socialist leader of France, Lionel Jospin commented:

If the Third Way lies between communism and capitalism, it is merely a new name for democratic socialism peculiar to the British . . . If, on the other hand, the Third Way involves finding a middle way between social democracy and neo-liberalism, then this approach is not mine.[2]

Certainly, the Third Way labelling was ill chosen as it implied that the New Labour project was equidistant between Thatcherism and old-style social democracy. As a marketing ploy, it may have been attractive to right-wing commentators but it proved a turn-off to many on the centre-left and was, in any case, an inaccurate description of New Labour practice. Blair and Brown accepted a number of Thatcherite reforms, such as the importance of financial discipline and the role of the market, industrial relations reform and the Conservative privatisations. But the Welfare to Work programme, the Sure Start scheme to help the poorest families with very young children, the Working Families Tax Credit, the minimum wage, rises in Child Benefit and, from 2000, the unprecedented increases in health and education spending were hardly Tory. As Tony Blair and the Third Way guru, Tony Giddens, admitted, what they were really talking about was 'modernising' or 'revising' social democracy. New Labour was, in fact, the heir to a long tradition of labour revisionism and ethical socialism.[3]

What New Labour was attempting to do was to combine, in a form relevant to the twenty-first century and the age of globalisation, social justice and cohesion, on the one hand, with an efficient, competitive economy, on the other.

Significantly, Gordon Brown was not involved in the Third Way debate. His most interesting theoretical contribution at this time was the essay 'Equality – Then and Now', which he wrote for an anthology in memory of Tony Crosland, the revisionist Labour thinker and politician. Brown was concerned to place equality in a modern context. He argued that 'what people resent about Britain is not that some people who have worked hard have done well. What angers people is that millions have been denied the opportunity to realise their potential.'[4] With its tax, employment and education policies, New Labour, he said, was trying to improve the situation. It was also in this essay that Brown laid down a marker for the future, when he said:

There have been left-of-centre politicians who have espoused socialism but fail to meet the test of credibility. There have been those who have presented themselves as credible by abandoning socialism. [Could he have been referring to the Prime Minister?] The real challenge of left of centre politics is to be socialist and at the same time credible. [In other words, watch this space.]

Mandelson famously remarked that New Labour had no objection to people becoming 'filthy rich', provided they paid their taxes. Interestingly he also said, in a new introduction in 2002 for *The Blair Revolution*, that 'equality is the essence of the left . . . New Labour's idea of equality is one that provides opportunity throughout the life cycle; that relies on real, active redistribution of opportunities in our society.'[5] If he had read this, Gordon Brown would have approved, though Tony Blair maybe would not.

New Labour had fought the 1997 election as being the 'safe' alternative to the unpopular Conservative Party. In 2001, it ran on its record of economic competence and, for the future, on its commitments on health and education expenditure. It was the crisis in the health service in the winter of 1999–2000 that shaped the direction of the government over the second term and beyond – a direction which was recognisably social democratic, even if New Labour did not always acknowledge it.

When, after a ten-month spell as Chief Secretary to the Treasury, Alan Milburn, a northern colleague of Tony Blair, returned to the Department of Health as Health Secretary in October 1999, he speedily came to the conclusion that the NHS needed a major investment of money as soon as possible. Brown had increased NHS funding but it was not nearly enough and certainly not as much as he claimed. Milburn persuaded the Prime Minister that they could not afford to wait until the next spending review in July 2000 but the Chancellor resisted on the plausible grounds that, without a strategy for making sure that the money was efficiently spent, it would be wasted.

However, at the beginning of 2000, Brown's hand was forced by a national influenza outbreak, a succession of horror stories about overcrowded hospitals, cancelled operations, patients being shuttled about the country in search of beds and then by Blair's television interview with Sir David Frost on 16 January. The key individual case was the treatment of the eighty-seven-year-old mother of Robert Winston, celebrated fertility expert, broadcaster and Labour life peer. She had to wait sixteen hours in a casualty department, when she was found a bed it was in a mixed-sex ward, which the government had promised to phase out, and was then not given drugs when she should have been. Winston told the *New Statesman* that Britain's health service was much the worst in Europe and, under New Labour, was actually deteriorating. Blair, deeply wounded by Winston's attack and aware of widespread public disenchantment with the government's performance on the NHS, realised that, whatever the Chancellor said, something had to be done – and done quickly.

In his Frost interview, he discarded the inaccurate claim that the health service had already had the biggest cash injection in history and accepted that the NHS would have to have massive extra resources. His most striking commitment, not cleared with Brown, was to bring health service spending up to the European average over five years. The next day's press rightly reported this as a massive new pledge to the NHS, which threw Brown into a fury. He accused Blair of going beyond what they had agreed. 'You've stolen my fucking budget,' he shouted at the Prime Minister.[6]

However, in his Budget speech two months later, the Chancellor was in fine form, announcing to Labour cheers that, from 2000 until 2004, spending on the NHS would grow by 6.1 per cent a year in real, inflation-adjusted terms:

Last year the equivalent of just over £1850 per household was spent on the NHS. By the year 2004 more than £2,800 will be spent on the NHS. Half as much again for health care, for every family in our country.[7]

There were also extra resources for education in the budget and later in the spending review. I reflected in my diary on the towering position of Brown, 'smouldering with repressed energy and passion like a modern Heathcliff', as he delivered his budget. But I also added that it was the Prime Minister in his Frost interview who had shaped Brown's new strategy: 'The truth is that this is a government which, to a considerable extent, is run by two people alone – Tony and Gordon.'[8]

The year 2000 was a turning point for New Labour. Until then, Brown and Blair had bent over backwards to follow the Tory line on tax and spend. Now, it was increasingly clear that the voters were demanding increased spending on public services, especially on health and education – and that the government would ignore this changed public mood at its peril. Even the Conservatives were forced to accept this shift in opinion, promising to match the government's spending increases for the NHS. The terms of the underlying political argument had changed in New Labour's favour.

Although, in the event, Labour won another massive victory in June 2001, the government and especially its leader experienced a difficult year in the run-up to the election. In a leaked memorandum of June 2000 published in the *Sunday Times*, Blair's political adviser, Philip Gould, warned, 'TB is not believed to be real. He lacks conviction, he is all spin and presentation, he says things to please people, not because he believes them; TB has not delivered.' He continued in the same vein, 'TB promised a new Britain, a transformed NHS and public services, and all we have got is more of the same.'[9] As if to bear out Gould's depressing message, Blair was slow-hand-clapped when he spoke to the Women's Institute. Foolishly, the Prime Minister had ignored the advice of his Special Assistant, Anji Hunter, not to make the speech too political. His enthusiastic description of how the government was improving the NHS merely played into the hands of Tory supporters in the audience.

In September 2000, a far more serious challenge, the fuel protest, came almost out of nowhere. At the end of August, French fishermen, lorry drivers and farmers, protesting at high fuel costs, blockaded oil refineries and the French government gave in to their demands. A month later, British self-employed road hauliers, supported by militant farmers, followed their example and, after panic-buying, the pumps ran dry. Following consultation with heads of the oil companies, Blair unwisely went on television to say that the situation would be back to normal 'within the next twenty-four hours'. Only after Blair had threatened the oil companies with emergency powers and Milburn had gone on television to say that the blockade was putting people's lives at risk was it called off. The government had not made any concessions but had hardly looked in control. There was a feeling of helplessness at Number Ten while Ed Balls, adviser to Gordon Brown, accurately if unhelpfully briefed that the government had lost the propaganda battle. However, Labour MPs also remarked on the 'deafening' silence of the Chancellor.[10] Labour's standing in the polls dropped and the Tories briefly went ahead. But at the Labour Party conference, both Blair and Brown made excellent speeches reasserting the government's authority and, by the end of the year, the Conservatives were trailing by twenty points.

The second crisis, the outbreak of foot-and-mouth disease, influenced the date of the general election. Blair had been inclined to hold the election on the same day as the local elections, 3 May 2001, after Gordon Brown's fifth budget on 7 March. In his budget, the Chancellor, in full electioneering mode, was able to say that, under Labour, the UK had the lowest inflation, the lowest long-term interest rates and the lowest unemployment for a generation and that, having achieved economic stability, Labour was now able to rebuild the public services, especially by investing in health and education. Both the budget and Gordon Brown received record opinion-poll endorsement.[11] The scene seemed set for an early general election.

However, against the background of a rapid spread of foot-and-mouth, Blair worried about appearing opportunistic and splitting town from the countryside. He was also focused on dealing with the disease. At the end of March, he decided to postpone the local elections – and, by implication, the general election – from 3 May until 7 June. Many Labour MPs argued for the earlier date. Mandelson, advising Blair from the sidelines, supported postponement. Brown could see the arguments both ways but left the decision to Blair. In the end, delay was probably the right decision. Once again, Blair had shown his feel for the national mood.

The Prime Minister, unimpressed by the Tory opposition under William Hague, was confident about the outcome of the election. Indeed, he compared the 2001 election to getting into the boxing ring and then finding there was no opponent.[12] In Mandelson's absence – after resigning from office, he also resigned from his election post – Brown was in sole charge of the campaign. At Millbank, relations between the two camps were strained. Brown took a cautious approach, focusing on the strength of the economy and investment in health and education. Blair wanted a more lively and radical campaign. In a confidential minute to his key aides, which he did not circulate to Gordon Brown, he set out the key themes he planned to expand in speeches during the election.

He opened the campaign in a London comprehensive school, stressing his commitment to improving education, and, at Trimdon Labour Club in his constituency, he put the case for New Labour as a 'modern, liberal, social democratic party', occupying the centre ground between 'crypto-Thatcherites' and 'Old-style Socialists'. Launching the manifesto in Birmingham, he announced that spending on health was to rise by 6 per cent in real terms over the next three years, on education by 5 per cent and transport by 20 per cent. A few days later, he said 'world-class public services', tailored to the consumer, was his aim in the second term. In Edinburgh, against Brown's advice, he spoke about the European Union, as being the best forum for Britain's international involvement. It was a good series of speeches but it did not add up to a detailed programme for the second term.

The result of the election was a 'historic' second landslide, with an overall Labour majority of 167. Throughout, Labour maintained substantial poll leads on effective leadership, economic competence, party unity and a sense of direction. Labour also had large leads on the issues which voters considered important, especially on health and education.

The Brown camp was especially delighted. One of his supporters said, 'The campaign was chaired by Gordon, fought to Gordon's agenda, and on his record as Chancellor. It was his victory. What particularly pleased him was to win it this time without any input from Mandelson.'[13]

Despite his victory, Blair was more downcast. He was disappointed by the turnout, which was only 59 per cent – down 12 per cent from 1997. The level of voting was especially low in the party's 'safe' working-class constituencies – an indication that New Labour had failed to get across its message to its working-class supporters. Blair was also concerned by the deterioration of his relations with Brown. At Labour's victory party at Millbank, it was noticeable that Labour's two leaders could scarcely bring themselves to shake hands or exchange a word in public.[14] Yet, though the state of their relationship did not bode well for the future, the truth was that it had been the Blair–Brown partnership that was mainly instrumental in achieving Labour's second landslide. If Brown had managed the economy well, Blair's charisma and communication skills had delivered the centre ground. The victory was a joint effort – the result of a partnership which they would find more and more difficult to sustain.

PART 4

THINGS GO AWRY

12

9/11, BUSH
AND AFGHANISTAN

On Tuesday, 11 September 2001, Tony Blair was working through lunch in his hotel suite on a speech he was about to deliver to the TUC annual conference at Brighton. He was concentrating hard because he wanted to be certain that his words on public service reform struck the right note. He was also intending to make some positive remarks about the euro and Britain's relationship with the European Union. Then at 1.48 p.m., he was interrupted by his aide, Anji Hunter, who told him that a plane had crashed into the North Tower of the World Trade Center at New York. 'Oh my God,' said Blair. Thinking it was an isolated accident, he turned to Alastair Campbell and remarked, 'I will have to refer to it at the beginning of my speech.' He then went back to his text, writing against the clock.

Then, at 2.03 p.m., a second plane hit the South Tower of the World Trade Center. When another aide broke the news to him, the Prime Minister switched on the TV and watched for himself as a third plane crashed into the south-west face of the Pentagon. It was clearly a terrorist attack on the United States. After consulting first Campbell and then Jonathan Powell in London, he cancelled his speech though, before leaving for London, he said a few characteristically well-chosen words to the trade union delegates:

> There have been the most terrible, shocking events in the United States of America in the last few hours. I am afraid we can only imagine the terror and carnage there, and the many, many innocent people who have lost their lives. This mass terrorism is the new evil in our world today.[1]

Blair returned immediately by train to London for emergency talks with his advisers, senior colleagues and security officials. While the US President, George W. Bush, on the advice of his Vice-President, Richard Cheney, circled aimlessly in his plane, Air Force One, over America, Blair provided reassurance and leadership by appearing on the six o'clock television news outside Downing Street. After expressing his sympathy with the victims of the terrorist attack on the United States and condemnation of those who had carried it out, the Prime Minister outlined the practical measures that the British government was taking to minimise the security risk to the UK, including enforcing a no-fly zone over London. His conclusion stressed the international significance of what had happened and offered British support:

> This is not a battle between the US and terrorism, but between the free and democratic world and terrorism. We therefore, here in Britain, stand shoulder to shoulder with our American friends in this hour of tragedy, and we, like them, will not rest until this evil is driven from our world.[2]

Almost instinctively, Blair had realised that 9/11 (as it came to be called) would have a major impact across the world and, above all, on the United States which, previously, had appeared virtually invulnerable to outside attack. The question he asked himself was how the United States would respond – particularly when the country was led by a right-wing Republican president. It would be disastrous if the world's only superpower decided to lash out unilaterally and indiscriminately. Blair was afraid that the United States might 'jump out of the international system',[3] ignoring the United Nations, NATO and the other international institutions, mainly developed under American leadership, since the Second World War. He immediately saw a crucial role for the United Kingdom in persuading the United States not to act unilaterally but to build an international coalition to fight the terrorists. At the same time, the Prime Minister would help convince other major countries and their leaders to support the United States. In other words, Britain would act as a bridge between the USA and other countries, above all members of the European Union. At the same time, Blair with all his experience, charisma and persuasive power, would be a pivotal player in this new and dangerous world.

9/11 was a key moment for Blair. It altered the way that he saw the world. As he told the Chilcot Inquiry into the UK's involvement in Iraq, by demonstrating the damage terrorists could inflict, it changed what he called the 'calculus of risk'. It also led directly to the war in Afghanistan, where Al Qaeda were harboured by the Taliban regime, and, later, to the conflict in Iraq. It had another effect on his premiership. At the beginning of his crucial second term, his attention was diverted away from his domestic agenda to these critical international issues. One of his aides said, '[G]etting meetings into his diary for domestic policy was a great struggle after 9/11.'[4]

Blair was, in truth, adopting a high-risk and exposed strategy. It depended not so much on the power of the United Kingdom, which was, after all, only a medium-sized European country, albeit an important one with world interests, but more on the Prime Minister's undoubted persuasive abilities. It assumed that, at one and the same time, he would be able to convince a conservative Republican president to behave multilaterally *and* persuade European leaders, with their own contrasting standpoints and interests, to back him. And it also presumed that he would be able to unite his political party and the British Parliament behind his bold approach. It was a tall order.

The British Prime Minister was very clear that, at this moment of extreme vulnerability for the United States, his first priority was to get alongside the US President – what one of his advisers described as the 'hug them close' approach to British–American relations. Blair had developed a close relationship with Bush's predecessor, the Democrat Bill Clinton, at first almost that of a younger brother with an older one but later turning into a more equal partnership. When Clinton came to the United Kingdom for his final visit as President, he gave Blair some advice about Bush. First, he warned him not to underestimate the Republican President-to-be, saying, 'He's a shrewd, tough politician and absolutely ruthless.' Second, he told him to 'get as close to George Bush as you have been to me'.[5] Blair's first meeting with Bush went well. To a senior colleague, Blair said about Bush, 'He is strong, straightforward, with an underlying seriousness. You know where you are with him. I like him.' Bush remarked about Blair, 'He's a pretty charming guy. He put the charm offensive on me.'[6]

Yet there were always going to be differences of approach between the new Republican administration and most European governments which even Blair would find it difficult to reconcile. In the run-up to the US election, Bush had stressed that it would be the American national interest rather than international agreements which would shape its relations with other countries. Although his Secretary of State, Colin Powell, was more cautious about the use of American power and more concerned to work with allies, Bush's views were reinforced by his Vice-President, Richard Cheney, and his hawkish Defense Secretary, Donald Rumsfeld, who both argued for a strong and unilateral assertion of American national interests, backed up, if necessary, by military force. Even before 9/11, the Bush administration had rejected the Kyoto Protocol on climate change and refused to sign up to the proposed International Criminal Court. 9/11 was bound to strengthen this assertive tendency. As Bush told the Joint Session of Congress on 20 September a few days after the attack, 'Every nation, in every region, now has a decision to make. Either you are with us, or you are with the terrorists.'

In that same speech, Bush singled out the British Prime Minister who was sitting in the so-called 'press' gallery next to the First Lady, Laura Bush. 'I am so honoured the British Prime Minister has crossed the ocean to show his unity with America.' He added in his demotic Texan drawl, 'Thank ya for comin', friend.'[7] Bush's tribute to Blair was the culmination of an extraordinary day for the British Prime Minister. He had breakfasted with President Chirac at the Élysée Palace, flown across the Atlantic to New York (during the flight he spoke by phone to Mohammad Khātamī, the reformist President of Iran), attended a service at St Thomas Church, Manhattan, for the British victims of 9/11, at which he read a passage from Thornton Wilder's *The Bridge of San Luis Rey*, and had then flown on to Washington. After travelling back to Europe overnight, Blair then attended an emergency summit of EU leaders in Brussels the following day.

In the next few months, Tony Blair became a sort of super envoy or special ambassador for George Bush. In the eight weeks after 11 September, he held fifty-four meetings with other leaders, almost one a day. He went on thirty-one flights and covered more than 40,000 miles.[8] Working closely with Bush and the American administration (unkind critics called him 'Bush's poodle'), he succeeded in assembling an impressively wide-ranging international coalition, including not only France and Germany and other EU countries but also Russia, Pakistan and other countries bordering Afghanistan. At the end of October, however, he went on a less successful visit to Syria, Saudi Arabia, Israel and Gaza. Against Foreign Office advice, he appeared at a Damascus news conference with President Assad of Syria. Assad proceeded to denounce Israel as a terrorist state and praise Palestinian suicide bombers as freedom fighters. Deeply embarrassed, Blair remained mute.

In his speech on 2 October 2001 to the Labour Party conference at Brighton, Blair once again made Britain's support for the United States clear. 'We were with you at the first – we will stay with you to the last,' he said dramatically. He stressed his unremitting hostility to Al Qaeda and the Taliban who 'aided and abetted' them. But the underlying themes were, as they had been in his 1999 Chicago speech, global interdependence and the justification for intervention. His peroration had an almost messianic tone to it. He talked of a fight for freedom and justice and proclaimed that 'the starving, the wretched, the dispossessed, the ignorant, those living in wanton squalor, from the deserts of North Africa to the slums of Gaza, to the mountain ranges of Afghanistan: they are our cause'. He concluded, in full hyperbolic mode, 'This is a moment to seize. The kaleidoscope has been shaken. The pieces are in flux. Soon they will settle again. Before they do, let us re-order the world around us.' This was going over the top. Despite Blair's fine words, Britain no longer had the capability. It was only the remaining superpower, the United States, which could do the re-ordering and then only on its terms.

What did Blair actually get in return for his fervent support of Bush? When he met Bush at the White House on 20 September, the US President had said, 'I agree with you that the job in hand is Al Qaeda and Taliban. Iraq we keep for another day.'[9] Though Blair was relieved to hear what Bush had to say, his intervention had not been crucial. Bush had already decided to concentrate on hunting down Al Qaeda and removing the Taliban. The United States had also gone to the United Nations to get a Security Council resolution approved condemning those responsible for 9/11 and countries which aided them, as well as supporting the implementation of Article 5 of the NATO Charter which set in motion the procedure for aiding fellow members under attack. But these were tactical responses to the attack, not an unexpected conversion to multilateralism. The United States made it known that it wanted to run the operation in Afghanistan itself though it permitted a minor role for other countries, above all the UK whose troops were involved in the conflict.

After a slow start, US air power and Special Forces, combined with the troops of the so-called Northern Alliance of Afghan warlords, succeeded in removing the Taliban regime. A new Afghan government led by Hamid Karzai and backed by an international peacekeeping force was put in place. But its writ did not run much beyond the capital Kabul. Afghanistan was still in a precarious and unstable state – as it still is today. And the Al Qaeda and Taliban leaders escaped into the mountains on either side of Pakistan's north-west frontier.

Other countries, including France and Germany, condemned 9/11 and supported the American effort in Afghanistan to destroy Al Qaeda and dislodge the Taliban. But, from the first, there was a difference of emphasis. For the United States, the 'war' against terrorism was the first priority. The continental Europeans, of course, believed that it was important but, for them, there were other priorities as well. And they were disturbed by the intemperate language which Bush sometimes used – for example, wanting the leader, Osama bin Laden, 'dead or alive' and about fighting 'a crusade against evil'.

In his speech at the Lord Mayor's Banquet on 12 November 2001, Blair extolled his policy of 'riding both horses', being alongside the US President and working closely with his European allies:

> We have buried the myth that Britain has to choose between being strong in Europe or strong with the United States. Afghanistan has shown vividly how the relationships reinforce each other; and that both the United States and our European partners value our role with the other.[10]

There was an element of wishful thinking here. As far as the Europeans were concerned, there was already resentment of Blair's assumption of the role of messenger between Europe and America, especially as they sometimes felt that the messages were going only one way. The German

Chancellor, Gerhard Schröder, remarked about 'the bridge' metaphor often used by Blair that the traffic across Blair's bridge always seemed to be in one direction.

In public, Bush was very complimentary about Blair, welcoming him to the White House on 7 November in glowing terms – there was 'no better person to talk to than Tony Blair. He brings a lot of wisdom and judgement.'[11] But the problem for Blair was that Britain was very much the junior partner, always following on behind. There was a real risk in attaching British policy so closely to the USA, especially when it was understood between Bush and Blair that Blair did not criticise American policy in public. The British Prime Minister may have been popular in the US but playing the role of the President's mouthpiece did not go down well in Britain or on the continent of Europe.

13

IRAQ

Emboldened by its success in Afghanistan, the US administration moved on to Iraq. In January 2002, in his annual State of the Union Address to Congress, Bush announced a new interventionist doctrine and warned of pre-emptive action. This was his 'axis of evil' speech in which, referring to North Korea, Iran and, above all, Iraq he said:

> States like these, and their terrorist allies, constitute an axis of evil ... [B]y seeking weapons of mass destruction, these regimes pose a global and growing danger. They could provide these arms to terrorists, giving them the means to match their hatred ... I will not wait on events, while dangers gather.[1]

Behind the scenes, Rumsfeld ordered the Pentagon to make contingency plans for an invasion of Iraq later in the year. *Time* magazine reported in March that Bush had poked his head into the White House office of his National Security Advisor, Condoleezza Rice, and told three senators sitting there, 'Fuck Saddam. We're taking him out.'[2] In Republican circles, this was hardly a surprising remark. After all, a Republican Congress had passed legislation supporting 'regime change' in Iraq as long ago as 1998 and, following 9/11, the so-called neo-conservatives in the administration were arguing for the removal of Saddam Hussein and installing a democratic regime.

If bellicose words about pre-emption and war in Iraq were popular in the United States, the 'axis of evil' speech created real alarm in other countries, especially in Europe. Hubert Védrine, the French Foreign Minister, said that US policy had become 'simplistic' while Chris Patten, the EU External Affairs Commissioner, said that the US was in danger of going into 'unilateralist overdrive'. For the Left, it was not so much Saddam Hussein but Bush who began to be seen as the threat to world peace. Blair's 'bridge' between the United States and Europe was in danger of breaking into two.

Blair himself favoured a tough line towards Saddam Hussein. Ever since the previous crisis over Iraq in 1997–98, he had believed that the Iraqi dictator was a dangerous man whom the international community would eventually have to confront. Although he never believed that there was evidence of links between Saddam Hussein and Al Qaeda, 9/11 underlined the potential dangers of leaving weapons of mass destruction in Hussein's hands. The difference between Blair and Bush was that, if possible, Blair wanted the response to Saddam Hussein to be a multilateral, international effort. This was, in part, because it would make it easier to sell the war both in Britain and on the continent. In part, it was because it fitted in with his theory of liberal interventionism, as outlined in his 1999 Chicago speech and repeated in his address at the Bush Presidential Library on 7 April 2002. In the latter speech, Blair said:

The international coalition matters. Where it operates, the unintended consequences of action are limited, the diplomatic parameters better fixed. The US and EU together is a precondition of such alliances. But it needs hard work, dialogue and some mutual understanding.

At the meeting between Blair and Bush at the President's Texas ranch in Crawford the previous day, Bush had made it clear that his policy was to remove Saddam. Contrary to what some have argued, Blair did not, at that stage, commit the UK to a war in Iraq. He did, however, stress the need to 'deal with Saddam', to bring him back into compliance with UN resolutions and to stop him developing weapons of mass destruction, a process that could – indeed, was likely – to lead to war. He also argued more broadly for using the UN, for a real effort by the US to broker a just peace between Israel and the Palestinians in the Middle East and to a commitment to rebuild the failed states which fostered terrorism.

On Blair's return to London, there was growing unease at Westminster that the United Kingdom was being sucked into war in Iraq by the United States. The Leader of the House, Robin Cook, noted in his diary that at Prime Minister's Questions, on 10 April, that 'there were a number of challenging points on Iraq made from our own side which have an uncustomary hard edge to them'. When, the next day, Blair reported to Cabinet on his visit to the US, Patricia Hewitt, the Secretary of State for Industry spoke of the need for 'UN cover for any military action on Iraq'. She was supported by Robin Cook who said that 'both Labour MPs and the British public will want to know that what we do has the support of the international community'.[3]

The next few months saw a battle for President Bush's ear. Number Ten, supported by the US State Department and former members of Bush's father's administration, argued for going to the United Nations. At the end of July, Blair sent his top foreign affairs adviser, David Manning, with the message to Bush that, without a UN resolution, Britain might not be able to join the US in Iraq. As Manning told the President, without international backing, 'we would be unable to do it'.[4] The American Vice-President, Richard Cheney, and the Defense Secretary, Donald Rumsfeld, were, however, strongly opposed to getting 'bogged down' at the UN. On the day after President Bush had agreed in principle with his advisers to go through the UN, Cheney, in a public speech, said that 'a return of the [weapon] inspectors would provide no assurance whatsoever of his [Saddam's] compliance with UN resolutions. On the contrary, there is a great danger that it would provide false comfort that Saddam was somehow "back in the box".'5 Such words as these only increased the growing opposition to war both in Britain and on the continent of Europe.

At the beginning of September, Blair flew to the US to try to clinch a deal on the UN route. On his arrival at Camp David, Blair was surprised to find Cheney sitting alongside Bush, either to test Blair's case or, more likely, for the President to lock the Vice-President into any agreement. To Cheney and his staff, Blair's support for multilateralism was a dangerous distraction. Cheney's chief of staff would say, 'Oh, dear, we'd better not do that or we might upset the Prime Minister.'6 However, at Camp David, Bush agreed to go to the Security Council to seek a further UN resolution, giving Saddam a last chance to comply. In return, the Prime Minister would back US-led military action if Saddam did not co-operate with the UN weapons inspectors.

Afterwards, critics accused Blair of deliberately deceiving the voters, a charge which he later vehemently denied:

> What I said to him [the President] was 'Look, if we can rescue this through the UN route' and he accepted that was so . . . The idea that we had some pre-arranged agreement that there was to be conflict, that the UN process was a charade, is completely and totally untrue.'7

It was certainly the case that, according to the deal, the United States would not go ahead with regime change, if Saddam complied with the UN. But Bush never expected Saddam to comply – he had never done so before. He was, nevertheless, prepared to go through the UN to help Blair and as a sop to international opinion, provided the UN got tough with Saddam.

In the short term, the Camp David deal provided Blair with the cover he needed to try to persuade his party and his European allies. The problem for the British Prime Minister was what happened if the UN route proved ineffective. The danger was that he would then be left exposed to going to war alongside a US President who was increasingly unpopular in Britain and on the Continent and without his main European allies.

On 12 September, Bush spoke to the United Nations General Assembly. Somehow the crucial sentence had somehow been left off the autocue – the British said, only half jokingly, that it had been sabotaged by Cheney – but the US President remembered it and said, 'We will work with the UN Security Council for the necessary resolutions.' These words and the emphasis on the UN helped limit the scale of a Labour backbench rebellion to fifty-six MPs at the end of an emergency Commons debate on 24 September. It was for the September debate that the dossier on Iraq's weapons of mass destruction was prepared by the intelligence agencies. Although the tabloids picked up the claim, highlighted in Blair's introduction, that Iraq had weapons of mass destruction that could be ready for use within 'forty-five minutes', the main evidence was drawn from the past and, above all, the chemical stocks unaccounted for when the UN inspectors left Iraq in 1998. Though the dossier showed that Saddam's record had been poor, it did not prove that he was an urgent threat.

The high point of Blair's pre-war diplomacy was the unanimous Security Council vote on 8 November 2002 behind UN Resolution 1441. This resolution called for tough inspections and full Iraqi compliance. But the apparent transatlantic unity hid a sharp division between the US view that, in the event of non-compliance, another vote was not needed before military action and the French and Russian view that further consultation was required. In the first three months of 2003, British efforts to reconcile the two sides failed. Blair's policy of a bridge between the United States and Europe was shown to be unrealistic, leaving the UK dangerously exposed.

Following the Iraqi government's 12,000-page response to the UN resolution, the US concluded that Saddam was not interested in a diplomatic solution and prepared for the war. Meanwhile the Franco-German position hardened against the war. Schröder had narrowly won a second term on 22 September, fighting his campaign on an anti-war ticket, while the French elections in May had greatly strengthened the position of Chirac who was now free to assert himself internationally. The Franco-German alliance, which previously had been in some disarray, was revived on the basis of joint opposition to the war. At a Franco-German summit in January, Chirac declared, '[W]ar is always an admission of defeat.'[8]

Rumsfeld's reply to the Franco-German initiative was to attack France and Germany as 'Old Europe' and to point to other European countries as being on the side of the US. Eight heads of European governments, including Blair, then signed an article in the *Wall Street Journal*, supporting the enforcement of Resolution 1441. This public spat may have shown that France and Germany could no longer always speak for Europe. But Rumsfeld's typically clumsy intervention effectively undermined any chance of sustaining transatlantic cooperation and damaged European unity, which had been a key objective of previous American administrations. As far as Blair was concerned, Rumsfeld's unwise response, which was as much a sign of desperation as of considered policy, threatened to undo all his efforts since 1997 to come closer to France and Germany.

In the weeks leading up to war, Blair became increasingly isolated. The massive demonstration in London of more than one million people on 15 February 2003 showed growing domestic opposition – public hostility which was replicated in other European capitals. On 26 February, 121 Labour MPs voted against the government after a debate on Iraq. At the UN, Blair tried to secure a majority for a second Security Council Resolution which would authorise the use of force and, in so doing, win over wavering MPs. But weeks of lobbying and telephoning ended in failure – in part because some delegates thought that the UN inspectors ought to have time to finish the job; in part because of the opposition of France, Germany and Russia; and in part because the Bush administration itself regarded a second resolution as completely unnecessary.

Then Chirac, giving a TV interview from behind his desk in the Élysée Palace, presented Blair with a face-saver when he said, in full Olympian style, 'My position is that, whatever the circumstances, France will vote "no" because she considers this evening that there are no grounds for waging war to achieve the goal we have set ourselves, that is to disarm Iraq.' The Number Ten publicity machine quickly put out the line that, by using the phrase 'whatever the circumstances', Chirac was unreasonably blocking the further resolution. There followed some unseemly French-bashing led by the Foreign Secretary, Jack Straw, and backed up by the tabloids. In the short term, it may have helped Blair get off the UN hook but at the cost of undermining his European policy. Faced by a fundamental choice, Blair opted for the United States rather than Europe – so much for 'the bridge'.

Blair now had to carry his Cabinet, his party and Parliament for his policy of going to war without a second UN resolution. There was only one Cabinet resignation though it was an important one – that of Robin Cook, former Foreign Secretary and reforming Leader of the House of Commons. Clare Short resigned over Iraq but only after the war was over. In his eloquent resignation speech, on 17 March, Cook said that 'neither the international community nor the British public is persuaded that there is an urgent and compelling reason for this military action in Iraq'. He continued:

On Iraq, I believe the prevailing mood of the British people is sound. They do not doubt that Saddam is a brutal dictator, but they are not persuaded that he is a clear and present danger to Britain . . . Above all, they are uneasy at Britain going out on a limb on a military adventure without a broader international coalition and against the hostility of many of our traditional allies.[9]

Brown, who had remained on the sidelines throughout the crisis, now gave Blair full support in Cabinet. If he had been against the war, it is doubtful whether Blair could have held the line. Straw, who had worked hard on trying to get the second resolution through the Security Council, concluded that the attempt would fail and advised Blair to plan for the possibility that the UK would stay out, only offering support after Saddam had been deposed. When Bush himself suggested much the same idea to Blair, he said, 'No thanks.' If Britain was going to join in, it had to be as a full, albeit junior, partner to the United States.

In the Commons debate on Iraq on 18 March, Blair made one of his most powerful speeches. After stressing Saddam's continued defiance of the UN over weapons of mass destruction and pointing to the danger of rogue regimes and terrorist groups coming together, he warned that failure to enforce Resolution 1441 risked forcing nations – that is the United States – down 'the very unilateralist path we wish to avoid'. He concluded:

> To retreat now, I believe, would put at hazard all that we hold dearest. To turn the United Nations back into a talking shop; to stifle the first steps of progress in the Middle East; to leave the Iraqi people to the mercy of events over which we would have relinquished all power to influence for the better; to tell our allies that at the very moment of action . . . Britain faltered. I will not be party to such a course.[10]

It was a veiled threat of resignation. At the end of the debate, 139 Labour MPs voted against the government – a massive rebellion but less than half the Parliamentary Labour Party. With the Tories voting in favour of military action, he always had a majority in Parliament. But, if he had not been able to carry a majority of his own party, he probably would have been forced to resign.

Twenty-four hours later, Britain went to war in Iraq. The 40,000 British troops had an important role in the south of the country, especially in securing control of Basra, but it was mainly a US operation run by the US. In three weeks, the conflict was over – Saddam's army simply melted away. But, if the war was quickly won, the peace was quite another matter.

It soon became clear that the United States government and, above all, the Pentagon had failed to prepare for what would happen in post-war

Iraq. There had been a plan drawn up in the State Department but it had been totally ignored by Rumsfeld. Saddam's regime, like his statue in Baghdad, may have been toppled but a massive effort was going to be required if Iraq was going to be rebuilt as a stable democratic modern state. There would need to be a sustained programme of nation building, backed by an intensive security drive, but both of these were far too long in coming. Iraq was deeply divided both religiously and ethnically. It was dogged by terrorism, insurgency and, at times, virtual civil war and, with its borders open to unfriendly countries, above all Iran, the difficulty of running the country threatened to overwhelm coalition forces.

Why did Blair involve his country in the Iraq war? His decision was shaped mainly by three factors. The first was that he believed that Saddam Hussein had to be confronted. His concern about Saddam and weapons of mass destruction predated the election of Bush and 9/11. It was Blair, after all, who had authorised British involvement in the Operation Desert Fox bomb and missile attacks on Iraq in December 1998 and the enforcement of the no-fly zones over southern and northern Iraq. After 9/11, his view was that the potential threat of Saddam, especially if it was linked to international terrorism, had significantly increased. Although, in terms of UN resolutions and international law, he was not able to argue directly for regime change, he strongly believed that the world would be a safer place without Saddam.

Second, Blair was convinced that the US should not be left alone to deal with difficult problems. Isolation would only encourage the unilateralist forces within the administration. That is why Blair was so anxious that the Iraq invasion should be an international one and why he made desperate attempts to get UN support for the US. If that failed, as it did, then at least Britain should stand 'shoulder to shoulder' with its major ally.

The third reason Blair went to war related to his own character. In a House of Lords debate on Iraq in September 2002, Roy Jenkins, in his last major speech, described Blair as, above all, a 'conviction' politician:

He is a little too Manichean for my perhaps now jaded taste, seeing matters in stark terms of good and evil, black and white, contending with each other, and with a consequent belief that if evil is cast down, good will inevitably follow.[11]

Blair's incipient moralism had been strengthened by what he saw as successful liberal intervention in Kosovo, Sierra Leone and Afghanistan – that is the idea of toppling bad rulers, securing conflict zones through military, mostly US, deployment and then gaining international support for reconstruction and democratic renewal. With his unabashed confidence in his own judgement and persuasive abilities, he brushed aside any doubts about potential difficulties in post-conflict Iraq or about the damage British involvement might do to his European strategy or to his government's and his own standing at home. He went to war in Iraq in 2003 because he believed it was the 'right thing' to do. Despite everything that happened subsequently, he told the Chilcot Inquiry that he would take the same decision again.

But there were substantial costs arising out of his decision to go to war. It was certainly a plus factor that a cruel dictator, Saddam, had been removed and, with him, the possibility of Iraq as a political threat. It was also good that a democratic government had replaced Hussein's regime. But the loss of life – probably amounting to over 100,000 among Iraqis – and the instability and insecurity that followed had also to be taken into account. Even now, seven years after the war, it is too soon to judge whether Iraq will ever become stable and securely democratic.

The Prime Minister's European policy was also a casualty of the Iraq war. Blair had believed that he could act as a mediator between the US and Europe and Iraq exposed the fallacy behind this idea. It also weakened his pro-European strategy, which had been a key point of New Labour's approach.

His relations with France and Germany had already deteriorated by the end of 2002. In October, Chirac and Schröder ganged up against

Blair by launching a surprise joint initiative on the future financing of the Common Agricultural Policy. A public row between Blair and Chirac then led to a postponement of a planned British–French summit. Then Rumsfeld's jibe about 'Old Europe' and the UK's campaign against France made matters worse. It also encouraged British euro-scepticism, which was hardly the best way to win a referendum on entry to the euro. Indeed, the combination of a Blair weakened by the war and euro-scepticism strengthened by European divisions made it all the more certain that Brown would win the battle to put off joining the euro (see next chapter).

At home, Blair and his government were weakened by the war. The failure to find weapons of mass destruction (WMD) in Iraq after the war led to accusations in the media and at Westminster that Blair had deliberately deceived voters and led the country to war on a false prospectus. There was also the issue of whether the government had 'doctored' the intelligence reports it had received. Two official reports – the Hutton and Butler inquiries – exonerated the Prime Minister of lying and improper behaviour. In other words, it was legitimate to criticise Blair's judgement but not his veracity. With respect to WMD, the failure of intelligence was not confined to the UK. The intelligence services of France, Israel and Russia, as well as those of the UK and the US, were amazed that no weapons of mass destruction were found while even Hans Blix, the leader of the UN inspection team, was surprised.

However, despite the findings of the Hutton and Butler inquiries, a large section of opinion, especially amongst the liberal intelligentsia, many of whom had joined the one-million-strong demonstration in London against the Iraq war, lost trust in Blair. Blair's personal ratings dropped and Labour suffered in the public opinion polls and at the local and European elections. The party entered the run-up to the 2005 general election in a less strong position than it had been in 2001. After Iraq, Blair's 'big tent' began to look a lot smaller and the long-term electoral prospects of New Labour significantly weaker. Iraq was a disaster for both Blair and his party.

14

THE BLAIR–BROWN WARS

L ooking back on the first term, the Prime Minister felt that he had wasted too much of it, partly because of the government's inexperience and partly because his main priority had been to win a second term. While relaxing in the garden of his constituency home on Election Day in 2001, he assured Alastair Campbell that 'it was all going to be different second term, that he was older, wiser, more experienced, would deal with the crap better, would be more focused on the things he needed to focus on'.[1]

One of the first decisions he had to make was what to do about Gordon Brown. As his Cabinet Secretary, Richard Wilson, said to him as he returned to Downing Street after his landslide election victory, 'You are now at the peak of your power. You may never be as strong again as you are now.'[2] If he wanted to move Brown, the beginning of the second term was the time to do it. Many of his advisers at Number Ten argued strongly for such a step. They had tired of what they saw as his rival centre of power at the Treasury and his high-handed obstructionism. Blair understood only too well the case for a change In his more optimistic moods, he considered persuading Brown to go to the Foreign Office, with the argument that it would give him the wider experience which he would need to be Prime Minister. But, after mulling it over, he decided to keep his Chancellor.

In the end, the counter arguments were more powerful. He knew Brown did not want to leave the Treasury. If he was moved against his wishes, he would probably resign and make trouble on the backbenches. It would, in any case, be difficult to explain to the Labour Party why he was sacking a Chancellor who had proved such a success and whose record had been a major factor in winning a smashing election victory. A combination of fear, guilt and perhaps also residual affection persuaded him to stay his hand. It was a decision – or, rather, a non-decision – which, as relations between the two men deteriorated during the second term, he may have come to regret.

If Blair hoped that the second term was going to be 'different', so did Brown. During it, he was expecting Blair to step down so that he could take over as Prime Minister. In the 2001 election campaign, Blair was often asked by the media about whether, if he was re-elected, he intended to serve a full term or whether he would stand down after two or three years in accordance with their so-called 'deal'. But he denied that there was such a deal, insisting that as 'Gordon and I both say whenever we're asked about this, there is no gentleman's agreement'.[3] In fact, though Brown did not directly contradict Blair's interpretation, he believed that there was indeed such a deal and he fully intended to make Blair stick to it.

After the election, Brown was in a very strong position. The polls showed that he was extremely popular. He had proved that he was unsackable – at least by this Prime Minister. And, in his first budget following the election on 17 April 2002, he made a bold attempt to seize hold of the public spending agenda by announcing the biggest rise in health spending since the NHS was set up – an increase of 7.4 per cent a year in real terms for five years. To pay for part of this unprecedented rise, he introduced a special 1 per cent National Insurance increase, a step which, according to public opinion polls, was supported by the voters. Brown's 2002 budget ushered in a sustained period of rises in public spending, especially on health, education and policing.

Public spending provided part of the backdrop to the explosive rows between Blair and Brown – the so-called TB–GBs as civil servants called them – which bedevilled the years between 2002 and 2005. There is no doubt that this conflict was, to a considerable extent, a battle of egos, in which the two most powerful men in the New Labour government jockeyed for political position. Brown's understanding of the deal made in 1994 was apparently that Blair would stand down in 2004, in time for a general election in 2005. This view of the deal was much encouraged by Brown's entourage who, of course, had a vested interest. Blair's Downing Street adviser, Sally Morgan, now Baroness Morgan, recounted how, in the summer of 2004, one of Brown's advisers, Ed Miliband, demanded of her, 'Why are you still here? Why haven't you packed up yet to go? There's a deal and he's got to go.' Morgan replied, 'I don't know anything of the sort.'[4]

Blair's attitude to his own possible resignation varied according to his political and psychological vulnerability. When he was feeling strong, he insisted that he was not going to be forced out by Brown. When he was feeling weak – either because of Iraq or because of hostility to public sector reform or because of both – he tended to prevaricate, suggesting a departure sometime in the future. During the second term, Brown kept demanding a date for Blair to go but was cautious about pressing too hard, in case it all ended in a bloody civil war which could fatally damage his inheritance.

But it would be wrong to conclude that the Blair–Brown rows were entirely about power. They were also about policy and strategic direction. Despite his pre-occupation with the fallout from 9/11 – first Afghanistan and then Iraq – Blair was acutely aware that he had at the most three years to make his mark on events before preparation would have to start for the next election. His new policy guru, Andrew Adonis, later Lord Adonis and Transport Secretary in Brown's government, wrote to him on 7 January 2002, saying:

2002 could well be your watershed – akin to 1946 for Attlee, 1969 for Wilson and 1984 for Thatcher – determining whether the government's early successes turn into historic achievements or a slow process of disintegration. Your seminal issues are international security, Europe and the public services.[5]

Domestically, the key issue for Blair was public service reform. The increasing spending in health and education was designed to bring expenditure in these areas up to European and the Organisation for Economic Co-operation and Development (OECD) levels. The Prime Minister wanted these and other services to become so good that not only would the taxpayer be prepared to pay for them but also the growing number of well-off people would continue to use them, even though they could afford the private alternative. In his view, this was also the best way of ensuring decent services for the less well-off, as well as keeping the New Labour coalition together. But improving public services was not only a question of money – it was also one of management, delivery and reform. When he appointed Alan Milburn to Health, Stephen Byers to Transport, David Blunkett to the Home Office and Estelle Morris to Education, he told them, at one of a series of special dinners at Number Ten, that he wanted them to stay in place for the whole Parliament to deliver public service reform. Although all of them, for different reasons, left office before the general election,[6] this showed Blair's intent, as did the establishment of the remarkably successful Prime Minister's Delivery Unit, headed by Michael Barber.[7]

During the second term, results in almost every aspect of public services improved. In health, waiting times were dramatically reduced for all kinds of surgery and for Accident and Emergency Departments. Mortality rates dropped steadily and care for patients with cancer and coronary disease got better. Primary school pupils could now read and write and do mathematics much better than their predecessors a decade ago and they compared well in reading and maths standards with the rest of the world. In the case of crime, the large volume crimes – vehicle crime and burglary – were much reduced. The chances of being a victim of crime were the lowest since records began in 1981.[8]

Most of these improvements, especially in NHS waiting times and literacy and numeracy in primary schools, came about as a result of a top-down implementation of change – what Tony Blair called 'flogging' the system. The Prime Minister wanted improvements to be self-sustaining. That is why he turned to a second model – that of 'quasi-markets'. The idea was to put the user of the service in the driving seat. This would, he hoped, lead to increased choice, productivity and efficiency. Through a combination of market incentives and government regulation, his aim was to reap the benefits of the market in terms of innovation and productivity while also safeguarding equity and other values essential to the public services.[9] This was the underlying point behind the Prime Minister's public service reform agenda – above all foundation hospitals, tuition fees, academies and the five-year plans – and it led to a fierce row on policy with his Chancellor.

Brown's position was best set out in his 2003 speech to the Social Market Foundation, entitled somewhat ponderously 'A Modern Agenda for Prosperity and Social Reform'. He began by making it clear that he was not against markets as such:

> Markets are part of advancing the public interest and the left are wrong to say they are not; but also markets are not always in the public interest and the right is wrong to automatically equate the imposition of markets with the public interest.

He then came out against markets in the NHS on the grounds that 'the consumer is not sovereign; use of healthcare is unpredictable and can never be planned by the consumer in the way that, for example, weekly food consumption can'. He added, however, that, 'where the private sector can add to, not undermine, NHS capacity and challenge current practices by introducing innovative working methods, it has a proper role to play – as it always has – in the National Health Service'.[10] In other words, in contrast to Blair, Brown was adopting a more cautious, less market-oriented approach to public service reform.

Foundation hospitals provided the first battleground for this ideological clash between the two men. The foundation hospital idea was the brainchild of the Health Secretary, Alan Milburn. Milburn wanted these hospitals to be non-profit-making companies which would have full managerial autonomy so long as they met clinical standards and were financially competent. He also proposed that, though state funded, foundation hospitals should have the ability to borrow money against their own assets. However, the Treasury told Milburn that these hospitals would not be able to raise money privately and that any debt taken on by them would have to come out of the health budget. Milburn's reply was that foundation hospitals should be treated like universities which were not classified as part of the public sector. Brown's response was that, if a hospital faced bankruptcy, the government would have to step in, thereby accepting liability while sacrificing political control. In briefings to Labour MPs, his acolytes raised the spectre of a two-tier service – one offering a premium service to those who could pay and the other a basic service to the rest. The gloves were off.

In August 2002, Milburn upped the stakes when he wrote an article for *The Times* publicly revealing for the first time the clash between the so-called 'transformers' who, like Milburn and, by implication, Blair, had, in his view, the courage to see that New Labour must be bolder in backing reform and the 'consolidators', presumably Brown and his allies, who were content to rely on increased public spending alone to deliver an improved service. Milburn argued that:

[p]atients need greater freedom to choose where and when they are treated and resources must follow . . . In Britain we have allowed choice over schools or health provision to be the exclusive preserve of those who can pay directly. Embracing diversity can extend choice beyond the ability to pay.[11]

Brown was so furious to be labelled an old-fashioned 'consolidator', particularly in an article in the Murdoch press, that, at the end of September, he sent the Prime Minister a paper, copied to every member of the Cabinet, setting his objections to Milburn's scheme in considerable detail. Blair, who thought that Brown's paper was a preliminary to leaks in press, ordered it to be suppressed. But the row spilled over into the 2002 Labour Party conference. In a briefing about Brown's speech, his chief aide, Ed Balls, categorically stated that NHS hospitals would remain in the public sector and that borrowing by foundation hospitals would be included in the public sector accounts.[12] In a counterblast, Milburn declared at a fringe meeting, 'A service employing one million people in thousands of hospitals and health centres . . . can't be run from Whitehall',[13] while the Prime Minister, in a passionate conference speech, backed radical public sector reform. 'At our best when at our boldest' was the Blair watchword.

These were fine words but, much to Milburn's disappointment, the battle ended in a compromise. On 9 October, Blair met Brown, Milburn and Prescott in Blair's 'den' at Number Ten. Brown and Milburn, sitting uncomfortably beside each other on the sofa, exchanged harsh words. Milburn accused Brown of playing politics and ignoring policy. Brown replied, referring back to Milburn's *Times* article, 'You shouldn't have written what you wrote in the summer.'[14] It was agreed that the best performing hospitals should be given more independence to manage their affairs, including the right to borrow from the financial sector. There was also to be a steady increase in the number of NHS operations being delivered by the private sector, thus helping reducing waiting times. But, on the crucial issue of central control of budgets, Brown won. The Treasury retained its

Left: Bush and Iraq loom large and disastrously in Blair's second term. Blair is in full persuasive mode as President Bush visits the Foreign Office in November 2003, while coalition forces are bogged down trying to 'win the peace' in Iraq.

Below: President Bush and Blair, looking presidential, appear on the world stage as Bush presents Blair with the Presidential Medal of Freedom – but only after Blair had left Number Ten. This was symbolic of how much of a liability this relationship had become to Blair at home.

Blair, the war leader, visits British troops in Basra for the fourth time since the March 2003 invasion. Blair's frequent visits to Iraq and Afghanistan became a poignant feature of his second and third terms.

Brown also visited Iraq. He may have brought the troops home but he had fully supported the decision to invade Iraq.

The perennial Blair–Brown diptych. This is Blair's last party conference as leader. Gordon's path to the premiership is practically secured but, as the photograph shows, resentment still lingers.

Brown smiles as, finally, the deal for the transfer of power is completed unopposed but the so-called Granita deal cast a long and shadow over Labour's second and third terms.

Cameras capture Sarah and Gordon Brown's joy as they take their new baby home. Fraser was a welcome little brother for their older son John.

In June 2007, the Blair family leaves Downing Street for the last time.

In 2008 Mandelson returns to Cabinet – again! It would prove to be third time lucky for Mandelson as he became the lynchpin of the Brown government. Brown had cold-shouldered him for fourteen years.

As the de facto deputy prime minister, Lord Mandelson rapidly exerted his strategic role in the Brown government, injecting it with much needed energy and direction.

Brown and Mandelson literally appear to be joined at the hip. Brown's premiership was saved by his Business Secretary's handling of James Purnell's resignation from the Cabinet in June 2009.

Brown exhibited great courage and resolve doing what he does best – saving the international financial system. Mandelson, seen here with Brown, and Chancellor Darling gave him great support.

The 2010 general election was dominated by the first-ever television debates between the party leaders. Afterwards, Gordon Brown was adjudged to have performed less well in each of the three debates than either Cameron or Clegg.

On the stump in Rochdale, Brown commits a gaffe. He is photographed here speaking to a lifelong but now wavering Labour voter, Gillian Duffy. Getting back into his car, he forgot that he was still mic'd up and was heard to call Mrs Duffy 'a bigoted woman'. Brown's remark was seized on by the media but Labour still won Rochdale.

New Labour's thirteen years in government ended in defeat. Here Gordon Brown says goodbye and leaves Number Ten with his wife and two sons.

ability to control the amount borrowed, the debt remained on the public sector balance sheet and whatever was borrowed would reduce the amount available for spending on other parts of the NHS.[15] Despite nine separate backbench rebellions, tacitly encouraged by the Brown camp, the Commons eventually agreed, by a majority of only seventeen, to the foundation hospital proposals, with the government having to rely on the votes of Scottish and Welsh MPs – despite the proposals only affecting hospitals in England. Earlier in June 2003, Milburn's sudden resignation to spend more time with his family – though Blair's failure to back him against Brown was also a factor – was seen as a setback for the Blairites and a cause for celebration by the Brownites who saw in him a potential rival to their man as Blair's successor.

The struggle over tuition fees was even fiercer than that over foundation hospitals. Early in the second term, Blair became convinced that the financing of universities should be put on a more sustainable footing. There were two basic arguments for finding a new source of funding – the massive expansion of higher education and the need to ensure that British universities did not fall behind the competition in the rest of the world. On coming into power in 1997, the government had introduced tuition fees capped at £1000 per annum. The 2001 Labour manifesto had stated that 'we will not introduce top-up fees and will legislate to prevent them'. However, after the 2001 election, a number of universities, including the so-called Russell Group of leading institutions, campaigned for the introduction of top-up or variable fees to supplement their income. Blair was persuaded by Andrew Adonis of the case for charging students top-up fees of up to £3,000 a year.

Once again, Brown was against. Instead, he favoured a graduate tax, rising progressively and linked to the income of graduates, to replace both up-front fees and loans for maintenance, which he believed deterred the less well-off going into higher education. However, when Treasury officials examined the graduate tax plan in detail, they discovered it was prohibitively expensive in terms of public spending, especially initially.

Brown then argued for delay, proposing a formal review of university funding and a decision after the next election when he hoped that he would be Prime Minister. The then Secretary of State for Education, Estelle Morris, was caught in the crossfire between the two big beasts of the Labour government. For months, there was no movement. Then, at the end of October 2002, Morris, who was also beset by a controversy about A-level standards, resigned, saying that she did not feel up to being a Cabinet minister. She was replaced by the party chairman, Charles Clarke, who was entirely confident about his own abilities.

Initially, Clarke was also in favour of a graduate tax but, after examining the options, he came out on Blair's side behind the idea of top-up fees. Brown now wrote another letter to Cabinet, arguing that top-up fees would deter less well-off students going into higher education. The battle over the issue then went, on 16 January 2003, to a Cabinet subcommittee chaired by John Prescott. Here, after fierce debate between Clarke and Brown, Clarke prevailed mainly because Brown did not have an alternative. The Cabinet Secretary, Andrew Turnbull, said, 'It was the first time that he [Brown] had been comprehensively defeated in an area of domestic policy.'[16] On 22 January, Clarke published a White Paper which allowed universities to charge tuition fees of up to £3000 a year, provided they signed agreements with a new government regulator to ensure that there was fair access to students from all backgrounds. The up-front annual fee of £1,100 was to be abolished. Graduates would repay loans at a rate of 9 per cent, later reduced to the equivalent of the rise in the retail price index, if they earned above £15,000 per year. Over the next year, while the implementing legislation was drafted, opposition to the proposals mounted, especially among students and Labour MPs, led by the Brownites, including Nick Brown.

If Brown suffered an unaccustomed defeat in Cabinet over top-up fees, he got his revenge over a more important issue – the euro. Blair had assured pro-European allies like Peter Mandelson and Charles Clarke, officials such as Stephen Wall and Roger Liddle at Number Ten and pro-European groups like Britain in Europe that joining the euro would be the big prize of his second term. Blair's problem was that, in October 1998, he had abdicated the decision of whether the conditions were right to join to his Chancellor. Without Brown's support, there was no way he could win a referendum on an issue where the majority of the press was against him.

There is evidence that, on a number of occasions during 2001 and 2002, Blair tried to persuade Brown to take a more sympathetic view of joining the euro. Blair's aide, Anji Hunter, suggested to Brown's aide, Sue Nye, that Blair would quit for Brown as long as he delivered on the euro, a message that was allegedly repeated by Blair to Brown at Downing Street on 18 December 2001.[17] According to Clare Short, the International Development Secretary and a supporter of Brown, Blair also told Short while they were away together on a tour of Africa that his departure from office would be speeded up if progress could be made on the euro. At a lunch a week later, Short recorded Brown as saying that 'he would not contemplate recommending that we join the euro in order to advance his own position rather than advance the economic interest of the country'.[18]

Brown's apparently high-minded response was also motivated by a shrewd assessment of his personal interest. Against a background in which the British economy was performing better than most of its continental rivals, he did not believe a referendum on joining the euro was winnable. Even if it was, Brown did not wish to preside, either as Chancellor or Prime Minister, over a British economy damaged by joining the euro at the wrong time. At the Treasury, the Chancellor commissioned an exhaustive analysis of the prospects of joining, on which twenty-five officials worked full-time on eighteen background papers at a cost of almost £5 million. The conclusion of the Treasury's assessment of the so-called first test was that 'a clear and unambiguous case for UK membership' had not been made and 'a decision to join now would not be in the national economic interest'.

When Blair was presented with the Treasury verdict on 1 April 2003, his first reaction was: 'This is all fine, but I don't accept it.'[19] Blair's argument was that the negative Treasury conclusion was not sustained by the supporting evidence and that, in any case, the decision was about more than economics. Brown's blunt reply was that Blair would have to accept the verdict and that he intended to publish it in the Budget the following week. The next day the two men clashed again. Most unusually for him, Blair lost his temper and told Brown, 'You will have to consider your position.' Brown responded, 'I'll do just that.' and left the room.[20]

However, both men pulled back. Blair did not wish to lose his Chancellor on an issue where Brown had popular backing and at a time when the Prime Minister was beginning to face a backlash over Iraq. For his part, it was not in Brown's interest to jeopardise his chances of succeeding Blair as Prime Minister. Without conceding the main conclusion of the Treasury exercise, Brown helped Blair save face. The announcement of the result of the assessment was delayed. Cabinet ministers were called in individually to discuss the assessment with Blair and Brown. There would be a review at the next budget on whether to conduct a future assessment in the light of fresh circumstances. But the reality was that Brown, who made the statement to the Commons on 9 June, had won. Bitterly, Mandelson told a lunch of female journalists that Blair had been 'outmanoeuvred' over the single currency because the 'obsessive' Brown thought politics '24 hours a day, seven days a week'.[21]

The period from the summer of 2003 to the summer of 2004 was the most difficult of Blair's premiership. Iraq began to go badly wrong; there was the Kelly suicide and the Hutton Inquiry; and there were the parliamentary battles over foundation hospitals and tuition fees. Blair was taking a battering from the media and, for the first time, the polls had turned against him. A Mori poll for the *Financial Times* carried out just before the 2003 party conference showed that half the public wanted him to resign. As Blair faltered, Brown was waiting in the wings. The 2003 party conference was the nearest the two men came to open warfare. As always,

Brown spoke on Monday morning. This year, he threw down the gauntlet to Blair, presenting himself, in contrast to the Prime Minister, as the unifier. In a deliberate contradiction of Blair's sound bite in his previous year's speech, Brown said, 'This Labour Party – we are best when at our boldest, best when we are united, best when we are Labour.' According to one of his allies:

> What Gordon was saying to the world was, 'I'm here, I'm ready, I've won . . .' He'd won on the battle of ideas, policy, personality and even publicity. He saw himself as palpably stronger than a shrunken and weakened Prime Minister. This was his moment.[22]

In fact, Brown had over-reached himself.

On Tuesday afternoon, Blair, at his most impressive when his back was to the wall, came back strongly. On Iraq, he said he would make the same decision if he had to make it again. He also justified public service reform by saying that what modern consumers wanted was excellence. Echoing Mrs Thatcher, he said, 'I don't have a reverse gear.' He reminded the party of how divisions had undermined Labour governments in the past. His crushing response to Brown was not to mention him at all. As usual, he managed to win the conference over.

After the party conference, relations between Blair and Brown continued to be fraught. The Brown camp were furious that, following Alastair Campbell's resignation in August 2003, Peter Mandelson had been bought back to reorganise the Number Ten operation. One Brownite comment was '[H]e's like a camp version of Rasputin: every time you think he's dead he comes back.'[23] The Blair camp were equally angry with Brown's main aide, Ed Balls. They had found his behaviour, especially over the euro, arrogant and thought it inappropriate for a young man in his thirties to address the Prime Minister in this way. Blair complained to Brown who refused to curb him.

On 5 November, Blair excluded Brown from the National Executive

Committee (NEC), though he nominated Douglas Alexander, who was a close ally of Brown. The next day the Chancellor gave a television interview in which he complained that he had been left out of the NEC and that he expected to be in charge of Labour's election campaign. The spat between Brown and Blair came on the same day that the Tories had at last got their act together and replaced the ineffective Iain Duncan Smith as their leader with Michael Howard who was at least a competent operator.

That evening Blair and Brown dined with the Deputy Leader, John Prescott, at his flat in Admiralty House. Prescott saw his role as mediating between the two men and had already chaired a number of difficult meetings between them. On this occasion, Brown asked Prescott to fetch him another chair, as his was too low and uncomfortable. Prescott then asked Blair whether he needed another chair as well. According to Prescott, Blair replied, 'No, it's all right. I'm used to Gordon looking down on me.'[24] The Brown camp claimed that it was at this meeting that Blair said, 'I'm not going to turn this round for a very long time; therefore I'm going to stand down before the election. I need your help to get me through the next year.'[25] Blair's account of the dinner was rather different. According to the Prime Minister, he said that he would agree to Brown succeeding him but only if the Chancellor gave him his full support over the next year. Significantly, Prescott backed the Brown version: 'It was at that meeting that Tony promised to go by the next election . . . But Tony maintained later that he hadn't said it. As far as I'm concerned, he did. Tony reneged on his promise.'[26] But Prescott also said that Blair's promises to Brown 'were ambiguous and on condition anyway'.[27] Publicly, it was announced that Brown should be allowed to attend NEC meetings whenever he chose and placed in charge of the election campaign. An uneasy truce ensued.

The year 2004 threatened to be an even more difficult year for Blair than 2003 had been. Godric Smith, the Number Ten spokesman remembered, 'We seemed to be coming to a "perfect storm" moment.'[28] The beginning of the year was certainly a time of great danger for the Prime

Minister as the higher education debate and the publication of the Hutton Report were to take place on consecutive days – 27 and 28 January. He was facing a big revolt on higher education – 160 MPs had already signed an early day motion opposing top-up fees. What was even more worrying for Blair was that leading acolytes of Gordon Brown, the former Chief Whip, Nick Brown, who had been sacked from the government the previous year, and the former whip, George Mudie, were heading the revolt.

The scale of the rebellion over top-up fees forced the Secretary of State, Charles Clarke, and the Universities Minister, Alan Johnson, to make concessions, especially to poorer students. Gradually they won over some of the rebels. Johnson said, 'It's a charm offensive. I do the charm and Charles does the offensive.'[29] On Monday 26 January, the outcome of the vote was still uncertain. The fate of the top-up fees legislation – and possibly of the Prime Minister himself – lay in the Chancellor's hands. At the last moment, Brown blinked, persuading his namesake, Nick Brown, as well as other rebels to change sides. The Brownites had already done enough to destabilise Blair but, if the legislation was lost, it would be Brown who would get the blame. As it was, the bill scraped through by only five votes, the largest backbench rebellion on a second reading since 1945.

The Hutton Inquiry, set up by Blair to look into the circumstances surrounding the death of Dr David Kelly, a government weapons expert, reported the following day. It exonerated the government of manipulating intelligence about weapons of mass destruction in Iraq, was unsympathetic to Kelly for talking to journalists and was highly critical of the BBC for saying that the government had 'sexed up' the so-called September dossier. Blair was able to demolish the new Tory leader, Michael Howard, who had made Blair's integrity a big issue. 'What you should understand,' he told Howard, 'is that being nasty is not the same as being effective. Opportunism is not the same as leadership.'[30]

Then Alastair Campbell, who was hugely relieved that his name had been cleared, unwisely went on a rampage against the BBC, calling for resignations. The BBC's chairman, Gavyn Davies, honourably resigned, while the BBC governors forced the Director-General, Greg Dyke, who should have accepted responsibility immediately, to go as well. However, public opinion, shocked by Campbell's outburst and stirred up by a hostile media, backed the BBC and not the government. The Hutton Report did not bring closure for the government. A few days later, Blair was forced by the announcement that the White House was reviewing American intelligence over Iraq to set up a similar inquiry under Lord Butler to look at the failure of British intelligence. The dark cloud that the Iraq war had brought with it remained as big as ever. Tessa Jowell, a close ally of Blair, called Iraq 'a shroud over the government'.[31]

By the spring of 2004, Blair's morale was so low that he came close to quitting. The security situation in Iraq was deteriorating and barbaric pictures of American soldiers abusing Iraqi prisoners were published round the world. While Labour MPs grumbled, the Prime Minister's poll ratings dived. His political position was so weak that, without telling the Cabinet, he reversed his previous decision not to hold a referendum on the new constitution proposed for the European Union. Sceptics were jubilant while his pro-European allies like Peter Mandelson, Charles Clarke and Alan Milburn were furious because they feared it would be lost. He was suffering from a heart condition, first diagnosed on October 2003. The pressure on their father affected his children. Leo, born at Number Ten, awoke at nights while his older children were deeply upset by Blair's unpopularity. There was also, as Cherie Blair remarked, the constant attrition from his neighbour, Gordon Brown, 'rattling the keys above his head'.[32]

According to one account,[33] Blair was so depressed that he told Brown, just after the budget on 17 March, that he was going to announce in May his intention to retire, to take effect in the autumn. Brown's reaction was that, if the Prime Minister made a pre-announcement, he (Brown) would have to campaign throughout the summer against other heavyweights such as Charles Clarke and John Reid. He, therefore, suggested that, instead of a pre-announcement, Blair should simply stand down in the autumn. The Prime Minister agreed to think about it over the Easter recess.

What actually happened over Easter was that Blair's friends and supporters in the Cabinet, including John Reid, Tessa Jowell, Lord Falconer, David Blunkett and Charles Clarke, got wind of Blair's 'wobble' and successfully persuaded him to stay. Mandelson told his friend, 'Don't be so daft. Buck up. Buck up . . . You're the best politician in this country by a mile. So just get on top of this.'[34] The most important influence in persuading Blair to stay on was his wife, Cherie, who reminded him that he needed, in the words of the song, to 'pick himself up, dust himself off and start all over again'.[35]

The clinching factors for Blair were the results of the local and European elections in June and the report of the Butler Inquiry in July. Labour did badly in the elections but the Tory performance was not impressive either – they polled below the crucial 40 per cent in the local elections and only a disappointing 27 per cent in the European elections. Philip Gould advised Blair that Labour could win another three-figure majority at the general election. The Butler Report criticised the Blair style of leadership and implied that the Prime Minister had exaggerated the strength of the evidence but cleared him of 'deliberate distortion and of culpable negligence'.

By 18 July, when Blair and Brown attended another Prescott dinner at Admiralty House, the Prime Minister had recovered his morale. He told Brown that, following the Butler Report, he needed to take a different approach. 'To go now would look like I've been defeated over Iraq.' He added that he would consider things over the summer. 'I need more time, I can't be bounced.'[36] So far had he recovered his confidence that he even considered bringing Mandelson back into the Cabinet for the third time but was told by senior ministers including Prescott and Straw that there would be uproar among Labour MPs if he came back. Blair promised Mandelson that he would give him a Cabinet job after the election.

However, despite the fact that it apparently meant the end of his political career at Westminster, Mandelson decided to accept Blair's alternative offer to become Britain's European Commissioner.

Blair turned instead to Alan Milburn, the former Health Secretary who had resigned the year before. Milburn shared Blair's views on public sector reform and could be relied upon to take a robust attitude to Gordon Brown. Blair brought Milburn back into the Cabinet as Chancellor of the Duchy of Lancaster, responsible for developing government policy and running the general election campaign. Brown saw Milburn's promotion as a direct slap in the face which, in reality, it was. 'Why's Milburn coming back? Is it about cooking the manifesto against me? This is symptomatic of the way you behave,' complained Brown, when Blair told him about the Milburn appointment.[37]

The speeches of the two men at the 2004 party conference at Brighton contained the usual coded messages. Brown said that 'there are values far beyond those of contracts, markets and exchange' and put himself forward as the man representing Labour values. Blair argued that 'choice' not through wealth but through equal citizenship, was what 'the modern Labour Party should stand for'. Much more important was Blair's announcement immediately after conference that he intended to fight the next election and serve a third term before retiring. When Blair had met Brown the previous day, 29 September, they had rowed again about the Milburn appointment. Blair replied that he had every right to bring his people in, especially the able Milburn. He also told Brown he had to stop working against him. But he did not tell the Chancellor about the announcement he was planning to make or about the minor operation to correct an irregular heartbeat he would undergo on 1 October. Brown, who had flown off to an IMF meeting in Washington, was furious that Blair had not told him directly that he was staying on as Prime Minister. His entourage likened Blair's behaviour to the staging of 'an African coup' while a rival was out of the country.

On his return from Washington, Brown furiously demanded why Blair had not told him of his intention to serve a third term, when they had spoken in Brighton. Blair prevaricated, pretending they had spoken about it before. It was probably then that Brown said to Blair, 'There is nothing that you could ever say to me now that I could ever believe.'[38] It looked as if Blair had finally torn up the deal he had made with Brown in 1994. His attempt to accommodate the restless and ambitious Brown was apparently over and he was now determined to win a mandate to push his own agenda. Brown, having failed to gain Blair's agreement to step aside in his favour, was now free to stake his own claim to lead the country.

However, until the election was won, Blair and Brown were still bound together. Blair initially tried to freeze Brown out of the campaign but was persuaded by Philip Gould and Alastair Campbell that, given that Brown's successful chancellorship was one of Labour's trump cards, Brown had to be part of the campaign. There was a price to pay for the Chancellor's support as the unfortunate Milburn was sidelined – another example of Blair failing to protect his allies – and Blair had to guarantee Brown's continuation at the Treasury. During the campaign, the two men were seen together as much as possible – in one election stunt, they were even photographed side by side, holding ice creams. Asked about Iraq, Brown gave his support to Blair: 'I not only trust Tony Blair but I respect Tony Blair for the way he went about that decision.'[39] The partnership had just about survived, even if the old friendship had gone.

Despite a tough and difficult election campaign, Labour won the 2005 election comfortably. But forty-seven seats were lost, cutting the government's majority to sixty-six. Iraq cost Labour votes. A post-election analysis found that a quarter of defecting Labour voters cited the war as a reason. With only 36 per cent of the vote, Labour had the lowest share of votes for a party winning the majority of seats since the 1832 Reform Act. New Labour had won a third historic term but was now on the defensive.

15
BLAIR'S LEGACY, BROWNITE COUP

Blair had hoped that winning the 2005 election would strengthen his political position in his last term as Prime Minister and give him a mandate for public service reform. However, given the slashed Labour majority and the downbeat reaction of the media to his victory, it was Brown and not Blair who emerged as the main victor of the election. The question that was increasingly asked not only by Brown but also by the Parliamentary Labour Party and the media was when Blair was going to go.

The reshuffle after the election was that of a weakened Prime Minister. He tried to take the Communities and Local Government Portfolio away from the empire of the Deputy Prime Minister John Prescott but Prescott refused to let it go. Despite misgivings about Straw's loyalty – Straw had been making overtures to Brown – he left him at the Foreign Office. Two Blairite allies, Milburn and Byers, rejected office. Chris Mullin wrote in his diary, 'The Friends of the Man know that the game is almost up.'[1]

However, Blair brought the rising star David Miliband into the

Cabinet as Communities and Local Government Minister under Prescott while his radical and controversial adviser, Andrew Adonis, became a junior Education Minister with a seat in the Lords.

There was no question of moving Brown from the Treasury. When the Prime Minister tried to make John Hutton Chief Secretary, the Chancellor simply refused to allow the appointment. After their co-operation during the election, Brown had apparently expected to be consulted about the government. Blair's response was, 'Gordon, it's got to be my reshuffle. I am Prime Minister.'[2] The Chancellor's ally, Nick Brown, described Brown's mood after the election: 'Gordon felt let down and frustrated and things settled at a low point.'[3]

At the Parliamentary Party meeting after the election, a tired-looking Blair, with Brown glowering beside him, reminded his MPs that Labour had just won a historic third term and that, if they remained united, they could win a fourth one. He promised that there would be a 'stable and orderly transition' and pleaded for 'the time and space to ensure that happened'. But, though his speech was warmly applauded by a majority, for the first time there were calls for his resignation from disgruntled members, including two former ministers. For example, Peter Kilfoyle said that the sooner he stood down the better off the party would be.

This low point for Blair immediately after the election was, however, succeeded by a brilliant summer period which lasted into the autumn and reminded MPs why they had supported him in the first place. The crucial event was the French referendum on the European Constitution at the end of May, which resulted in a substantial victory for the 'no' campaign. Three days later, the Dutch voted the same way in their referendum. Paradoxically, the 'no' votes in two of the founding members, which effectively scuppered the European Constitution, strengthened rather than weakened Blair. At home, he was able to escape the commitment, unwisely conceded at a moment of maximum political frailty, to the holding of a UK referendum which he would have almost certainly lost. In the Europe Union, the results of the two referenda were more of a setback for the French President, Jacques Chirac, and the German Chancellor, Gerhard Schröder, than for the British Prime Minister. In his immediate response to the French 'no' vote, Blair described it as a wake-up call for EU leaders to reconnect with the voters. As he quickly realised, the demise of the EU constitution gave the UK, which assumed the EU Presidency in the second half of 2005, an opportunity to set out a new, more pragmatic direction for Europe.

First, however, he had to survive a Franco-German ambush, orchestrated by the Luxembourg Prime Minister, Jean-Claude Juncker, President of the June European Council meeting in Brussels. The issue to be decided was the EU budget for the next seven years – a decision made more urgent by the accession the previous year of new members from Eastern and Central Europe. The Franco-German plan, put forward by Juncker, was to make the UK give up its rebate – or at least a substantial proportion of it – to help pay for the enlarged EU. With the exception of support from Sweden and the Netherlands, the British Prime Minister found himself isolated. But he refused to accept Juncker's proposals which meant that the row over the budget would have to be resolved during the British presidency.

Then, in his presidency speech to the European Parliament on 23 June, Blair boldly seized the initiative. 'The people are blowing trumpets around the city walls. Are we listening?' he cried. The choice, he argued, was not between a 'free market' Europe and a 'Social' Europe. Noting the twenty million unemployed in Europe and productivity lagging behind that of the United States, he said that what was required was not the abandonment of the European Social model but its modernisation – a combination of economic growth *and* social protection. Yes, Britain was prepared to compromise on its rebate but only as part of a wider reform of the EU agenda, including the Common Agricultural Policy. Blair's speech, arguably his finest about the EU, was given a standing ovation by MEPs.

As if inspired by his European triumph, Blair then showed outstanding powers of leadership in early July – first, in lobbying delegates in Singapore to decide which city would host the 2012 Olympic Games; second, at the G8 (+5) summit on 7 and 8 July which the British Prime Minister chaired at Gleneagles Hotel in the Scottish Highlands; and third, following the 7/7 bombings in the heart of London, in rallying the nation.

Blair flew out to Singapore on 2 July and the next day held thirty-four individual meetings in support of London with key International Olympic Committee (IOC) delegates who were to choose the winning city on 6 July. Lord Coe, former Olympic champion and chairman of the London's bid, praised Blair's skill.[4] 'He never asked them for their votes. Often he would just talk to them about issues unrelated to the Olympics, and was just very attentive and warm with them.' Blair's personal charm, assisted by the energy of his wife, Cherie, was in marked contrast to the lordly approach of the French President, Jacques Chirac, who was supporting Paris's bid. After flying back to the UK, the Prime Minister had arrived at Gleneagles, when he heard the news via the Number Ten switchboard that London had narrowly beaten Paris by four votes. He danced out into the hotel gardens, leaving Jonathan Powell to worry, 'What if the cameras see him?'[5] The almost universal judgement was that Blair's intervention had made the difference.

It was next morning before the official opening of the G8 summit and after a walk with the US President, George W. Bush, in the hotel gardens that the Prime Minister first received news of what appeared to be a terrorist attack on London. Breaking short his pre-summit bilateral with the President of China, the Prime Minister decided to proceed with the official opening of the summit and await further information. However, it soon became clear that it was a serious attack, with four bombs detonated on the London Underground and, an hour later, a further bomb exploding on the Number 30 bus as it went round Tavistock Square. There had been many deaths as well as a considerable number of injured. Briefed by Blair, the leaders of the world debated what to do. The Prime Minister of Italy, Silvio Berlusconi, suggested that they should all fly down to London. The US President sensibly pointed out that, if they all went, security personnel would have to be diverted to guard them. The British Prime Minister should go alone while they got on with the conference. Before Blair left by helicopter for London he made a well-judged statement on television, supported by all the G8 leaders, as well as the other world leaders who had been invited to the summit, including those from China, India, Brazil, South Africa and Mexico and representatives from Africa:

> The purpose of terrorism is just that. It is to terrorise, and we will not be terrorised . . . [I]t is our determination that they will never succeed in destroying what we hold dear in this country and in other civilised nations throughout the world.

Although his presence in London was not operationally necessary, the Home Secretary, Charles Clarke, had suggested that he return to the capital to show that he was in charge, advice which accorded with his own instincts. In the early afternoon, Blair took over the chair of COBRA (Cabinet Office Briefing Room A), the Cabinet office emergency organisation. It was the biggest attack on London since the Second World War – fifty-six had been killed and seven hundred injured. It also emerged that the four bombers were all British citizens, a fact which shocked Blair deeply. His critics claimed that it was his policy in Iraq which made Britain more vulnerable to terrorist attack. After visiting New Scotland Yard to thank the police, he flew back to the G8 summit at Gleneagles, where he delivered another statement: 'We will not allow violence to change our society or our values. Nor will we allow it to stop the work of this summit.'

The Gleneagles meeting was arguably one of the most successful of all the G8 summits, seeming to mark a new direction both in tackling poverty in Africa and in facing up to climate change. The summit had been very well prepared by the British. Blair and Brown worked very closely together on debt relief and aid to Africa, showing just how good they could be when they acted as a team. Blair leant heavily on President Bush, who promised to double US aid to Africa and, for the first time, publicly recognised the human contribution to global warming. To underline their commitment, the final communiqué was signed by the leaders in front of the international media. In a dramatic week, Blair had shown what an effective prime minister he could still be.

Invigorated by his August family holiday at Cliff Richard's Barbados home (as usual his holidays were criticised by the tabloid press), Blair remained in confident, upbeat form at the party conference. While, in his Monday speech, Brown talked about the need to restore 'trust' and announced that he would tour, presumably as heir apparent, all the regions of Britain to 'listen, hear and learn', on Tuesday Blair reminded delegates that he was 'the first leader in the Labour Party's history to win three full consecutive terms in office', with the emphasis on the 'full'. It was clear from his stress on 'choice' and public service reform, especially of education, that he was planning a busy work programme, likely to last for a least a couple of years. The Brownite camp who hoped that Blair would step down in 2006, was furious and also infuriated by a comment from Cherie Blair. On being asked when the Blairs would be leaving Number Ten, she cried, 'Darling, we are a long, long way from that.'6

The presidency of the EU, held by the UK over the second half of 2005, was a success for the Prime Minister. After an EU Council at Hampton Court at which European leaders unusually discussed policy issues, including energy and research and development, Blair focused on resolving the EU budget crisis. Brown urged that Britain should refuse to do a deal on the British rebate, until the French agreed to reform the Common Agricultural Policy (CAP). Though Blair had some sympathy with this line of argument, he also considered that, as the chief supporter of EU enlargement, the UK had a moral responsibility to help pay for it. At the EU Council meeting that took place in Brussels from 15–16 December, he formed an alliance with the new German Chancellor, the Christian Democrat Angela Merkel. Blair agreed to a reduction in the British rebate in return for a fundamental review of all EU spending by 2009. The British concession opened the way to a general agreement which ensured that EU resources went not only to existing members but also to the new and less wealthy members from Central and Eastern Europe. When accused in Parliament of giving away the British rebate, he reminded euro-sceptics that enlargement had to be paid for and that, even after the concession, the rebate would still rise in value.[7]

If the last half of 2005 had proved unexpectedly fruitful for the Prime Minister, 2006 was arguably the least successful of all his years in office. His authority drained away as his Cabinet ministers began to look to a future without him. Labour MPs became restive, as the Tories, under a new and more promising leader, David Cameron, staged a strong recovery. With a reduced majority, it became more difficult to get legislation, above all the flagship Education and Inspections Bill, through Parliament. And the 'cash for peerages' issue hung like a pall over Blair's last fifteen months in office.

The fate, on 9 November 2005, of the 'ninety-day' clause for detention without trial for terrorist suspects was an indication of the Prime Minister's deteriorating political position. The government had already given MI5 and the police extra resources to deal with terrorism with tangible results. Up to twenty terrorist plots were thwarted during Blair's premiership.[8] Anti-terrorist laws had been rushed on to the statute book in 2001 following 9/11. Now, after 7/7 and the failed bombing attempt a fortnight later, Blair decided to introduce further anti-terrorist legislation. The key proposal was the 'ninety-day' clause – a big increase on the fourteen-day limit – which, Blair claimed, was demanded by the police.

There was strong opposition, including from the Lord Chancellor and the Attorney General, while the Chief Whip, Hilary Armstrong, warned Blair that the clause faced defeat in the Commons. But the Prime Minister told MPs, 'Sometimes it is better to lose and do the right thing than to win and do the wrong thing.'[9] The government went down by 323 votes to 290, with forty-nine Labour MPs voting with the opposition parties.

A compromise proposal of twenty-eight days detention without trial was passed – still the longest in the western world. Earlier in his premiership, Blair would have been more pragmatic. Now he was the conviction politician at the end of his career and was no longer prepared to compromise. The other point was there was now a significant bloc of Labour MPs ready to defy him, even if it meant voting with the Tories.

The Education and Inspections Bill a few months later was even more controversial among the Labour ranks. In part, this was because of the way the White Paper describing the legislation was oversold by Blair who deliberately exaggerated its radical nature. The introduction, written by the Prime Minister, said, 'Our reforms must build on the freedoms that schools have increasingly received, but extend them radically . . . The local authority must move from being the provider of education to being its local commissioner and the champion of parent choice.'[10] Blair wanted an educational system in which schools were largely autonomous. The role of local authorities would be reduced to encouraging choice. He argued that choice and competition between schools would drive up standards.

The reality was that, though schools were to be allowed more freedom (including owning their own assets, employing their own staff and, within strict limits, setting their own admissions arrangements), under the proposals, local authorities would continue to control most of the funding and teachers' pay would be set centrally.

Opposition mounted when Blair's Deputy Prime Minister, John Prescott, who had himself failed the eleven-plus, warned the Cabinet on 15 December 2005 that the proposals would lead to a division between first- and second-class schools. In an interview in the *Sunday Telegraph*, he also told Susan Crosland, widow of the former Labour Education Secretary, Tony Crosland, that he feared that city academies, which had been set up under the Learning and Skills Act of 2000, could become grammar schools by another name.[11] In January 2006, the former leader of the Labour Party, Neil Kinnock, publicly criticised the proposals as 'at best a distraction and at worst dangerous'[12] and chaired a critical meeting addressed by the former Education Secretary, Estelle Morris, and attended by Alastair Campbell and his partner Fiona Millar.

When the Education Bill was published at the end of February, the Conservatives announced that they would be supporting it. Although Tory backing would ensure that the bill would go through, the danger was that it would encourage more Labour MPs to vote against. The Chancellor lay low, neither opposing the legislation nor giving it more than token support. He was probably content to see Blair weakened by another substantial revolt. In the event, the second reading of the Education Bill was passed on 15 March by 458 votes to 115. Fifty-two Labour MPs rebelled and twenty-five abstained, which meant that the bill had only passed because of Conservative support. The timetable motion for the discussion of the bill which the Tories opposed was carried by a mere ten votes. The Prime Minister could no longer rely on his own MPs to back his public service reform programme.

Over the next few months, the Blair premiership suffered a series of setbacks. On the same day as the crucial votes on the Education Bill, Jack Dromey, the Treasurer of the Labour Party and husband of Harriet Harman, issued a statement announcing an inquiry into the securing of loans by the Labour Party. Although the Labour Elections and Referendums Act of 2000 had forced parties to declare donations of over £5000, loans did not have to be disclosed. In the run-up to the 2005 election, Blair, worried that the Tories, who were raising money by loans, would outspend Labour, authorised his fundraiser, Lord Levy, to start taking loans for Labour, though it was hardly in line with the party's declared policy of maximum transparency.

At his press conference the following day, 17 March, the Prime Minister admitted that the House of Lords Appointments Commission, set up by Blair to scrutinise nominations for peerages, had not been told about the loans (in total £14.7 million) which four of his nominees had made to the Labour Party. An SNP Member of Parliament then asked the

Metropolitan Police to investigate whether any breach of the 1925 Honours (Prevention of Abuses) Act had occurred. To the surprise of Number Ten, the Metropolitan Police then launched an inquiry into the affair. In 2007, the inquiry was broadened to conspiracy to pervert the course of justice allegations against Lord Levy and Ruth Turner, Blair's Director of Government Relations. Both Levy and Turner were arrested – Turner after a dawn raid on her house. Blair himself was interviewed by the police three times. Not until 20 July 2007 – nearly a month after Blair had stepped down from office – did the Crown Prosecution announce that there was no case to answer. All the same, the lengthy inquiry severely damaged the Prime Minister especially as it was assumed by a badly informed media that leading figures at Number Ten would be bound to face charges. Blair's lamentable failure to tackle the issue of party financing (above all state funding) earlier in his premiership made him vulnerable to charges of 'sleaze' when he sought to raise money from rich businessmen.

If March 2006 was a bad month for Blair, April was even worse. The tabloids were able to draw an unfortunate if unfair parallel with John Major's government when, on Wednesday 25 April – Blair's 'Black Wednesday' – three humiliating events occurred on the same day. The Home Secretary, Charles Clarke, had to admit the error of the Home Office in failing to consider a thousand convicted foreign criminals who had been released for deportation – thus undermining the Prime Minister's claim to be tough on crime. The Health Secretary, Patricia Hewitt, was jeered when she addressed a conference of the Royal College of Nurses (RCN), at Bournemouth, because the RCN had just published a survey saying that 13,000 nursing jobs might be lost. And the Deputy Prime Minister, John Prescott, admitted to the *Daily Mirror* that he had been having an affair with his diary secretary.

The local elections on Thursday 4 May were especially poor for Labour who finished on 26 per cent (the worst performance since Michael Foot), behind the Liberal Democrats on 27 per cent and the Conservatives, under their new leader, David Cameron, on 40 per cent. Brown went on Radio 4's *Today* programme at 8 a.m. on Friday 5 May. His more aggressive supporters were urging him to deliver the *coup de grâce*. On air, he described the events of the previous two weeks as 'a warning shot for the government' and rather lamely said, 'We have got to renew ourselves . . . it must start now.' His indecision infuriated Ed Balls, who repeatedly shouted at Brown, 'You bottled it!'[13] Once again, Brown's caution and his fear that a disputed succession could end in a 'bloodbath' led him to stay his hand.

For his part, Blair resorted, for the last time, to the device so favoured by Prime Ministers in trouble – he reshuffled his government. He dismissed the unfortunate Charles Clarke from the Home Office, replacing him with John Reid. As consolation, he offered Clarke the Defence job but Clarke refused and went to the backbenches, thus bringing an end to a promising political career. Jack Straw was moved from Foreign Office to become Leader of the House. To her and everyone else's surprise, he made Margaret Beckett Foreign Secretary though some of his advisers had been urging him to put the young David Miliband in Straw's place. Only a year later, it was Brown rather than Blair who was to promote Miliband to the Foreign Office. Two young Brownites, Ed Balls and Ed Miliband, were promoted to the government. But overall the reshuffle failed to give his administration a fresh look and, once he had carried it out, his last bolt was shot.

Then, at a tense party meeting on Monday 8 May, a number of MPs said that uncertainty about the succession was damaging the party. In an attempt to calm the situation, Blair said he would leave his successor 'ample time' before the next election, which only encouraged dissidents to ask how long was 'ample'. A more effective move was the briefing from Number Ten that, if Blair was deposed, he would not support Brown as his successor. Brown was reminded that, without Blair's backing, he would find it more difficult to win votes in Middle England. For the moment, the Brownites stayed their hand.

Despite the tension between Blair and Brown, they did manage to come to a decision over the crucial issue of the future of pensions. A commission, headed by Adair Turner, had proposed that the link between pensions and earnings be restored, to be paid for by raising the retirement age. Brown strongly resisted the restoration of the link but was, in the end, persuaded by a combination of Blair and the Work and Pensions Secretary, John Hutton, that, subject to the affordability of the fiscal position, 'the earnings link should be restored by 2012'. An official commented that 'at some level Blair and Brown still retained this capacity to do business and come up with a reasonable sane conclusion'.[14]

In September, the two men, following the so-called 'September Coup', finally came to a showdown over the succession. In July Blair had weakened his position by his stubborn refusal, against the advice of his officials, to condemn Israel's retaliatory strike into Lebanon in pursuit of Hezbollah terrorists. Chirac had spoken for most Labour MPs (and many Israelis) when he condemned the attack as 'completely disproportionate'. Blair backed the US in not calling for an immediate ceasefire. To make matters worse, at the G8 summit in St Petersburg, Blair was heard on an accidentally 'live' microphone apparently asking Bush's permission to go to Lebanon in a peace-keeping role, only to have his offer casually rejected by the US President. The charge made over Iraq that Blair was Bush's 'poodle' was revived once again. At the last Cabinet before the summer recess, David Miliband, who had never criticised Blair in Cabinet before, said that the Prime Minister's refusal to call for a ceasefire was causing uproar in the PLP, while Jack Straw issued a public statement warning that disproportionate action only escalated an already dangerous situation.

Before Blair left for his Caribbean holiday, his closest advisers told him that he had to be more precise about how long he intended to go on as Prime Minister. They argued that uncertainty merely provided ammunition for his critics. Prescott also told Blair that, unless he made an announcement as to when he was going by the time of party conference, he would himself resign and blame Blair.[15] However, on his return from holiday, Blair gave an interview to Philip Webster and Peter Riddell of *The Times* in which he repeated that he would 'leave ample time for [his] successor'. He then said, 'People have to accept that as a reasonable proposition and let me get on with the job.' *The Times* ran the interview on Friday 1 September under the headline 'Blair defies his party over departure date'.

It was the *Times* interview which triggered what Prescott called 'The Corporals' Revolt'. The revolt not only involved Brownites but also two disgruntled Blairites, Sean Simon and Chris Bryant, who had missed out on promotion to office. It was headed by Tom Watson, a junior Defence Minister who was a supporter of Brown. Brown himself may not have been directly involved though he certainly knew it was taking place. On Monday 4 September, Watson visited Brown and his wife at their North Queensferry home in Scotland to present, Watson later insisted, a *Postman Pat* video to Fraser, the Brown's recently born younger son. The plotters' plan was to circulate first to the 2001 intake, then to the 1997 and 2005 ones, a letter calling on Blair to go. In the meantime, the Prime Minister was on a two-day tour of the North of England but his senior staff back at Number Ten put together a fight-back strategy. First, the Environment Secretary, David Miliband, went on the *Today* programme on Tuesday to say that Blair would carry on for no more than a year. Second, they organised a counter letter, signed by sixty MPs, which warned colleagues not to turn an 'orderly transition into a crisis of regicide'.

On Wednesday morning, the Prime Minister and the Chancellor had an angry confrontation at Number Ten. Blair expressed his fury at the attempted coup and at Brown's failure to condemn it. The Prime Minister reminded the Chancellor that he had told him that he would leave by next summer. Brown replied that Blair had broken a number of promises about going that he had made in the past. This time he wanted a public announcement of the departure and a commitment by Blair that nobody else from the Cabinet would stand against him. Blair said that he could not stop colleagues standing. The meeting ended inconclusively with Brown threatening the Prime Minister with further trouble.

Later that morning, the junior minister, Tom Watson, resigned, followed by six parliamentary private secretaries. When Blair met Brown for a second meeting at 2 p.m., this time in the garden of Number Ten, both men had calmed down. Blair agreed to announce publicly that he would stand down by next summer though he refused to give his endorsement to Brown or to try and stop others from standing. The two men also agreed to work more closely together. Being driven away from the meeting, Brown was caught on camera with a smile on his face which he later attributed to talking to his aide, Sue Nye, about his baby son, Fraser.

On the face of it, the Chancellor was the gainer. Although the Prime Minister may have already decided in his own mind to step down by the summer of 2007, the coup forced him to announce his departure publicly, which he did, with characteristic grace, the following afternoon in a North London school. He began by apologising on behalf of the Labour Party for the last week: 'It has not been our finest hour, to be frank.' He went on to confirm that, though he would have 'preferred to do this in [his] own way', the next party conference would be his last as leader and Prime Minister. And there was a sting in the tail for the plotters: 'We can't treat the public as bystanders in a subject as important as who is the Prime Minister.'[16]

By the end of the week, parliamentary opinion had turned sharply against the Brownites. On Saturday, the BBC lunchtime news reported that 'the question today is not now how long can Tony Blair hang on but is Gordon Brown fit to be Prime Minister'. When news trickled out that the Chancellor's chief ally, Ed Balls, and another close acolyte, Ian Austin, had been involved in the plot, it provoked a backlash against Brown who, in desperation, rang around his mostly sceptical Cabinet colleagues to try to convince them that his hands were clean. John Prescott, who believed that his own resignation threat would, by itself, have been enough to persuade Blair to go, thought the coup was completely unnecessary. The former Home Secretary, Charles Clarke, who never rated Brown, denounced him as being 'totally, totally uncollegiate', a 'control freak' and having 'psychological issues'. On Sunday the Chancellor, by then very much on the defensive, issued a somewhat implausible denial: 'There is no truth in the suggestion that there was an attempted coup. The suggestion was sad, regrettable and has caused a great deal of grief.'[17] It was certainly true that the events of September, which had flushed out a public announcement of his retirement from Blair, had also, as polls showed, inflicted serious damage on Brown.

Brown was very much on his best behaviour at party conference, promoting himself as Prime Minister in waiting. He praised Blair saying, 'It has been a privilege for me to work with and for the most successful ever Labour leader and Labour Prime Minister.' Its healing impact was unfortunately spoiled by Cherie Blair's comment, 'Well, that's a lie.', which was overheard by a journalist. Mrs Blair's gaffe, however, helped provide a witty opening line for her husband's speech. After thanking his wife and children for their support, he said, 'I mean, at least I don't have to worry about her running off with the bloke next door.' Without endorsing him, Blair was as fulsome about Brown as Brown had been about him: 'I know New Labour would never have happened, and these election victories would never have been secured, without Gordon Brown. He is a remarkable man, a remarkable servant to this country.'

Blair's final party conference speech was a huge success, reminding his party what a superb communicator he was and what a difficult act he would be to follow. He extolled New Labour's achievements, set out the direction to follow and the challenges ahead and gave his party some practical advice: 'There is no rule that says the Tories have to come back. David Cameron's Tories, my advice: get after them.' Brushing off the criticism that he was only remaining to secure his personal legacy, he replied that there was only one legacy 'that has ever mattered to me – a fourth term election victory'.

In fact, there *was* a 'legacy project' which would help inform and direct

Blair's last nine months in office. There was undoubtedly an element of vanity, even hubris in the 'legacy' idea. A leaked memorandum in April 2006 written by Ben Wegg-Prosser, head of Blair's Strategic Communications Unit and former aide to Mandelson, gave an unfortunate impression:

> As TB enters his final phase, he needs to be focusing way beyond the finishing line, not looking at it. He needs to go with the crowds wanting more. He should be the star. He won't even play that last encore.[18]

Yet there were also solid achievements in his final months in office of which Blair could feel proud of. The most notable was the breakthrough in Northern Ireland – an achievement that, in itself, justified his staying on as Prime Minister – which led to the establishment, or reestablishment, on 8 May 2007 of the power-sharing executive with the arch Unionist Ian Paisley, as First Minister, and the former IRA terrorist Martin McGuinness, as Deputy First Minister. Speaking at Stormont, Blair said, 'Look back and see centuries marked by conflict, hardships and even hatred among the peoples of these islands. Look forward and we see the chance to shake off those heavy chains of history.' For nearly a decade, Blair had focused his skill, energy and dedication on bringing peace to Northern Ireland. Now, just as he left office, he was rewarded by the astonishing spectacle of Paisley and McGuinness, the 'Chuckle Brothers' as they were sometimes called, sharing power at Stormont.

At the June 2007 European Council, Blair played a leading role in negotiating a replacement for the Constitutional Treaty which had been so decisively rejected in 2005 by the voters of France and the Netherlands. His key demand was that the member states should agree not a 'constitution' but an 'amending' treaty which would not justify holding referenda in the UK or any other European state. He also successfully protected his so-called 'red lines', the areas on which Britain would not accept EU control. These were the charter of fundamental rights, common law, social security legislation and foreign policy. At the G8 + 5 summit earlier that month, Blair had a partial success in persuading his fellow leaders, including Bush, to declare that the starting point for future negotiations on climate change would be the goal of halving global emissions by 2050.

However, though he flew out in May 2007 to thank the 5,000 British troops still left in the Basra area, Iraq was unfinished business, with Basra city at the mercy of militias and criminal gangs. Even as he fraternised with British soldiers at Basra airport, there was a mortar attack which landed near the aircraft waiting to fly the Prime Minister back to Kuwait. Asked by a British journalist how long it would take 'for it not to be a mess', he replied, 'I dunno. You can't tell. It will resolve itself, it just will. People will get sick of killing.'[19] Blair's answer was a sad commentary on the Iraq intervention – the great failure of his premiership.

The outstanding domestic issue left to resolve was the succession. At times, Blair appeared to be contemplating an alternative to Brown. There was the tough Home Secretary, John Reid, but he did not have enough support in the party. More promising was a representative of the younger generation, David Miliband. However, Miliband did not think he was ready for the job and nor did he relish the idea of a bloody election battle against the Brown camp. In the end, Blair felt that Brown had to be his successor. For a complex mixture of reasons, a combination of guilt, friendship and admiration, he believed that the Chancellor deserved his turn. But he wanted Brown to accept public service reform. After the latter came in March to the launch of the first of the so-called policy reviews (set up by the Prime Minister to try and commit Brown to a New Labour agenda) and talked the language of public service reform ('greater choice, greater competition and greater local accountability'), Blair decided to give Brown the benefit of the doubt and the endorsement he craved. On 1 May 2007, the tenth anniversary of the victory which brought New Labour to power, Blair told a meeting in Edinburgh, 'Within the next few weeks, I won't be Prime Minister. In all probability, a Scot will become Prime Minister . . . someone, who, as I've always said, will make a great Prime Minister for Britain.'[20]

On 10 May, Blair flew to his constituency and announced that he would be tendering his resignation to the Queen on 27 June, reminding his supporters in one sentence of his government's achievements. 'There is only one government since 1945 that can say all of the following: more jobs, fewer unemployed, better health and education results, lower crime and economic growth in every quarter.' After a whirlwind 'legacy' tour, which took in the United States, Iraq, Africa and the continent of Europe and as well as the G8 + 5 and European Council summits, Blair said goodbye to the House of Commons, leaving MPs, if not exactly 'wanting more', as the Wegg-Prosser memorandum suggested, but unprecedentedly clapping with the Tories, led by Cameron, joining in the applause. The first New Labour premiership, which had lasted ten years and two months, was over.

PART 5

BROWN'S TURN

16

BROWN IN TROUBLE – MANDELSON RETURNS

As always happens in the British parliamentary system, the Blair regime went out through the back door – actually through the basement, handing back their passes as they went – while the new Brown team came in through the front door. After their visit to the Palace, Gordon and Sarah Brown got out of the prime ministerial Jaguar in Downing Street and Brown then proceeded to say a few well-rehearsed words in front of Number Ten. He promised to be 'strong in purpose, steadfast in will, resolute in action' and repeated his old school motto: 'I will try my utmost.' Though he had been Chancellor of a government which had been in power for a decade, he made a bold attempt to promote himself as the Prime Minister of change:

This will be a new government with new priorities. I have heard the need for change, change in our NHS, change in our schools, and change with affordable housing, change to build trust in government, change to protect and extend the British way of life.

Then the door to Number Ten opened, the Browns entered and were clapped in by the same staff who had clapped the Blairs out.

After thirteen years of waiting, Gordon Brown had at last achieved his goal of the premiership. The question was what was he going to do with it? Brown had prepared for the transition carefully. The Cabinet Secretary, Gus O'Donnell who had been his Permanent Secretary at the Treasury, had organised a series of briefings with civil servants, defence staff and intelligence chiefs. Tony Blair, with whom he had resumed something of his old friendship, had given him advice on Prime Minister's Questions. Brown consulted Blair about the making of his Cabinet. Colleagues remarked that, if only they had worked as closely together over the last ten years as they did in the last few weeks of Blair's premiership, New Labour might have achieved so much more.

Brown promised a new government – and, to some extent, it was. Six members of the Cabinet were under forty. David Miliband became the youngest Foreign Secretary since David Owen, James Purnell was made Culture Secretary, and Andy Burnham Health Secretary. Three bright Brownites, Ed Balls (Department for Children, Schools and Families), Ed Miliband (Cabinet Office) and Douglas Alexander (Department of International Development Secretary) were brought into the Cabinet. A Blairite loyalist, Jacqui Smith, became the first female Home Secretary, Alistair Darling, a friend of Gordon Brown but also popular across the political spectrum for his unassuming ways, was appointed as Chancellor of the Exchequer. But if there was a welcome freshness about some of the promotions, it was also noticeable that there was no room for any of the Blairite 'big hitters'. There was no David Blunkett, Charles Clarke, Alan Milburn or John Reid. And, of course, there was nobody with the weight of Brown to challenge the new Prime Minister. In the Blair Cabinets, there had been two centres of power. Now, there was only one – that of Gordon Brown.

In his version of Blair's 'big tent', Brown brought in distinguished outsiders (GOATS or Government of all the Talents) into his administration. These included Sir Alan West, the former First Sea Lord, who became Security Minister, Professor Sir Ara Darzi, a surgeon who was appointed Health Minister, Sir Mark Malloch Brown, UN Deputy Secretary General, who served for two years at the Foreign Office, and later, Paul Myners, former Chairman of Marks & Spencer who Brown made City Minister. All of them proved good ministers and they also improved the quality of the House of Lords. A less successful choice was the Trade Minister, Digby Jones, former Director General of the CBI, who left after sixteen months.

If a number of his government appointments won praise, his Number Ten team, organised for Brown by Ed Balls, was criticised in Whitehall and Westminster as being undermanned and, with a few exceptions, not up to the required standard. Two of the more effective of his former aides, Balls and Alexander, were now running departments, while Ed Miliband was in charge of the Cabinet Office. Almost all of Blair's political staff were either dismissed or left to find other employment and a great deal of experience went with them. Brown, who was well known as a demanding taskmaster, had to operate without a proper Chief of Staff, Director of Communications or even a speech-writer. The Cabinet Secretary warned the new Prime Minister not to bring his spin doctor, Damian McBride, into Number Ten because of the hostility his aggressive briefings aroused amongst ministers. Brown ignored the warning and later McBride had to be dismissed for improper behaviour.[1] If Brown was to be an effective Prime Minister, he badly needed the support of an experienced and high-quality team at Number Ten. But, for at least the first year or so of his government, he lacked such a team.

There was one person who could have helped the new Prime Minister and that was the British European Commissioner, Peter Mandelson. But Brown had still not forgiven him for what happened in 1994, and Mandelson was still angry with Brown. Earlier in the year, Mandelson told journalists, 'I don't know whether this is going to come as a disappointment to him, but he can't actually fire me. Like it or not, he will have to accept me as a commissioner until November 2009.'[2] He added that he would not be seeking a second term.

Gordon Brown was inheriting a difficult situation. He did not yet know that the economy, whose excellent record under his stewardship was his main claim to be Prime Minister, was about to erupt into the biggest crisis since the 1930s. But, as the opinion polls turned against Labour, he was faced with the unenviable task of renewing in government the New Labour project with both a shrinking pool of experienced and talented ministers and a tarnished party reputation, as the detrimental electoral fall-out from Iraq and the cash for honours affair took their toll. Roy Jenkins had often spoken of the danger of being a 'tail-end Charlie' at the end of a long period of government, a prime minister like Eden after Churchill, Home after Macmillan, Callaghan after Wilson or Major after Thatcher. Brown desperately wanted to avoid their fate.

Brown's pollster, Deborah Mattinson of Opinion Leader Research, identified his strengths and weaknesses in the eyes of the voters. On the plus side, they saw him as a formidable politician. However, they also saw him as scheming, bullying and somewhat to the Left of Blair.[3] If Brown was to win over the electorate, he had to accentuate the positives and minimise the negatives.

Brown did, indeed, bring some significant strengths to the premiership. He was clever, tough, single minded and a formidable negotiator. He had the experience of holding down the second most important job in the government for a decade. He had shown remarkable persistence in sustaining his superior claim to the top post, beating off rival claims, as well as refusing to be moved from the chancellorship, which he had seen as the best launching pad for Number Ten. And, with his late marriage to Sarah Macaulay, a former public relations executive, Brown now had a devoted partner and two young sons, John and Fraser (their daughter, Jennifer, died soon after birth), who brought warmth and colour to his life. With them, the private smile and twinkle which charmed his friends were much in evidence.

On the face of it, Brown was well prepared for the top job but he took time to get used to being Prime Minister. The Treasury is not necessarily the best training ground for Number Ten. The Chancellor has a dozen big decisions to take a year – the Prime Minister has as many in a month, sometimes in a week. This suited Blair's instinctive style of decision making. Brown, who preferred to weigh all the options before coming to a decision, found the sheer flow of business coming into Number Ten a big problem. What made things even more onerous was that he was, by nature, a 'control freak' – he liked to take as many decisions as possible himself. The combination of Brown's style of working and an inferior team at Number Ten meant that decisions were delayed or sometimes not taken at all. Always a ferocious worker, Brown tried to compensate by toiling all hours of the day and night. Not surprisingly, he often became exhausted which did nothing for his temper or morale.

Compared to Blair, he was a poor communicator. In his set-piece speeches as Chancellor, Brown commanded the House of Commons. He could also make impressive addresses at conference and to party activists. But he appeared stilted on television. Whereas Blair had an easy conversational and persuasive style which connected well with the voters, Brown tended to become declamatory and to use jargon which turned them off. He could appear wooden, even robotic. His advisers tried to turn his weakness into a strength by devising the slogan 'Not flash – just Gordon', a plausible, if defensive, response to the fluent Tory leader David Cameron, who was modelling himself on Blair.

From the end of June to the end of September 2007, Brown enjoyed a short honeymoon. A series of emergencies – terrorist incidents, floods and an outbreak of foot-and-mouth – showed the new Prime Minister in command, very much the strong national leader, robust in a crisis. His critics at Westminster were impressed. The media gave him a good write-up. And the polls responded favourably. In the last few months of Blair's premiership, Labour ran behind the Tories. Now Labour went ahead with Brown perceived as a better leader than Cameron. Inevitably, speculation grew about an early election. Why should Brown not capitalise on the favourable polls and win a personal mandate at a general election?

Brown's handling of 'the election that never was' was a disaster. Even though he had not made up his own mind, he allowed his closest advisers – Alexander, Balls and Miliband – to keep the story running, in part to unsettle the Tories. Then, during the Labour Party conference, election fever got out of hand – so much so that most Labour MPs and much of the press became convinced that there *was* going to be an election. However, instead of destabilising the Conservatives as Brown had hoped, it united them. At their conference the following week, the shadow Chancellor, George Osborne, enthused delegates and rattled the government by promising to exempt all but millionaires from inheritance tax. A confident Cameron then made an hour-long speech without notes, upbraiding Brown for brazenly flying off to Iraq during the Tory conference to announce troop withdrawals in order to seize the headlines from the Tories and confidently daring the Prime Minister to call an election.

In the end, it was Brown who blinked. The polls at the end of the Tory conference were predicting at best a narrow Labour majority. Brown, who did not want to do down in history as the shortest serving premier in modern political history, decided against a general election. Despite attempts by his spin doctors to blame his young advisers, the Prime Minister was crucified in the press as a 'bottler'. At a stroke, the image that he had been carefully developing as a calm and decisive leader was destroyed. From this time onwards, Brown was more often than not portrayed as incompetent and indecisive.

There was an argument for holding an election. If he had announced that he was going to have one during his conference speech, it could have galvanised his own party and knocked the Conservatives off balance. It would have been a gamble but some Labour MPs and a number of senior Tories thought that Labour would have won.

There was an even stronger case for not holding an election. As his childhood friend, Murray Elder, reminded Brown, Labour had only been ahead in the polls for a short time and certainly not long enough for that to be a reliable indicator. The defeat of Labour's Prime Minister, Harold Wilson, in 1970, who called an election on the basis of a few months' poll lead, was a warning. But, if Brown had ruled out an election during his conference speech and when the polls were going his way, he could have put himself forward as a national leader who wanted to get on with governing the country.

Brown's great mistake was his procrastination. By allowing election fever to gather momentum, he was forced to make the decision from a position of weakness rather than strength. His close ally, Nick Brown, then Deputy Chief Whip, said:

> The sense of it being on and it being off was a watershed looking back at it . . . Because I think people felt that if there wasn't going to be an election, the speculation should have been damped down earlier than it was.[4]

By the end of October, the Tories were ahead in the polls. Brown's own ratings tumbled and a whole host of misfortunes seemed to beset his government. On Friday 14 September, Britain had its first run on a bank for more than a century when queues began to form at branches of Northern Rock, the fifth-largest mortgage lender in the country. It was a powerful and disturbing sign that credit was drying up (see next chapter). In November, two computer disks belonging to the Revenue and Customs (HMRC) with the personal and banking information of nearly half the population, went missing and were never found. The chairman of HMRC was forced to resign amid tabloid and opposition outrage. Then came the so-called 'donorgate' affair, when the *Mail on Sunday* revealed that, contrary to the party funding law introduced by the government in 2000, Labour's third-biggest donor had used intermediaries to channel money to the party. Though he had not done anything illegal, the party's General Secretary was forced by Brown to resign.

Somewhat unfairly, Brown, who had seemed so dominant only two months before, now became a figure of derision. The Commons erupted in mirth when Vince Cable, Liberal shadow Chancellor and Deputy Leader, said at Prime Minister's Questions (PMQs): 'The house has noted the Prime Minister's remarkable transformation in the last few weeks from Stalin to Mr Bean.'[5] The Tory leader, David Cameron, who was finding it increasingly easy to score over Brown at PMQs, hit the mark when he said, 'For ten years, you plotted and schemed to have this job – and for what? No conviction, just calculation, no vision, just vacuum.'[6]

There was a feeling, even among Labour loyalists, that Brown had no strategy. In 1997, he had brought a fresh approach to the Treasury. As years went by, his agenda seemed to be shaped as much by his ambition to be Prime Minister and his opposition to Blair as by policy. Now that he had become Prime Minister, his direction seemed uncertain. He had promised 'change'. But 'change' to what? Was he going to build on what New Labour had achieved – a sort of Brownite consolidation? Or did he intend to branch out, as he sometimes hinted, in a new more radical direction? It was not clear. Too often, Brown seemed prisoner of the latest headline, pushed about by events. As Peter Mandelson told the BBC in April 2008, 'Jumping on passing bandwagons, hobby horses or marginal issues is not the way, in my view, for any government to present itself if it is going to sustain its support in the country.'[7]

In April 2008, the fiasco over the abolition of the 10p tax band further undermined Brown's reputation and threatened to bring about a humiliating defeat for his government in the Commons. When Brown had presented his last budget in 2007, he had cut the basic tax rate by 2p and had financed this tax cut by abolishing the 10p tax band, a change which came into effect in April 2008. Frank Field MP had warned the then Chancellor that, as a consequence of the abolition, millions would be worse off but he did not listen. By the spring of 2008, Labour MPs had woken up to the impact of abolition of the 10p band on some of their least affluent constituents while the Treasury Select Committee had also confirmed that abolition would leave many low-income households worse off. The celebrated *Guardian* columnist Polly Toynbee wrote, '[I]n one iconic error Brown has blown away his most admirable reputation – a 10-year record of directing money to the poorest.'[8] At first, Brown refused to give way but then was forced into capitulation. On 23 April, his Chancellor, Alistair Darling, announced a compensation package for more than five million losers. *The Times* talked about 'the humbling of a Prime Minister'.[9]

In May, Labour's local election results were appalling – the worst for forty years. The Mayor of London, Ken Livingstone, was beaten by the Conservative candidate, Boris Johnson. At the end of the month, the Tories won a parliamentary by-election from Labour for the first time since 1978. In July, Labour lost another by-election – this time, in Scotland to the Scottish Nationalists. Labour MPs grew restive. There were mutterings the Cabinet. At the end of July in a *Guardian* article, Foreign Secretary David Miliband called for 'a radical new phase'.[10] It was widely perceived as a veiled attack on the Prime Minister. At the end of August, the *Guardian* published an interview with the Chancellor, Alistair Darling, in which he said that economic conditions were 'the worst they've been in 60 years',[11] an accurate judgement which infuriated Brown who was predicting that the financial crisis would be over in six months. Darling later complained that Number Ten briefed against him: 'The forces of hell were unleashed.'[12] He was referring to the unattractive antics of Damian McBride and Charlie Whelan who, though working for the Unite union, informally assisted Brown. It was an unhappy time.

In the run-up to the 2008 party conference, a number of junior ministers openly called for a leadership contest. Leading ministers refused to condemn them. The Chief Whip, Geoff Hoon, said, 'I simply don't think at this stage it's appropriate.' while the Business Secretary, John Hutton, commented, 'I'm not going to criticise any of my colleagues who want Labour to do better.'[13]

But, on 15 September, Brown's premiership was saved by the collapse of Lehman Brothers, the major US investment bank (see next chapter).

In his conference speech, the Prime Minister said that this was 'the week the world was spun on its axis, and old certainties turned on their heads'. Suddenly, Brown's assertion that he was the only person qualified to lead Britain through the financial crisis looked credible. Swatting the two Davids, Cameron and Miliband, aside he added, 'Everyone knows that I am in favour of apprenticeships, but this is no time for a novice.' To the astonishment of Westminster, Brown then bolstered his position by bringing Peter Mandelson back into the Cabinet, as Business Secretary, in the reshuffle following party conference.

During the four years he had served as Britain's European Commissioner, Mandelson had grown in stature. No longer in the shadow of Blair, in Brussels he assumed weightier responsibilities than most of the British Cabinet.[14] Formidably well briefed, Mandelson consistently made the positive case for globalisation and free trade. As European Commissioner, he held the trade portfolio and, when the Doha Development Round of the World Trade Organisation (WTO) talks collapsed, some blamed him for their failure although it was not his fault but that of the USA and India. However, despite his position in Brussels, he still hankered after a return to British politics.

The reconciliation between Brown and Mandelson, who had hardly spoken to each other for fourteen years, began when the Prime Minister went to Brussels in March 2008 and met Mandelson. They had a friendly, hour-long conversation. In July, Mandelson, who had been having lunch with Sir Jeremy Heywood, the newly appointed Permanent Secretary at Number Ten, went back with him to see Brown, at the Prime Minister's invitation. This time, they had an even longer conversation. They began to speak to each other in the intimate way they used to do before the big bust-up in 1994. With nothing to lose, Mandelson was able to be completely frank both about Brown's dire situation and about his mistakes and faults. Soon, they were talking frequently on the phone and Mandelson was dropping in to see the Prime Minister when he came to London. Then, on 2 October during a light lunch, Brown asked

Mandelson to join the Cabinet. Mandelson replied that he would have to consult Blair first. When he heard the news, the former Prime Minister burst out laughing and said that, at a time of national economic crisis, Mandelson had no alternative but to accept. So Mandelson took Blair's advice and became Business Secretary and Baron Mandelson of Hartlepool and Foy.

Why did Brown bring Mandelson back into the Cabinet and why did Mandelson accept? One reason was to unify the Cabinet and the party. If the arch Blairite was back, then it would be more difficult for Blairites to rebel against Brown. Without being a threat to Brown, Mandelson also added colour and clout to a Cabinet which was widely criticised for its drabness. At the same time, he could offer blunt advice and say things to the Prime Minister that nobody else could. Maybe, just maybe, Mandelson, with his strategic intelligence, could help rescue the government and the New Labour project which they, together with Blair, had created many years before.

For his part, Mandelson longed to be back at Westminster. He was excited to become a Cabinet minster again, a job which he had greatly enjoyed. To be asked to return after the humiliation of his two resignations was indeed a vindication. 'Third time lucky', as he told reporters in Downing Street. He also felt the obligation to help out when both the New Labour project and the country were in such deep trouble.

The new Business Secretary proved good at his job. He listened to advice and took clear decisions. At first, he focused on getting banks to lend to industry. He also set up schemes to provide capital for small businesses. In January 2009, he announced a £2.3 billion rescue package for the car industry, though the most immediately effective measure was the car scrappage scheme announced in May, which gave drivers a £2,000 inducement to swap their old cars for new ones. He began to develop a more active industrial policy, helping Sheffield Forge Masters with plant for civil nuclear reactors and Nissan with research for its electric car to be produced at Sunderland. He tried to introduce private capital into

Royal Mail but was forced to abandon the plan in the face of opposition from Labour MPs.

The impact of Mandelson on the Brown government was, however, far wider than merely departmental. If his government was to be rescued, Brown desperately needed somebody of real political and intellectual authority to whom he could turn for advice and support. Mandelson quickly emerged as de facto Deputy Prime Minister. He was able to draw fire away from Brown during minor political crises; he also had the drive to push focused policy agendas through Whitehall *and* the strategic vision to give the administration the sense of direction it so badly needed.

At the heart of his new role was his relationship with Brown. The relationship worked because, first, it was based on a shared experience, going back over twenty years. Even though after 1994, Mandelson had been cast out in Brown's 'outer darkness', the latter still found time to call the former and offer his condolences after Mandelson's mother, Mary, had died. Second, because of this closeness, Mandelson was able to tell Brown the truth about his political weaknesses, while also trying to offer constructive solutions as to how these can be remedied. Third, Brown knew that Mandelson's motives were largely disinterested. He had no designs on Brown's job and, with the possible exception of the Foreign Office, had no ambitions for any other job in the government. He was driven rather by a dedication to the New Labour project in particular and to the Labour Party in general.

In June 2009, Mandelson saved Brown. The Labour Party did disastrously in the local elections, being beaten in third place by the Liberal Democrats. In the European elections, it polled under 16 per cent of the vote and finished third behind the United Kingdom Independence Party. As polls closed at 10 p.m. on Thursday 4 June, James Purnell, the young Blairite Work and Pensions Secretary, resigned, saying that Labour could not win under Brown. If he had been joined by David Miliband, Alan Johnson and one or two other members of the Cabinet, the Prime Minister would have been finished. Mandelson was called out of a dinner engagement to Number Ten to help shore up Brown's tottering authority. Desperately he worked the phones. Despite rumours that they were to be moved, Miliband stayed on as Foreign Secretary and Darling as Chancellor, while Johnson was locked into the new Cabinet as the new Home Secretary. Mandelson was given the titles of Lord President of the Council and First Secretary of State, confirmation of his paramount role in the government. Brown survived partly because there was no obvious successor. Brown told a meeting of the Parliamentary Labour Party the following Monday that he had his strengths and his weaknesses – and that he would try to address his weaknesses.

Mandelson's speech to the 2009 Labour Party conference at Brighton in September was a tour de force and, for the first time, he was given a standing ovation. It was witty, moving and rousing. Accepting that Labour was the underdog in the coming election, he said to the cheering delegates, 'If *I* can come back . . . *we* can come back.' Afterwards Blair exchanged text messages with him about finally being loved by the party. It had taken a political and economic crisis to turn the former 'Prince of Darkness' into a conference hero. The question was was it too late?

17

CREDIT CRUNCH – BROWN HELPS 'SAVE THE WORLD'

On 21 March 2007, Gordon Brown delivered his last budget as Chancellor before becoming Prime Minister. In it, he repeated, with more than a touch of hubris, the words he had spoken, to the intense irritation of the Tory opposition, more than a hundred times in the Commons between 1997 and 2007: 'We will never return to the old boom and bust.'[1] On the face of it, he was justified in being proud of the record of the economy under his stewardship. 'I can report the British economy is today growing faster than all the other G7 economies – growth stronger this year than the euro area, stronger than Japan and stronger even than America,' he proclaimed. For more than a decade, the British economy had grown with national output increasing by a third. What was equally remarkable was that inflation, in the past the UK economy's Achilles heel, had gone up annually by only 1.5 per cent. Living standards rose steadily. Public spending had increased by 4 per cent in real terms between 1999/2000 and 2007/08 (with much of it going into health and education), faster than the long-run growth rate of the economy – 2.75 per cent according to the Treasury estimate.[2] The budget was in deficit but Brown estimated that the public borrowing would be less than 3 per cent of GDP. He boasted that '[j]ust as our monetary discipline is the foundation of our economic growth, our fiscal discipline is the foundation of the strength of Britain's finances'.

If, as Mervyn King, the Governor of the Bank of England, said in a 2007 lecture, the monetary framework introduced by Brown in 1997 was a significant factor in the stability in inflation and output growth experienced by the UK over the decade,[3] it was also true that the years between the early 1990s and the recession of 1998–99 were, despite some minor setbacks, relatively benign ones generally for the world as a whole. A number of factors, including productivity gains, low interest rates, low commodity prices and the rise of the Chinese and Indian economies, combined to produce what economists have called the 'Great Moderation'. However, the financial markets which underpinned the global system carried within them the seeds of their own degeneration.

The Deputy Governor of the Bank of England, Charlie Bean, described what happened well:

> Underestimation of risk born of the 'Great Moderation', loose monetary policy in the United States and a perverse pattern of international capital flows together provided fertile territory for the emergence of a credit/asset-price bubble. The creation of an array of complex new assets that were supposed to spread risk more widely ended up destroying information about the scale and location of losses, which proved to be crucial when the market turned. And an array of distorted incentives led the financial system to build up excessive leverage, increasing the vulnerabilities when asset prices began to fall.[4]

When Brown gave his final Mansion House speech as Chancellor on 20 June, in the week before he became Prime Minister, he was clearly totally unaware of the troubles which were about to descend on the UK's financial services and on the banking system in particular. 'Over the ten years that I have had the privilege of addressing you as Chancellor, I have been able year by year to record how the City of London has risen by your efforts, ingenuity and creativity to become a new world leader,' he proclaimed in glowing terms. Hailing 'the beginning of a new golden age for the City of London', he went on to state:

> The financial services sector in Britain, and the City of London at the centre of it, is a great example of a highly skilled, high value added, talent-driven industry that shows how we can excel in a world of global competition. Britain needs more of the vigour, ingenuity and aspiration that you already demonstrate that is the hallmark of your success.[5]

Brown was accused by critics of having made a 'Faustian' pact with the City.[6] In return for low tax rates,[7] a blind eye was turned to the mushrooming bonus culture (bonus payments nearly tripled between 2001 and 2008); there was a 'light touch' regulatory regime; and London celebrated its role as the world's financial centre and home to two thirds of the global secondary bond market and 40 per cent of the over-the-counter derivatives market. Meanwhile, the Chancellor was happy that the growing financial services sector was making a major positive contribution to the UK balance of trade and paying as much as a quarter of UK corporation tax receipts.[8] Apart from support for a 'light touch', Brown had little interest in regulation while Ed Balls, his City Minister from May 2006 to June 2007, boasted about the UK's system of 'increasingly light touch and risk-based regulation which had made London a magnet for international business'.[9] Meanwhile the Conservative opposition was arguing for even less regulation.

There is no evidence that the Chancellor and his City Minister ever showed any concern about the explosive and unsound growth of many British banks. In the 1970s, the UK banking sector had a balance sheet of 50 per cent of United Kingdom GDP but, by 2007, it was four times more than UK GDP. Only Switzerland and Iceland, before its collapse, had a higher ratio.

As the Bank of England's October 2008 Financial Stability Report observed, major UK banks almost tripled their assets between 2001 and 2007. This remarkable growth was driven by a rapid rise in lending, leading to sharp and dangerous increases in leverage ratios – assets relative to equity – at some banks. What happened was that the combination of a fall in risk-free returns and large amounts of mainly Asian capital looking for a home in western markets led to a demand for new so-called 'financial instruments' offering a higher return. As well as lending to households and businesses, banks increased their lending to other banks which then purchased ever more exotic financial instruments, as risk was sliced up and repackaged. In the Governor of the Bank of England's judgement, 'the effect was to replicate the original risky loans many time over'.[10] It was a recipe for disaster. The House of Commons Treasury Select Committee concluded, 'The culture within parts of British banking has increasingly been one of risk taking leading to the meltdown that we have witnessed. Bankers have made an astonishing mess of the system.'[11]

Throughout the first half of 2007, there were ominous signs that America's 'sub-prime' mortgage market – the lending of money to borrowers who could not afford to repay – was collapsing. The sub-prime bubble had helped spawn a $6.5 billion so-called 'mortgage securities market' in which banks across the world were involved. On a flimsy base, a vast global superstructure was erected. Not surprisingly, when the base collapsed, it brought the superstructure down as well. In February, HSBC, the UK-based global bank, announced it was making provisions for $10.5 billion of losses by its US mortgage subsidiary. Hedge funds failed in the United States. Then, on 9 August 2007, BNP Paribas announced it was suspending withdrawals from three investment funds because they could no longer be properly valued. The European Central Bank stated that it stood ready to supply liquidity and the Federal Reserve followed suit the following day. Looking back, a year later, Larry Elliott of the *Guardian* wrote:

> As far as the financial markets are concerned, August 9 2007 has all the resonance of August 4 1914. It makes the cut-off point between 'an Edwardian summer' of prosperity and tranquillity and the trench warfare of the credit crunch – the failed banks, the petrified markets, the property markets blown to pieces by a shortage of credit.[12]

In Britain, Northern Rock, a former building society which had become a thrusting mortgage bank, was immediately in deep trouble. The bank had an unorthodox business model which had enabled it to become, by early 2007, the fifth-largest mortgage lender in the country. The special features of its model were, firstly, the so-called 'Together' mortgage, which enabled applicants to borrow six times their annual income and up to 125 per cent of the value of the property and, secondly, the financing of the bank's loans not from the savings of retail customers – by the end of 2006, down to 22 per cent – but from a constant flow of borrowing from the wholesale money markets. As the credit crunch bit, Northern Rock was unable to raise new financing from the wholesale markets and was on the edge of insolvency.

The plight of Northern Rock revealed both the ambiguities of the institutional reforms introduced by Gordon Brown in 1997 and the inexperience of the three main players. The Chancellor had set up a tripartite system – the Treasury, the Bank of England and the Financial Services Authority – to deal with 'systemic' risk. But the arrangements did not make it clear what the role of the Bank of England was and who had the final say. Alistair Darling was a new Chancellor who hesitated to overrule the Governor of the Bank of England, Mervyn King. The governor was a fine economist but with little experience of financial markets. He had underestimated the credit crisis in August and, because of arguments of 'moral hazard' (that is, that banks should not be rescued from their own follies), refused to put up Bank of England funds to bail out Northern Rock. The chief executive of the Financial Services Authority (FSA), Hector Sants, thought that Northern Rock should be given the funds but was in no position to insist as the FSA had failed, in the words of the Commons Treasury Select Committee, 'in its duty as a regulator to ensure Northern Rock would not pose a systemic risk'.[13]

Markets continued to plunge and then, following a scoop by the BBC's Business Editor, Robert Peston, that Northern Rock was to be given an emergency loan by the Bank of England, there was a run on the bank on 14 September, as customers withdrew their deposits from Northern Rock. Following a hesitation of four days after news of the bank's difficulties broke, the Chancellor finally announced that all existing deposits would be guaranteed by the authorities – a move which stemmed the run. Commenting later on the authorities' slow response, the Deputy Governor, Sir John Gieve, described their footwork as 'leaden', adding, 'We did not need two days of queues in the streets.'[14] Richard Lambert, Director-General of the Confederation of British Industry, was highly critical, remarking that 'a run on a bank is something that happens in a banana republic'.[15]

But stopping the bank run did not solve the problem of what to do with Northern Rock. For five long months, the government, while continuing to prop up the bank, searched for a 'white knight', a private sector buyer to take it over. Brown and Darling were extremely reluctant to accept the solution of nationalisation that was put forward by a number of prominent people, ranging from the Labour Chairman of the Commons Treasury Select Committee, John McFall, the Liberal Democrat economic spokesman, Vince Cable, and the Cabinet Secretary, Sir Gus O'Donnell, to the *Economist* newspaper, because they feared being attacked by the right-wing press. However, private sector buyers all wanted a substantial 'dowry' from the government to take the bank off their hands. In the end, on 17 February 2008, Alistair Darling was forced to announce that Northern Rock was being taken into temporary public ownership, following an assessment by Treasury officials that the private sector bids did not represent good value for the taxpayers' money.

Predictably, the Conservative leader, David Cameron, said on the BBC that 'the nationalisation of Northern Rock is a disaster for the British taxpayer, a disaster for this government and a disaster for the country' but failed to propose any alternative. In fact, it was by no means certain that the taxpayer would lose out. It was possible that, when the bank was eventually sold back to the private sector, taxpayers would get their money back. From the point of view of Brown and Darling, dealing with Northern Rock, albeit clumsily and hesitantly, provided an invaluable dress rehearsal for a far more serious situation – bailing out the whole British banking system.

Presenting his first budget, Alistair Darling repeated Brown's complacent line that 'Britain is better placed than other economies to withstand the slowdown in the world economy'.[16] But it quickly became clear that the credit crunch was having an impact on the real economy, especially in the housing market. Banks did not want to lend – either to their customers or to other banks. Mortgages were more difficult to get, property prices were falling and consumer confidence was down. Highly dependent on consumer spending and the housing market, the British economy was on the edge of recession.

By 2008, the United States' financial markets were in deep trouble. In March, Bear Stearns, America's fifth-largest bank, got into terminal difficulties and was sold at a knock-down price to JP Morgan. In September, the US government had to bail out Freddie Mac and Fannie Mae, the two government-sponsored mortgage enterprises. A week later, in a disastrous move, it allowed the investment bank, Lehman Brothers, to fail – the largest corporate bankruptcy the world had ever seen. The fall of Lehman was a massive shock to the global financial system and turned the credit crunch into a world financial crisis. As Professor Paul Krugman, winner of the 2008 Nobel Prize in Economics, concluded, 'Letting Lehman fail basically brought the entire world capital market down.'[17]

The reaction in the United Kingdom was immediate. The London Stock Exchange fell to a three-year low. It rapidly became clear that a number of banks were in deep trouble. The shares of Halifax Bank of Scotland (HBOS) fell by 34 per cent and a merger with Lloyds Bank, encouraged by the government, emerged as a strong possibility. The Royal Bank of Scotland (RBS), Britain's second-largest bank, was also in difficulties – its shares were declining rapidly and it was running out of money. On the 27 September, the FSA announced that Bradford and Bingley, a former building society, no longer met the legal conditions for operating as a deposit taker and, after a frantic weekend, the Treasury put together a rescue package. The deposit part of the business was transferred to the Spanish bank, Santander, while the remainder of the business, mainly comprising its mortgage lending, was nationalised. Having learned the lessons from Northern Rock and now with more legal powers, the government acted swiftly and decisively.

Increasingly, however, Brown and Darling and their advisers were coming to the conclusion that, if they were to prevent a complete banking collapse, they needed to put together a comprehensive response. The story of the next two weeks was about the emergence of a rescue plan for the British banking system, the principles of which were to be followed across the world. The key idea was the recapitalisation of the banks.

A number of people were 'sponsors' of recapitalisation, including: Mervyn King, who had gone from an extremely cautious position to arguing for recapitalisation of all the banks; Adair Turner, the new chairman of the FSA; Shriti Vadera – known by some of her colleagues as 'Shriti the Shriek' – a former investment banker who had become Brown's chief adviser on City matters; and Paul Myners, a Labour supporter from the City who had just been appointed City Minister to oversee the negotiations with the banks. But it was the politicians, Brown, Darling and Mandelson, and above all Brown, who had to take the responsibility for the negotiation, launching and selling of the plan. The Prime Minister fully understood that he was taking a major political gamble but the costs of inaction were far greater than action. A crucial meeting took place on Sunday 5 October between Brown, Darling and King when a decision was taken to go ahead with the recapitalisation package.

The main problem was to persuade the bankers to accept the money. Admitting that they needed government support meant acknowledging that they had brought their businesses to the verge of collapse. Another Peston leak – that RBS, Lloyds and Barclays were talking to government – both sent shares plummeting and forced the bankers' hand. On Wednesday 8 October, a package of £50 billion recapitalisation money was announced for the major British banks, together with £450 billion in liquidity and credit guarantees. This was the biggest rescue plan by any Western government since 1945 and was accompanied by the largest (half a point) internationally co-ordinated cut in interest rates ever. But it was still not enough to calm the markets which continued to plunge.

It took a weekend, 11–12 October, of intense negotiations, with the Prime Minister and the Chancellor flying out and in – Brown to and from a meeting of European leaders in Paris and Darling to and from a G7 meeting in Washington – to produce a more specific bailout package for the banks in most trouble (RBS, Lloyds and HBOS). At 6.25 a.m. on Monday 13 October, before the markets opened, the Treasury announced a £37 billion recapitalisation sum for RBS and Lloyds and HBOS, with £20 billion of it for RBS. In return, the taxpayer took shares of 57 per cent in RBS and 43 per cent in Lloyds–HBOS. The rescued banks also agreed to lend money to businesses and limit bonus payments. The government introduced a further package in January to remove so-called 'toxic' assets from the banks' books and increase the Treasury shareholding in RBS. Brown, Darling and Myners were later criticised for allowing the disgraced head of RBS to escape with a pensions pot of £16 million and for not taking a tougher line on bonuses. But the overriding issue was that they and their advisers had saved the country from a total banking collapse when the economy would have literally run out of cash.

Where the UK led, the rest of the world followed suit, broadly following the scheme first announced by Brown and Darling. Paul Krugman, under the headline 'Gordon does Good' in the *New York Times*, wrote:

> Brown and Alistair Darling . . . have defined the character of the world-wide rescue effort, with other wealthy nations playing catch up . . . The Brown government has shown itself willing to think clearly about the financial crisis, and act quickly on its conclusions. And the combination of clarity and decisiveness hasn't been matched by any other Western government.[18]

Peter Mandelson said about Brown, 'He was the market leader in taking action which others have followed. Nothing will detract from his place in history in taking that action.'[19]

But saving the banks was only the beginning. In the second half of 2008, the near collapse of the financial system fed through into the wider global economy. World trade plummeted, output fell and unemployment rose sharply across the world. The UK, with a proportionally larger financial sector, was severely hit and, over the course of the recession, the British economy fell by around 6 per cent. In the 1930s, the reaction of world leaders was to slash public spending, contract their economies and resort to 'beggar my neighbour' protection, all of which combined to lead to the Great Depression. This time it was different. Gordon Brown, exploiting his position as chairman of the G20 countries – which included China, India, Brazil, Indonesia, Mexico and Turkey as well as the G8 countries – summoned a conference in London at the beginning of April 2009. His big coup was persuading the glamorous Barack Obama, the newly elected US president, to come, thus ensuring that all the other leaders would come as well. Together, they agreed a plan for a concerted fiscal expansion of 5 trillion dollars.

Much of this vast figure was the combined deterioration in fiscal balances caused by the recession though one of Obama's first actions as President was to get Congress to support a $789 billion 'stimulus'. Other countries, including even Germany, whose Chancellor, Angela Merkel, had derided fiscal stimuli 'as a senseless race to spend billions', also introduced smaller 'stimulus' packages. In November 2008, the British government had not been able to inject more than £20 billion into the UK economy, mainly through a temporary reduction in VAT, because of the growing size of public borrowing (see last chapter). However, in contrast to what happened in the 1930s, in 2009 the response of governments could be described as 'Keynesian'.[20] Instead of cutting back, they supported their economies either by injecting extra spending or sustaining public borrowing or, in most cases, both. At Pittsburgh six months later, the G20 leaders were able to congratulate themselves on their success at London in April 2009:

> At that time, our countries agreed to do everything necessary to ensure recovery, to repair our financial systems and maintain the global flow of capital. It worked. Our forceful response helped to stop the dangerous, sharp decline in global activity and stabilize financial markets. Industrial output is now rising in nearly all our economies. International trade is starting to recover . . . and confidence has improved.[21]

In reply to a jibe by David Cameron in December 2008 about the failure of the UK bank rescue to unfreeze credit markets, Brown said, to Tory jeers, 'We not only saved the world . . .' He probably meant to say 'saved the world's banks'. In his decade as Chancellor, Brown may have made mistakes over regulation and supervision and have generally been too inclined to see the City through rose-coloured spectacles but there is a strong case for saying that Brown's contribution as Prime Minister, both over bank recapitalisation in October 2008 and then at the G20 London summit in April 2009, was an essential ingredient in ensuring that the world recession of 2008–09 did not become a world depression. Maybe he really did help 'save the world'.

18

BROWN'S LAST STAND

On 6 April 2010, after seeing the Queen at Buckingham Palace to ask for the dissolution of parliament, Gordon Brown called an election for 6 May. Since Brown's indecision about calling an election in the autumn of 2007, Labour had, except for a short period after the rescue of the banks in 2008, trailed the Tories by a wide margin in the opinion polls. Thursday 6 May 2010 was just about the last practical date on which a general election could be called within the statutory five-year period, coinciding, as it did, with the local elections. Appealing for a fourth term for New Labour, Brown opened his campaign in front of 10 Downing Street, flanked by his Cabinet and insisting that 'Britain is now on the way to economic recovery. And now is not the time to put it at risk'.

There was a good reason for the Prime Minister choosing to surround himself with his Cabinet. The poll numbers put him well behind Cameron as the most popular party leader. Brown wanted to demonstrate that, in plumping for Labour, the electors were not just voting for him but also for an experienced team, above all for the Chancellor, Alistair Darling, and the Business Secretary, Peter Mandelson. Darling's steady, unflappable performance as Chancellor had helped the UK stave off a banking collapse and come out of a major recession. It also lent credibility to the government's deficit reduction plan (see below). Mandelson's authority gave weight to Labour's recovery programme while his strategic skills and experience were invaluable as chairman of the campaign strategy committee and of Labour's morning press conference.

Significantly, the ex-Prime Minister, Tony Blair, joined the Labour campaign, in support of his old friend and rival Gordon Brown. Speaking at Trimdon Labour Club in his former constituency of Sedgefield, Blair praised his successor for his leadership during the economic crisis and skilfully, in what Michael White of the *Guardian* called a 'master class',[1] took the Conservatives apart for their opportunism. Analysing a number of Tory policy areas, he asked:

> Why the confusion? The benign explanation is that the policy makers are confused, not just the policies. The less benign one is that one set of policies represents what they believe in; the other was that they think they have to say to win.

Blair suggested that this was why the polls had narrowed. For at least one more time, the three architects of New Labour were together again.

Brown's main case in the election was that he and Alistair Darling were bringing the UK out of recession and that only they were competent enough to complete the task smoothly while protecting the massive investments that the Labour government had made in health and education. In November 2008, the Conservatives, who had previously committed themselves to match government spending totals, switched policy and now said that the priority was to reduce the explosion in public spending as quickly as possible – although, in their campaign, their position softened again. They blamed the government, with shadow Chancellor, George Osborne, claiming that, '[i]n the end, all Labour Chancellors run out of money and all Labour governments bring this country to the verge of bankruptcy'.[2]

If Gordon Brown could be criticised for allowing public borrowing to rise too fast on the basis of over-optimistic forecasts, especially in the last two or three years of his chancellorship, it was nevertheless true that by far the largest part of the deficit was caused by the impact of the recession on output and tax revenues. Reducing the deficit too fast could tip the economy back into recession, as happened in Japan in the 1990s and in the United States in the 1930s. The government's plan was to reduce the deficit by £100 billion (or over half) over four years, the deepest cut since the Second World War. But, because they were still uncertain about the recovery, they delayed the start of the fiscal tightening – a decision which was supported by a number of economic authorities.[3] The debate about the speed of the deficit reduction and about which party could best be trusted to ensure the recovery and protect the most vulnerable should have been at the heart of the election debate but, in the campaign, the issue was largely ignored.

There were other important issues too. In education and health, the advantage was clearly with Labour, who had transformed the two services by a decade of steady investment and modernisation to the benefit of pupils and patients. Law and order and immigration were traditionally Tory issues and were likely to remain so, even though the Labour record on crime was impressive, with crime falling every year while the party was in office and violent crime standing at half what it was a decade ago.

Highlighted by the parliamentary expenses scandal, trust in politicians and the political system had become an urgent question. Although Labour, Conservative and Liberal Democrat MPs were involved in the scandal and all three party leaders tried to 'out-tough' each other in their response, inevitably more blame was attached to the government than to the other two parties. To tackle the 'trust in politics' issue, Gordon Brown proposed, in addition to new rules on MPs' expenses, a programme of parliamentary reform, including recall for errant MPs, election of the House of Lords and a referendum on the alternative vote (AV), a system to ensure that MPs were elected by a majority vote in their constituency.

Commentators suggested that the Prime Minister's somewhat belated initiative was designed to appeal to Liberal voters.

Europe had been a big issue at both the 1997 and 2001 elections, though the commitment by all three main parties to a referendum on the European Constitutional Treaty had muted it at the 2005 election. Brown had been criticised for his clumsy handling of the signing of the Lisbon Treaty in 2007 – when he flew to Lisbon but missed the signing ceremony – and of the negotiations in November 2009 over the President of the European Council and EU 'High Representative' (or foreign minister). But the French President, Nicolas Sarkozy, and the German Chancellor, Angela Merkel, came to respect him for both his leadership in the world financial crisis and his reliability as a British ally. That was more than could be said for David Cameron who, to appease anti-EU Tories, insisted on leaving the mainstream centre-right grouping in the European Parliament, which included both Merkel's and Sarkozy's parties, and setting up a more euro-sceptic and far right-wing grouping.

At the 2005 election, Iraq was a salient issue for both the media and Liberal voters. An election-day poll for *Sky News* found that one in four Liberal Democrat voters said they would have voted Labour 'but did not do so because of Iraq'.[4] However, British troops had now been withdrawn from Iraq. In February 2010, with barely concealed relief, Brown said:

> People know we're out of Iraq now and we've got a government in Iraq that's able to manage its own security . . . Our time ended with successful local elections which put local people in control of their own security.[5]

The Chilcot Inquiry into the Iraq war, which the Prime Minister set up, held most of its hearings, including those of Blair and Brown, in public but was not going to report until after the election.

British troops, 9500 of them, were still fighting in Afghanistan, supporting the US surge to push the Taliban out of Helmand Province. In 2009, the Prime Minister stated:

In 2001 the case for intervention in Afghanistan was to take on a global terrorist threat and prevent terrorist attacks in Britain and across the world. In 2009 the overriding reason for our continued involvement is the same – to take on, at its source, the terrorist threat, and prevent attacks here and elsewhere.[6]

Despite a majority of voters believing that the war was unwinnable[7] and criticism of Brown for sending ill-equipped troops, the three main political parties still supported British intervention in Afghanistan.

On 13 April, Labour published its manifesto. As befitted the times, it was a sober document, making no rash spending commitments. Peter Riddell of *The Times* commented that it was a typical manifesto for a government which had been in power for thirteen years, in that each Cabinet minister could point to a favourite programme being included. However, it made clear Labour's commitment to economic growth, while, at the same time, aiming to reduce the deficit. It promised to protect Labour's greatest achievements in power – the progress in health and education. Significantly the manifesto continued Labour's emphasis on reform of public services – this time, through a welcome synthesis of Blairite and Brownite ideas. It was Blairite in that the manifesto backed diversity of provision through foundation hospitals and academy schools and Brownite in that it also supported new individual guarantees in both health and education. The stress on an active industrial policy showed Mandelson's influence. Polly Toynbee of the *Guardian* summed up the manifesto by saying that 'anyone who has ever voted Labour will find plentiful reminders here of good reasons why', as well as 'a vision of the future'.[8]

The underlying clash at the 2010 election was between two contrasting arguments. The first was that it was better to stay with an experienced team that was helping to get the UK out of recession. The second was that it was 'time for a change'. In any election, 'time for a change' is a powerful cry, especially after a government has been in power for a long time. As Tony Blair said in his Sedgefield speech:

[T]he tough thing about being in government, especially as time marches on, is that disappointments accumulate, the public becomes less inclined to give the benefit of the doubt, the call for a time for change becomes easier to make, prospect of change becomes more attractive.[9]

On the other hand, as Blair also pointed out, 'time for a change' was a vacuous slogan which begged the question, 'To what?' From the beginning of 2010, the Tories were exposed to a series of probes designed to reveal that the Conservatives, in contrast to Labour, lacked experience, were unreliable and did not understand economics. In the polls, Brown may have consistently run behind Cameron but his sheer toughness and resilience in the face of adversity, combined with Tory weakness, seemed to make some impression. As one of his critics wrote in the *Guardian*, 'Brown's failings as a leader were obvious and well-documented. But so were his strengths, his grinding energy, his puritanical high standards over money throughout the expenses crisis, and his unflagging seriousness.'[10]

The question remained, as the election campaign started in earnest, was Brown leading New Labour's last stand or was he, together with his two able lieutenants Mandelson and Darling, contriving to put together a counter-attack sufficiently strong enough to give the party a majority or, more likely, to take it into a hung parliament?

CONCLUSION

Labour's result in the May 2010 general election, in which no party got an overall majority, was its second-worst performance since 1918. With 29 per cent of the poll, it was only a shade ahead of Michael Foot's 27.6 per cent in the disastrous defeat of 1983.

But, paradoxically, although Labour suffered a net loss of ninety-one seats, there was almost a feeling of relief amongst its supporters. Following the apparent Liberal Democrat surge in the opinion polls after the first television debate of the election campaign, there had been a fear in Labour ranks that the party could actually finish third in the popular vote, thus undermining its claim to be the alternative governing party. However, the Liberal Democrats ended up 6 percentage points behind Labour – although their share of the vote increased by 1 per cent – and, overall, they lost five seats. And, if the Tories had a net gain of ninety seats, they did not achieve outright victory. In that sense, David Cameron failed to 'seal the deal' with the British electorate for which he had hoped.

Labour fought a defensive campaign which only really came alive in the last few days. Though Gordon Brown performed competently in the three television debates which were such an important feature of the national campaign, he was adjudged by immediate polls to have lost out to Clegg and Cameron. To the delight of the media, he also made the only gaffe of the election when he was heard, over an open microphone which he had forgotten to remove, calling a potential Labour voter in Rochdale a 'bigoted woman'. However, it is interesting to note that, despite the incident, Labour still won in Rochdale.

In the closing stages of the election, a few Labour Cabinet ministers, including Ed Balls, who subsequently held on to his Yorkshire seat by just over a thousand votes, raised the issue of tactical voting for Liberal Democrat voters in Labour/Tory marginals and Labour voters in Liberal/Tory marginals. However, Brown and Mandelson were non-committal, preferring to concentrate on last-minute efforts to shore up the Labour vote while, on the day before the election, Blair reminded *Guardian* readers that 'the Lib Dems are not going out to people and saying "Vote Labour", they are trying to take seats off us'. The former Labour leader urged people to make up their own minds and back the party they believed in.[1]

In the five days following the election, Gordon Brown remained as caretaker Prime Minister. It was often overlooked that it was not only his constitutional right but also his duty to stay on to provide a government while coalition bargaining took place. It was clear that, if there was to be a coalition, the post-election parliamentary arithmetic pointed to a Tory–Liberal administration. Adding the Conservative and Liberal Democrat seats together produced a total of 363, a comfortable overall majority, while a Labour–Liberal Democrat arrangement could only muster 315 seats and would have needed the additional support of smaller parties, such as the Scottish National Party (SNP), Plaid Cymru (PC) and the Social Democratic and Labour Party (SDLP).

Although the Labour Party agreed to the Liberal Democratic request to enter into formal talks, with Brown announcing his intention to resign before the next party conference, the momentum was always with the

Conclusion

Conservative–Liberal Democratic negotiations. On Tuesday 11 May, the two parties reached an agreement to form a Tory–Liberal coalition, the first British coalition since Churchill's wartime government. Gordon Brown made a dignified and moving farewell speech outside Number 10 and tendered his resignation to the Queen. The New Labour era was over.

It left a substantial legacy. The sustained growth in the British economy – at least until the 'credit crunch' crisis – made possible steady and substantial increases in investment in health, education, policing and other public services. The statistics were impressive. In the NHS, there were 44,000 more doctors and 89,000 more nurses than in 1997 and, in schools, there were 42,400 more teachers and 123,000 more teaching assistants. There were nearly 17,000 more police officers and 16,800 more community officers.

Money also went into buildings. In the health service, 100 new hospitals, 100 walk-in centres and over 650 one-stop primary care centres were built. In education, nearly 4,000 schools were built, rebuilt or refurbished. Over 200 new academies were opened, usually replacing under-performing schools. Under the Sure Start programme for under-threes, 3,380 Children's Centres were set up.

Investment in health and education was accompanied by substantial improvements in outputs. Waiting times were the lowest since the NHS began. An average eighteen-month wait for hospital treatment in 1997 was reduced to a maximum wait of eighteen weeks from referral to treatment, with average wait even shorter. Over three quarters of GP practices offered extended opening hours for at least one evening or weekend session a week. Deaths from cancer, stroke and heart attacks fell substantially.

Educational standards rose – 80 per cent of eleven-year-olds reached the expected level in English and 79 per cent in maths, compared with the 1997 figures of 63 per cent for English and 62 per cent in maths. The numbers gaining five or more good GCSE exams were up by nearly 24 per cent since 1997. As promised in 1997 by Labour, there were free nursery places for all three- and four-year-olds. At the other end of the educational ladder, more young people attended university than ever before, including an increase in the number of students from the poorest homes. Apprenticeships more than tripled under Labour.

Although polls showed that voters believed that crime had risen, overall crime was, in fact, down 36 per cent since 1997 – domestic burglary was down 54 per cent and violent crime down 41 per cent. The Association of Chief Police Officers (ACPO) claimed that the risk of being a victim of violent crime was now at its lowest for thirty years.

Real progress was made in tackling poverty as defined in terms of a family living on less than 60 per cent of average earnings. In 1997, 3.4 million children and 2.9 million pensioners were living in poverty and, during the lifetime of the Labour government, about 500,000 children and 900,000 pensioners were lifted out of poverty. The introduction of the minimum wage, opposed by the Conservatives, and tax credits had also made a big difference in reducing poverty at work.

Labour ministers made much of their commitment to a fairer society. However, there was considerable debate about how much was achieved. A report by the Institute of Fiscal Studies in 2010 showed that, as a result of tax and benefit changes introduced by the Labour government, the poorest 10 per cent of households were better off in terms of income by 12.8 per cent, while the richest 10 per cent were worse off by 8.7 per cent.[2] But, at the same time, inequality in wealth, strengthened by powerful economic forces, continued to grow. Polly Toynbee and David Walker, often harsh critics of New Labour, concluded that, 'at best, Labour stopped inequality in the UK getting worse.'[3]

In his speech in front of 10 Downing Street on becoming Prime Minister on 11 May 2010, David Cameron said, in a generous farewell to Gordon Brown, 'Compared with a decade ago, this country is more open at home and more compassionate abroad.'[4] However, critics attacked Labour for its civil liberties record including its failed attempts to increase the number of days allowed for the detention of suspects without trial to ninety, under Blair, and forty-two, under Brown, and its plan to introduce identity cards. But, on the other side of the balance sheet, the Freedom of Information Act, the Human Rights Act, the signing up to the EU Social Chapter (including the right to join a union), civil partnerships for same-sex couples and, above all, the greater tolerance and diversity, as shown by the 2010 British Social Attitudes report, had also to be taken into account. Devolution of power to Scotland and Wales was a success while, thanks in part to Blair, peace was at last brought to Northern Ireland.

In foreign policy, the disastrous intervention in Iraq (British combat troops were withdrawn in 2009) and the long-running war against the Taliban in Afghanistan continued to cast their shadows. It should not be forgotten, however, that, under Blair and Brown's leadership, debt relief and international development became political priorities, while the Labour government was the first government ever to commit to a law that 0.7 per cent of GDP should be given in foreign aid. The Labour government played a leading role in building an international coalition to tackle climate change. Despite mistakes and shortcomings, UK relations with its EU partners were closer in 2010 than in 1997. As former Foreign Secretary, David Miliband, said, 'In everything from trade negotiations to the training of the Afghan police to sanctions on Iran or the greening of our economies, the European Union helps us achieve our foreign policy ambitions.'[5]

A backhanded tribute to New Labour and its record in office was how the other parties have had to respond to its agenda. For the Tories, Cameron talked about compassionate Conservatism, backed gay rights and accepted the need to reduce poverty, while the Conservative–Liberal Democrat coalition began by stressing its progressive credentials. Writing in the *Financial Times*, Max Hastings said, 'Mr Cameron knows that Britain is today a social democratic country.'[6] In that sense, like Attlee's 1945–51 governments, the influence of New Labour was likely to last beyond its period in government.

This is not to argue that the New Labour model should be preserved either in its Blair version or in its later Brown version. The world has moved on. The global financial crisis, its impact on the UK economy and the need to cut the budget deficit without undermining the social fabric will dominate politics in the next few years. It is against this background – and in the context of opposition – that Labour's new generation of leaders will need to regroup, revise and renew. Both New Labour's successes and failures will be relevant to their reappraisal.

Writing in 2005, Peter Riddell described New Labour as both post-Thatcherite and social democratic: 'post-Thatcherite in accepting the new framework of economic policy created in the 1980s and social democratic in the sense of trying to improve public services for all and broaden social opportunities.'[7] As we have seen above, the social democratic legacy is a powerful one. In the difficult years ahead, the task will be to try to preserve that legacy, albeit in a form relevant to a more austere age. It is the neo-Thatcherite, market-orientated approach which will need re-examination.

For a decade, New Labour's economic policy, guided by the Chancellor, Gordon Brown, was remarkably successful. Sustained growth in output produced the flow of resources necessary to finance the massive investment in public services, especially education and health. In March 1997, the *Guardian*'s economic editor Larry Elliott noted that Jean-Philippe Cotis, the chief economist of the Organisation for Economic Cooperation and Development (OECD), described Britain as 'a "Goldilocks" economy – getting the balance of strong growth and law inflation just right. "It is in fact surprising how stable the UK economy has been. It is doing very well."'[8] This was the calm before the storm. From the first quarter of 2008 to the third quarter of 2009, there was a 6.2 per cent decline in output, the largest fall for over seventy years.

It is wrong to pin the blame for credit cruch on Gordon Brown. The financial crash was a world phenomenon which began in the United States. But Brown could certainly be criticised for basing his spending plans on overambitious growth predictions. And the main reason the UK was so badly hit by the global economic crisis was because of the importance of financial services (especially banking whose assets had doubled between 2001 and 2007) in the British economy. An additional factor was that, with the encouragement of Brown and Balls, the City was too lightly regulated so that there were few warning signs of what was to come. In the future, there must not only be tighter regulation but also a rebalancing of the British economy.

The Third Way guru, Lord Giddens, pointed to a deeper issue. It was right, he argued, that Labour should become more business friendly and recognise the importance of the City but it was a fundamental error to allow the change in Labour's attitude to evolve into 'a fawning dependence, with the result that the UK was transformed into a kind of gigantic tax haven'. He went on: 'Blair and Brown should have made it much clearer than they did that recognising the virtues of markets is quite different from prostrating oneself before them.'[9]

Geoff Mulgan, the former head of the Downing Street Strategy Unit (DSSU), went further by claiming that there was a problem about New Labour's whole approach. It was, above all, an electoral project, according to Mulgan, which made it harder to take on the most powerful interests – the London media, the super rich, big businesses and the City – that stood in the way of progressive reform.[10] Without necessarily accepting Mulgan's criticism, the successor generation of Labour leaders will have to be careful of how they treat these powerful groups in future. If 'fairness not favours' is right for the unions, it certainly ought to be good enough for these other interests as well.

New Labour was always more than an electoral device, even if its development as a social democratic governing project, combining social justice and enterprise, took time to emerge, but it rightly believed in the importance of winning elections. After all, its rise to power followed four successive election defeats by the Conservatives and eighteen years of impotent opposition. It became the most successful electoral machine in Western Europe, winning three successive elections and thirteen years in office. Its defeat in 2010, though substantial, was, in the end, not life threatening.

Conclusion

Labour has been given the opportunity to rebuild in opposition. It must take it.

A top priority must be to reassemble New Labour's successful coalition of voters. At its zenith, it was an alliance of Labour's Celtic and northern heartlands with the upwardly mobile voters of the midlands and the south, of unskilled, skilled, white-collar and professional employees, a remarkable combination of compassion and aspiration. By 2005, New Labour was already losing seats in the south and, in 2010, it was defeated – as some warned might happen[11] – because it could not hold on to the majority of its suburban marginals in the south and the midlands. Despite being in power for thirteen years, the impact of a severe recession, the parliamentary expenses scandal and an unpopular Prime Minister, Labour retained the backing of most of its core voters. But it lost much of its skilled and white-collar support – employees earning between £20,000 and £30,000 a year or 'modest income' Britain[12] – who felt pressurised by a squeeze on their living standards, by housing problems and by massive immigration especially from Central and Eastern Europe. Labour's new leaders will have to analyse the causes of its defeat and devise a plan to put things right next time.

There is also the issue of relations with the Liberal Democrats. There is little point in either party spending time blaming each other for the breakdown in coalition talks. The parliamentary numbers always made a Labour–Liberal Democrat coalition a long shot. Of course, if the Conservative–Liberal Democrat coalition falters in its professed aim of providing strong, progressive government, then the Labour opposition should be the first to criticise. But Labour must also be ready to offer a warm welcome to disillusioned Liberal Democrats who seek a radical home. That includes adopting a favourable stance to proportional representation and constitutional reform as a matter of principle rather than deathbed conversion à la Brown. And, if political circumstances change, Labour should not rule out a progressive alliance with the Liberal Democrats.

It may be that we are entering a new era in which voters demand much more cooperation between the parties and less adversarial politics. Labour must be open to such a shift in attitudes.

A damaging fault of New Labour was its style, especially in its early years in power, and its method of governing. The emphasis on spin and media management when it first came to power was understandable, given its inexperience and the power of the media. But, by creating the impression that New Labour was only about presentation, it proved counterproductive. When results began to improve at the end of the first term and the beginning of the second, the government found it difficult to get journalists and voters to believe them.

The two-headed way of running New Labour was even more of a problem. In government, the celebrated 1994 deal between Blair and Brown led to an almost dual administration, with two heads and two camps. It might have been better for New Labour and the country if, instead of a deal in 1994, there had been a trial of strength in the leadership election between the two men, followed by a more normal way of running the government when the party won the 1997 general election. The Blair–Brown partnership worked well in the first term when the complementary skills and abilities of Blair and Brown, with the support of Mandelson's strategic direction, provided a highly effective combination. In the second term, relations between Blair and Brown deteriorated with Brown continually pressing Blair to stand down. As a result, instead of concentrating on providing joint solutions to public sector reform, too much time and energy was taken up with rows between the two men and their entourages. Though Blair had a brilliant Indian summer, the beginning of the third term was dominated by Brown's unremitting drive for power. In the end, after a short honeymoon, Brown proved less at home at Number Ten than he had been at the Treasury. He saved the country from a banking collapse and internationally led the fight against global recession but was unable, despite the help of Mandelson, to convince the voters that Labour deserved a fourth term. Indeed, his unpopularity was a major reason for Labour's defeat.

Conclusion

Tony Blair, Gordon Brown and Peter Mandelson were the people who contributed most to New Labour. All three had their faults and made mistakes. Blair had to live with the decision to invade Iraq. After 2008, Brown had to listen to Conservative MPs shouting derisively, 'The end of boom and bust!', the slogan which he had so hubristically repeated in Parliament in the years before. And Peter Mandelson had to suffer the humiliation of resigning twice – even if, the second time, he was blameless.

However, they were three exceptional politicians with substantial achievements to their credit. Tony Blair took the initial decision to revise Clause 4 of Labour's constitution. He was an outstanding Prime Minister, who won three elections victories and helped bring peace to Northern Ireland. Brown was a creative Chancellor who presided over ten years of economic growth and channelled resources into education and health and into reducing poverty. As Prime Minister, he helped rescue the global banking system. Mandelson, a key architect of New Labour who masterminded the 1997 landslide, was a first-rate minister and, in 2008, saved Brown's premiership. Together, they created New Labour, brought it to power and sustained it in government.

Could they have done better? Like the Attlee administrations of 1945–51, they helped to make Britain a fairer and more civilised place. But, if Blair, Brown and Mandleson had combined more effectively, New Labour could have achieved more.

NOTES

Introduction

1 Radice, Giles, *Diaries, 1980–2001* (London, 2004), 2 March 1990.

2 Macintyre, Donald, *Mandelson and the Making of New Labour* (London, 2000), p. 592.

1 Provenance and Upbringing – Tony Blair

1 *Observer*, 2 October 1994, quoted in Rentoul, John, *Tony Blair, Prime Minister* (London, 2001), p. 13.

2 Rentoul: *Tony Blair, Prime Minister*, p. 8.

3 Ibid., p. 9.

4 Ibid., p. 4.

5 Ibid., p. 4.

6 Ibid., p. 3.

7 Quoted in Seldon, Anthony, *Blair* (London, 2004), p. 7.

8 Rentoul: *Tony Blair, Prime Minister*, pp. 16, 20.

9 Ibid., p. 17.

10 Ibid., p. 19.

11 Ibid., p. 24.

12 Ibid., p. 20.

13 Seldon: *Blair*, p. 27.

14 Rentoul: *Tony Blair, Prime Minister*, p. 34.

15 Ibid., p. 39.

16 Naughtie, James, *The Rivals* (London, 2001), p. 17.

17 Rentoul: *Tony Blair, Prime Minister*, p. 37.

18 Ibid., p. 35.

19 Seldon: *Blair*, p. 40.

20 Rentoul: *Tony Blair, Prime Minister*, p. 43.
21 Ibid., p. 48.
22 Seldon: *Blair*, pp. 49–50.
23 BBC Radio 4, *Desert Island Discs*, 23 November 1996.
24 Seldon: *Blair*, p. 55.
25 Ibid., p. 55.
26 Ibid., pp. 69–80.
27 Ibid., p. 105.

2 Provenance and Upbringing – Gordon Brown

1 Routledge, Paul, *Gordon Brown* (London, 1998), pp. 22–24.
2 *The Times*, 15 May 1993.
3 Ibid.
4 Murray Elder interview, 13 August 1997, in Routledge: *Gordon Brown*, p. 26.
5 Ibid., p. 37.
6 Ibid.
7 Ibid., p. 39.
8 Ibid., pp. 39–40.
9 Ibid., p. 54.
10 Ibid., pp. 46–47.
11 Naughtie: *The Rivals*, p. 14.
12 *Harpers and Queen*, August 1992. This account is drawn from Routledge: *Gordon Brown*, pp. 243–63.
13 Quoted in Routledge: *Gordon Brown*, p. 22.
14 Naughtie: *The Rivals*, p. 22.
15 Brown, Gordon (ed.), *The Red Paper on Scotland* (Edinburgh University Student Publication Board, 1975).
16 Routledge: *Gordon Brown*, p. 76.
17 Ibid., p. 96.
18 Ibid., p. 111.

3 Provenance and Upbringing – Peter Mandelson

1 Interview, *The Chair*, BBC2 1997, quoted in Macintyre: *Mandelson and the Making of New Labour*, p. 12.
2 Macintyre: *Mandelson and the Making of New Labour*, p. 13.
3 Ibid., p. 6.

4   Quoted in Macintyre: *Mandelson and the Making of New Labour*, pp. 6–7.
5   Macintyre: *Mandelson and the Making of New Labour*, p. 9.
6   Ibid.
7   Ibid., p. 17.
8   Ibid., p. 18.
9   Ibid., p. 38.
10 Ibid., p. 47.
11 Ibid., p. 41.
12 Ibid., p. 46.
13 Ibid., p. 51.
14 The author was Shirley Williams's Parliamentary Private Secretary from 1978 to 1979.
15 Macintyre: *Mandelson and the Making of New Labour*, pp. 55–56.
16 Ibid., pp. 56–57.
17 Ibid., p. 64.
18 Ibid., p. 66.
19 Radice: *Diaries, 1980–2001*, 27 September 1981.
20 Macintyre: *Mandelson and the Making of New Labour*, p. 70.
21 My interview with Roger Liddle.
22 Macintyre: *Mandelson and the Making of New Labour*, p. 75–76.

4 Kinnock's Young Men

1   Radice: *Diaries, 1980–2001*, 10 June 1983.
2   *Hansard*, 27 July 1983.
3   *Hansard*, 27 July 1983.
4   *Hansard*, 6 July 1983, col. 320.
5   Naughtie: *The Rivals*, p. 26.
6   Quoted in Rentoul: *Tony Blair, Prime Minister*, (London, 2001), p. 118.
7   *Hansard*, 7 July 1984.
8   Clark, Alan, *Diaries* (London, 1994), 8 December 1983.
9   Interview with Gordon Brown, in Routledge: *Gordon Brown*, p. 130.
10 Macintyre: *Mandelson and the Making of New Labour*, pp. 88–93.
11 Ibid., p. 102.
12 Butler, David and Dennis Kavanagh, *The British General Election of 1987* (Basingstoke, 1988), p. 24.
13 Rentoul: *Tony Blair, Prime Minister*, pp. 133–34.
14 Campbell, John, *Pistols at Dawn* (London, 2009), p. 352.

15 Radice: *Diaries, 1980–2001*, 1 August 1987.

16 The others were Peter Shore, Peter Archer and Barry Jones. Denis Healey stood down. Apart from the question of merit, the shift from Solidarity to Tribune members occurred in part because of the retirement of Labour MPs who backed Solidarity.

17 Radice: *Diaries, 1980–2001*, 21 November 1985.

18 *Hansard*, 1 November 1988, cols 821–26.

19 Radice: *Diaries, 1980–2001*, 2 March 1990.

20 *Hansard*, 29 November 1989, cols 727–34.

21 *Hansard*, 29 January 1990, col. 55.

22 Macintyre: *Mandelson and the Making of New Labour*, p. 175.

23 Ibid., pp. 218–19.

24 Ibid., p. 237.

25 Ibid., p. 238.

26 Radice: *Diaries, 1980–2001*, 12 April 1992.

5 John Smith's Brief Reign

1 Radice, Giles, 'Southern Discomfort' (London, Fabian Society pamphlet no. 555, 1992) np.

2 Rentoul: *Tony Blair, Prime Minister*, p. 179.

3 Ibid., p. 180.

4 Radice: *Diaries, 1980–2001*, 12 April 1992.

5 Macintyre: *Mandelson and the Making of New Labour*, p. 268.

6 Ibid., pp. 268–69.

7 Ibid., p. 275.

8 Ibid., p. 274.

9 John Smith was a member of the GMB.

10 Radice: *Diaries, 1980–2001*, 29 September 1992.

11 Quoted in Macintyre: *Mandelson and the Making of New Labour*, p. 275.

12 *Hansard*, 24 September 1992, cols 93–108.

13 Rentoul: *Tony Blair, Prime Minister*, p. 188.

14 Quoted in Rentoul: *Tony Blair, Prime Minister*, p. 200.

15 Ibid., p. 200.

16 Ibid., p. 201.

17 Seldon: *Blair*, p. 180.

18 Ibid., p. 663.

19 *Evening Standard*, 28 July 1992.

6 The Blair–Brown Deal

1 *Independent,* 13 July 1996, quoted in Rentoul: *Tony Blair, Prime Minister*, p. 221.
2 Quoted in Routledge: *Gordon Brown*, p. 190.
3 Seldon: *Blair*, p. 186.
4 Radice: *Diaries, 1980–2001*, 13 May 1994.
5 Naughtie: *The Rivals*, pp. 58–59.
6 Ibid., p. 62.
7 Macintyre: *Mandelson and the Making of New Labour*, pp. 295–96.
8 Radice: *Diaries, 1980–2001*, 20 May 1994.
9 Naughtie: *The Rivals*, p. 66.
10 Routledge: *Gordon Brown*, p. 202.
11 Ibid., p. 205.
12 Macintyre: *Mandelson and the Making of New Labour*, p. 296.
13 Campbell: *Pistols at Down*, p. 363. Accounts of the Granita agreement are contained in Naughtie: *The Rivals*, Peston, Robert, *Brown's Britain* (London, 2005), Routledge: *Gordon Brown* and Seldon: *Blair*.
14 Routledge: *Gordon Brown*, p. 206.
15 Peston: *Brown's Britain*, pp. 66–68.
16 Naughtie: *The Rivals*, p. 72.
17 Radice: *Diaries, 1980–2001*, 1 June 1994.

7 The Triumph of New Labour

1 Gould, Philip, *The Unfinished Revolution* (London, 1998), pp. 202–03.
2 Radice: *Diaries, 1980–2001*, 27 July 1994.
3 Campbell, Alastair, *The Blair Years* (London, 2007), 11 August 1994.
4 Seldon: *Blair*, pp. 217–18.
5 Gould: *The Unfinished Revolution*, p. 218.
6 Pimlott, Ben, *Harold Wilson* (London, 1992), p. 227.
7 Blair, Tony, *New Britain* (London, 1996), pp. 38–39.
8 Campbell: *The Blair Years*, 4 October 1994.
9 Radice: *Diaries, 1980–2001*, 4 October 1994.
10 Campbell: *The Blair Years*, 4 October 1998.
11 Hattersley, Roy, *Observer*, 15 January 1995.
12 Seldon: *Blair*, p. 225.
13 Rentoul: *Tony Blair, Prime Minister*, p. 262.
14 Ibid., p. 261.

15 Radice: *Diaries, 1980–2001*, 23 July 1996.
16 Macintyre: *Mandelson and the Making of New Labour*, p. 313.
17 Ibid., p. 319.
18 Ibid., p. 331.
19 Rentoul: *Tony Blair, Prime Minister*, p. 275.
20 Ibid., p. 275.
21 Seldon: *Blair*, p. 237.
22 Gould: *The Unfinished Revolution*, pp. 270–71.
23 Keegan, William, *The Prudence of Mr Gordon Brown*, (Chichester, 2003), pp. 148–49.
24 Ashdown, Paddy, *The Ashdown Diaries* (London, 2000), 24 October 1995.
25 Rentoul: *Tony Blair, Prime Minister*, p. 276.
26 Ibid., p. 277.
27 Major, John, *The Autobiography* (London, 1999), p. 696.
28 Mandelson, Peter and Roger Liddle, *The Blair Revolution* (London, 1996), p. 1.
29 Butler, David and Dennis Kavanagh, *The British General Election of 1997* (Basingstoke, 1997), p. 250.
30 Peter Mandelson, interview.

8 Learning the Ropes

1 *Hansard*, 14 May 1997.
2 Riddell, Peter, *The Unfulfilled Prime Minister* (London, 2005), p. 42.
3 Rentoul: *Tony Blair, Prime Minister*, p. 394.
4 These included James Purnell, later to become Secretary of State for Work and Pensions in Brown's Cabinet, Roger Liddle, Blair's European adviser who later served in both Mandelson's and the President of European Commissions' cabinets, and Geoffrey Norris, Blair's adviser on industry, who was to go on to advise both Brown and Mandelson.
5 Macintyre: *Mandelson and the Making of New Labour*, pp. 388–89.
6 Ibid., p. 401.
7 Independent Commission on Electoral Reform.
8 *Hansard*, 27 October 1997.
9 Macintyre: *Mandelson and the Making of New Labour*, p. 399.
10 Radice: *Diaries, 1980–2001*, 23 March 1998.
11 Ibid., 26 September 2000.
12 Ibid., 7 May 1997.

13 Seldon: *Blair*, p. 320. Lord Kerr, as he now is, confirmed this comment to me.

14 Rentoul: *Tony Blair, Prime Minister*, p. 345.

15 Ibid., p. 369.

16 Radice: *Diaries, 1980–2001*, 16 November 1997.

17 Ibid., 10 December 1997.

18 Rentoul: *Tony Blair, Prime Minister*, pp. 377–78.

19 Ibid., p. 561.

20 Ibid., p. 405.

21 *Hansard*, 27 June 2007.

22 Radice: *Diaries, 1980–2001*, 31 March 1998, 30 June 1998.

23 Riddell: *The Unfulfilled Prime Minister*, pp. 131–32.

24 Radice: *Diaries, 1980–2001*, 22 June 1999.

25 Ibid., 6 June 1999.

26 *Hansard*, 23 March 1999.

27 Riddell, Peter, *Hug Them Close* (London, 2003), pp. 118–20.

28 Riddell: *The Unfulfilled Prime Minister*, p. 134.

9 Super Chancellor

1 Naughtie: *The Rivals*, pp. 282–83.

2 Peston: *Brown's Britain*, p. 116.

3 The Chancellor wrote a formal letter to me, in my capacity as Chairman of the Treasury Select Committee, suggesting an enhanced role for the Committee in examining the performance of the Bank (Appendix 3, First Report of the Treasury Committee, Session 1997–98).

4 *Hansard*, 20 May 1997.

5 Radice: *Diaries, 1980–2001*, 2 July 1997.

6 Peston: *Brown's Britain*, p. 282.

7 Treasury Select Committee, Eighth Report, 1997–98.

8 Peston: *Brown's Britain*, p. 169.

9 Rawnsley, Andrew, *Servants of the People* (London, 2000), p. 81.

10 Routledge: *Gordon Brown*, blurb.

11 Rawnsley: *Servants of the People*, p. 145.

12 *The Times*, 28 January 1998.

13 Rawnsley: *Servants of the People*, p. 150.

14 Ibid., p. 152.

15 Rentoul: *Tony Blair, Prime Minister*, p. 384.

16 Radice: *Diaries, 1980–2001*, 25 January 1998.

17 Campbell: *The Blair Years*, 23 July 1998.
18 Radice: *Diaries, 1980–2001*, 6 January 1999.
19 Ibid., 27 January 1999.

10 Mandelson Resigns – and Resigns Again

1 Macintyre: *Mandelson and the Making of New Labour*, p. 464.
2 Ibid., p. 480.
3 Ibid., p. 341; the gist of the conversation was confirmed by Roger Liddle.
4 Rawnsley: *Servants of the People*, pp. 213–14.
5 Ibid., p. 214.
6 Macintyre: *Mandelson and the Making of New Labour*, p. 507.
7 Rawnsley: *Servants of the People*, p. 327.
8 Radice: *Diaries, 1980–2001*, 27 April 1999.
9 Rawnsley: *Servants of the People*, p. 350.

11 Second Landslide

1 Blair, Tony, 'The Third Way' (London, Fabian Society pamphlet no. 588, 1998), np.
2 Jospin, Lionel, 'Modern Socialism', (London, Fabian Society pamphlet no. 592, 1999), np.
3 Diamond, Patrick (ed.), *New Labour's Old Roots* (Exeter, 2004), pp. 1–2.
4 Leonard, Dick (ed.), *Crosland and New Labour* (Basingstoke, 1999), pp. 35–48.
5 Mandelson and Liddle: *The Blair Revolution* (London, new edition, 2002), p. xxxii.
6 Rawnsley: *Servants of the People*, pp. 330–40.
7 *Hansard*, 21 March 2000.
8 Radice: *Diaries, 1980–2001*, 21 March 2000.
9 Riddell, *The Unfulfilled Prime Minister*, p. 49.
10 Radice: *Diaries, 1980–2001*, 18 September 2000.
11 Butler, David and Dennis Kavanagh, *The British General Election of 2001* (Basingstoke, 2002), p. 75.
12 Seldon: *Blair*, p. 461.
13 Butler and Kavanagh: *The British General Election of 2001*, pp. 240–41.
14 Seldon: *Blair*, p. 677.

12 9/11, Bush and Afghanistan

1 Seldon, Anthony and Peter Snowdon, *Blair Unbound* (London, 2007) p. 5.

2 Ibid., p. 15.

3 Stephens, Philip, *Tony Blair: The Making of a World Leader* (London, 2004), p. 271.

4 Seldon: *Blair Unbound*, p. 47.

5 Riddell: *Hug Them Close*, p. 2.

6 Ibid., pp. 137–39.

7 Meyer, Sir Christopher, 'Blair's War' (PBS *Frontline* (WG BH Boston), 2002), quoted in Seldon: *Blair Unbound*, p. 55.

8 Riddell: *Hug Them Close*, p. 161.

9 Ibid., pp. 160–61.

10 Ibid., pp. 171–72.

11 Ibid., p. 168.

13 Iraq

1 Riddell: *Hug Them Close*, p. 173.

2 Kampfner, John, *Blair's Wars*, (London, 2003), p. 152.

3 Cook, Robin, *The Point of Departure* (London, 2003), 10, 11 April 2002.

4 Kampfner: *Blair's Wars*, p. 193.

5 Riddell: *Hug Them Close*, pp. 208–09.

6 Stephens: *Tony Blair: The Making of a World Leader*, p. 295.

7 Ibid., pp. 293–94.

8 Ibid., p. 311.

9 *Hansard*, 17 March 2003.

10 *Hansard*, 20 March 2003.

11 *Hansard*, House of Lords, September 2002.

14 The Blair–Brown Wars

1 Campbell: *The Blair Years*, 7 June 2001.

2 Seldon: *Blair Unbound*, p. 32.

3 Rawnsley: *Servants of the People*, p. 488.

4 Seldon: *Blair Unbound*, pp. 276–77, confirmed by Sally Morgan.

5 Ibid., p. 68.

6 Byers resigned in May 2002; in August 2002 Morris resigned; Milburn left office in June 2003; while Blunkett was forced to resign in December 2004.

7 Barber, Michael, *Instruction to Deliver* (London, 2008), np.

8 Ibid., pp. 268–69.

9 Ibid., pp. 336–39.

10 Peston: *Brown's Britain*, pp. 302–06.

11 Ibid., p. 298.

12 Ibid., p. 301.

13 *The Times*, 2 October 2002, quoted in Seldon: *Blair Unbound*, p. 242.

14 Ibid., p. 243.

15 Peston: *Brown's Britain*, pp. 301–02.

16 Rawnsley, Andrew, *The End of the Party* (London, 2010), p. 232.

17 Seldon: *Blair Unbound*, p. 206.

18 Robert Peston, *Brown's Britain*, p. 229.

19 Ibid., p. 237.

20 Ibid., p. 238.

21 Rawnsley: *The End of the Party*, p. 196.

22 Seldon: *Blair*, p. 684.

23 Seldon: *Blair Unbound*, p. 230.

24 Prescott, John, *Docks to Downing Street* (London, 2009), pp. 314–15.

25 Seldon: *Blair Unbound*, p. 230.

26 Prescott: *Docks to Downing Street*, p. 315.

27 Rawnsley: *The End of the Party*, p. 229.

28 Seldon: *Blair Unbound*, p. 247.

29 Rawnsley: *The End of the Party*, p. 233.

30 *Hansard*, 28 January 2004.

31 Westminster House, 6 June 2004.

32 Blair, Cherie, *Speaking for Myself* (London, 2008), pp. 368, 370.

33 Peston: *Brown's Britain*, pp. 337–50.

34 Interview with Mandelson, quoted in Rawnsley: *The End of the Party*, p. 265.

35 Blair: *Speaking for Myself*, p. 370.

36 Peston: *Brown's Britain*, p. 343.

37 Seldon: *Blair Unbound*, p. 296.

38 Peston: *Brown's Britain*, p. 349.

39 *Sunday Times*, 1 May 2005.

15 Blair's Legacy, Brownite Coup

1 Mullin, Chris, *A View from the Foothills* (London, 2009), 4 May 2005.

2 Seldon: *Blair Unbound*, p. 347.

3 Quoted in Seldon: *Blair Unbound*, p. 347.

4 Ibid., p. 361.

5 Rawnsley: *The End of the Party*, p. 329.

6 *BBC News*, 27 September 2005.

7 *Hansard*, 19 December 2005.

8 Rawnsley: *The End of the Party*, p. 338.

9 *Hansard*, 9 November 2005.

10 'Higher Standards, Better Schools for All: More Choice for Parents and Pupils', DFES.

11 *Sunday Telegraph*, 18 December 2005.

12 *Guardian*, 12 January 2006.

13 Seldon: *Blair Unbound*, p. 452.

14 Ibid., p. 465.

15 Prescott: *Docks to Downing Street*, p. 324.

16 See accounts by: Seldon: *Blair Unbound*, p. 490; Rawnsley: *The End of the Party*, p. 397; Boulton, Adam, *Memories of the Blair Administration* (London, 2008), p. 285. Confirmed by both Blair and Brown advisers.

17 *News of the World*, 10 September 2006.

18 Seldon: *Blair Unbound*, p. 488.

19 Boulton: *Memories of the Blair Administration*, p. 112.

20 Rawnsley: *The End of the Party*, p. 442.

16 Brown in Trouble – Mandelson Returns

1 Rawnsley: *The End of the Party*, p. 468.

2 *Independent*, 23 March 2007.

3 Rawnsley: *The End of the Party*, p. 461.

4 Ibid., p. 511.

5 *Hansard*, 28 November 2007.

6 *Hansard*, 10 October 2007.

7 *BBC News*, 27 April 2008.

8 *Guardian*, 11 April 2008.

9 *The Times*, 24 April 2008.

10 *Guardian*, 30 July 2008.

11 *Guardian*, 30 August 2008.

12 *Independent*, 21 February 2010.

13 Rawnsley: *The End of the Party*, p. 568.

14 *The Economist*, 9 October 2008.

17 Credit Crunch – Brown Helps 'Save the World'

1 Q 2891, Treasury Select Committee, 19 March 2009.

2 Institute of Fiscal Studies 2009, 2009 Budget IFS.

3 King, Mervyn, 'The MPC [Monetary Policy Committee] Ten Years On', np.

4 Bean, Charles, 'The Great Moderation, The Great Panic and the Great Contraction' (Schumpeter Lecture, Annual Congress of the European Economic Association, 2009), quoted in Smith, David, *The Age of Instability* (London, 2010), p. 220.

5 Speech given by the Chancellor of the Exchequer at the Mansion House, 20 June 2007.

6 *New Statesman*, 7 January 2010.

7 Peston, Robert, *Who Runs Britain* (London, 2008), pp. 7, 8.

8 International Financial Service Research, 2009.

9 Balls, Ed, speech given to the British Bankers Association, 11 October 2006, quoted in Rawnsley: *The End of the Party*, pp. 483–84.

10 Mervyn King, speech given to CBI Nottingham 20 January 2008.

11 House of Commons, Treasury Select Committee Report, 21 April 2008.

12 Quoted in Smith: *The Age of Instability*, p. 107.

13 House of Commons Treasury Select Committee Report 2008.

14 Smith: *The Age of Instability*, pp. 119–20.

15 Ibid., p. 124.

16 *Hansard*, Chancellor's statement, 12 March 2008.

17 Smith: *The Age of Instability*, p. 168.

18 Krugman, Paul, 'Gordon Does Good', *New York Times*, 13 October 2008.

19 Quoted in Rawnsley: *The End of the Party*, p. 597.

20 Skidelsky, Robert, *Keynes: Return of the Master* (London, 2009), pp. 18–20.

21 Pittsburgh Summit communiqué.

18 Brown's Last Stand

1 White, Michael, *Guardian*, 31 March 2010.

2 *Hansard*, 24 November 2008.

3 House of Commons Treasury Select Committee Report, 6 January 2010.

4 Butler, David and Dennis Kavanagh, *British General Election of 2005* (Basingstoke, 2005), p. 191.

5 *Independent*, 21 February 2010.

6 House of Commons Foreign Affairs Committee, 2009.

7 *Independent*, 28 July 2009.

Notes

8 Toynbee, Polly, *Guardian*, 13 April 2010.
9 Blair, Tony, speech given at Sedgefield, 30 March 2010.
10 *Guardian*, 6 April 2010.

Conclusion

1 *Guardian*, 5 May 2010.
2 Institute of Fiscal Studies, March 2010.
3 Toynbee, Polly and David Walker, *Better or Worse? Has Labour Delivered?* (London: 2005), pp. 49–50.
4 *Guardian*, 12 May 2010.
5 Reeves, Rachel, *Why Vote Labour* (London, 2010), np.
6 *Financial Times*, 15 May 2010.
7 Riddell: *The Unfulfilled Prime Minister*, p. 205.
8 Elliott, Larry, economics editor, *Guardian*, 12 March 2007.
9 Giddens, Anthony, *New Statesman*, 17 May 2010.
10 Mulgan, Geoff, *Prospect*, May 2005.
11 Radice, Giles, *Progress Magazine*, March 2008.
12 Byrne, Liam, *Guardian*, 14 May 2010.`

BIBLIOGRAPHY

A NOTE ON SOURCES

I have drawn on conversations and interviews, published and unpublished diaries, autobiographies and biographies and other works about or involving New Labour and its protagonists. As well as the books and articles cited here, other sources are to be found in the notes.

DIARIES

Ashdown, Paddy (2000, 2002). *The Ashdown Diaries*, 2 vols, London: Penguin.
Campbell, Alastair (2007). *The Blair Years: Extracts from the Alastair Campbell Diaries*, London: Hutchinson.
Clark, Alan (1994). *Diaries*, London: Phoenix.
Cook, Robin (2003). *The Point of Departure*, London: Simon & Schuster Ltd.
Mullin, Chris (2009). *A View from the Foothills: The Diaries of Chris Mullin*, London: Profile Books Ltd.
Radice, Giles (2004). *Diaries 1980–2001*, London: Weidenfeld & Nicolson.

AUTOBIOGRAPHIES AND BIOGRAPHIES

Barber, Michael (2008). *Instruction to Deliver*, London: Methuen.
Beckett, Francis (2007). *Gordon Brown*, London: Haus Publishing.
Blair, Cherie (2008). *Speaking for Myself*, London: Little, Brown.
Boulton, Adam (2008). *Memories of the Blair Administration*, London: Simon & Schuster Ltd.
Bower, Tom (2001). *The Paymaster*, London: Simon & Schuster Ltd.
—— (2004). *Gordon Brown*, London: HarperCollins.
Brown, Colin (2005). *Prescott: The Biography*, London: Politico's Publishing Ltd.
Campbell, John (2009). *Pistols at Dawn*, London: Jonathan Cape Ltd.

Bibliography

Macintyre, Donald (2000). *Mandelson and the Making of New Labour*, London: HarperCollins.

McSmith, Andy (1994). *John Smith*, London: Mandarin.

Major, John, (1999). *The Autobiography*, London: HarperCollins.

Naughtie, James (2001). *The Rivals*, London: Fourth Estate.

—— (2004). *The Accidental American*, Basingstoke: Macmillan.

Oborne, Peter and Simon Walters (2004). *Alastair Campbell*, London: Aurum Press Ltd.

Peston, Robert (2005). *Brown's Britain*, London: Short Books Ltd.

Pimlott, Ben (1992). *Harold Wilson*, London: HarperCollins.

Pollard, Stephen (2005). *David Blunkett*, London: Hodder & Stoughton Ltd.

Powell, Jonathan (2009). *Great Hatred, Little Room*, London: Vintage.

Prescott, John (2009). *Docks to Downing Street*, London: Headline.

Pym, Hugh and Nick Kochan (1998). *Gordon Brown: The First Year in Power*, London: Bloomsbury.

Rentoul, John (2001). *Tony Blair, Prime Minister*, London: Little, Brown.

Riddell, Peter (2005). *The Unfulfilled Prime Minister*, London: Politico's Publishing Ltd.

Robinson, Geoffrey (2000). *The Unconventional Minister*, London: Michael Joseph Ltd.

Routledge, Paul (1998). *Gordon Brown*, London: Simon & Schuster Ltd.

—— (1999). *Mandy*, London: Simon & Schuster Ltd.

Seldon, Anthony (2004). *Blair*, London: The Free Press.

Seldon, Anthony and Peter Snowdon (2007). *Blair Unbound*, London: Simon & Schuster Ltd.

Short, Clare (2004). *An Honourable Deception?*, London: The Free Press.

Sopel, Jon (1995). *Tony Blair*, London: Michael Joseph Ltd.

Stephens, Philip (2004). *Tony Blair: The Making of a World Leader*, London: Viking Books.

OTHER WORKS

Balls, Ed and Gus O'Donnell (eds) (2002). *Reforming Britain's Economic and Financial Policy*, Basingstoke: Palgrave Macmillan.

Blair, Tony, (1996). *New Britain*, London: Fourth Estate.

—— (1998). 'The Third Way', London, Fabian Society pamphlet no. 588.

Butler, David and Dennis Kavanagh (1988). *The British General Election of 1987*, Basingstoke: Palgrave Macmillan.

—— (1997). *The British General Election of 1997*, Basingstoke: Palgrave Macmillan.

—— (2001). *The British General Election of 2001*, Basingstoke: Palgrave Macmillan.

—— (2005). *The British General Election of 2005*, Basingstoke: Palgrave Macmillan.

Bibliography

Diamond, Patrick (ed.) (2004). *New Labour's Old Roots*, Exeter: Imprint Academic.

Giddens, Anthony (1998). *The Third Way*, Cambridge: Polity Press.

Gould, Philip (1998). *The Unfinished Revolution*, London: Little, Brown.

Hennessy, Peter (2000). *The Prime Minister*, London: Penguin.

Hughes, Colin and Patrick Wintour (1990). *Labour Rebuilt*, London: Fourth Estate.

Kampfner, John (2003). *Blair's Wars*, London: The Free Press.

Keegan, William (2003). *The Prudence of Mr Gordon Brown*, Chichester: John Wiley and Sons Ltd.

Leonard, Dick (ed.) (1999). *Crosland and New Labour*, Basingstoke: Palgrave Macmillan.

Jospin, Lionel, Chris Evans et al. (1999). 'Modern Socialism', London: Fabian Society pamphlet no. 592,.

Mandelson, Peter and Roger Liddle (1996, new ed. 2002). *The Blair Revolution*, London: Faber and Faber; new ed., London: Politico's Publishing Ltd.

Marquand, David (2008). *Britain Since 1918: The Strange Career of British Democracy*, London: Weidenfeld & Nicolson.

Peston, Robert (2008). *Who Runs Britain?*, London: Hodder Paperbacks.

Radice, Giles (1988). *Labour's Path to Power: The New Revisionism*, Basingstoke: Palgrave Macmillan.

—— (1992). 'Southern Discomfort', London: Fabian Society pamphlet no. 555.

Radice, Giles (ed.) (1996). *What Needs to Change*, London: HarperCollins.

Rawnsley, Andrew (2000). *Servants of the People*, London: Hamish Hamilton.

—— (2010). *The End of the Party*, London: Viking.

Reeves, Rachel (2010). *Why Vote Labour*, London: Biteback.

Riddell, Peter (2003). *Hug Them Close*, London: Politico's Publishing Ltd.

Scott, Derek (2004). *Off Whitehall*, London: I.B.Tauris & Co Ltd.

Skidelsky, Robert (2009) *Keynes: The Return of the Master*, London: Allen Lane.

Smith, David (2010). *The Age of Instability*, London: Profile Books Ltd.

Toynbee, Polly and David Walker (2001) *Did Things Get Better?*, London: Penguin.

—— (2005). *Better or Worse?: Has Labour Delivered?*, London: Bloomsbury Publishing plc.

Young, Hugo (2008). *The Hugo Young Papers*, London: Penguin.

INDEX

The index is presented in letter-by-letter alphabetical order, so that 'Blair–Brown relationship' files before 'Blair, Cherie' and 'taxation' before 'tax credits'.

Index

Index

Index

Index

Index

Index

Index